FOREIGN POLICY CRISES

Appearance and Reality in Decision Making

Thomas Halper

Coe College

WITHDRAWN

Charles E. Merrill Publishing Company
A Bell & Howell Company
Columbus, Ohio

FOR MY PARENTS

Merrill Political Science Series

Under the general editorship of

John C. Wahlke
Department of Political Science
SUNY at Stony Brook

ISBN: 0–675–09719–3

Library of Congress Catalog Card Number: 72–163441

1 2 3 4 5 6 7 8 — 76 75 74 73 72 71

Printed in the United States of America

Preface

The purpose of this book is to investigate the relationship between appearance and reality in foreign policy crisis decision making in order to deepen our understanding of presidential decision making. My thesis, bearing on this relationship, consists of three parts: first, the factors tending to distort the President's perceptions of domestic and international political reality are everywhere (from communications problems in a huge bureaucracy to preconceived notions in his own brain), cumulatively powerful in affecting his decisions, and to a significant extent probably immune to efforts at elimination of error; second, Presidents define situations as "crises" if they are perceived as constituting serious and immediate threats to national or presidential appearances of strength, competency, or resolve, even if these situations do not pose substantial dangers to national security and are seen as not posing such dangers; third, Presidents are willing and, in the short run at least, generally able to mislead the public regarding the nature of and their response to crises, if Presidents feel that national or personal interests make such deceptions desirable.

By "appearance," I mean the decision makers' and public's perception of actual events at the time; by "reality," I mean the events as we have now, with the benefit of hindsight, come to know them. It is plain, even without becoming excessively epistemological, that these simple, straightforward definitions cannot banish a deeper practical problem. And that practical problem is, of course, how does the investigator determine what individuals perceived and what in fact took place.

From my location on the outside, let me concede at once, it is impossible to know for sure. Different people, as Hobbes said, do not wear the same skin, and the problem of invading the privacy of another's skull must remain insuperable. I can hardly pretend, then, that my view of the visions of decision makers, attentive publics, or mass publics is necessarily accurate and complete. All I can really do, of course, is to present

my perceptions of these views. Nor, by the same token, can I be certain
that the information I accept as "reality" is adequate for that purpose.
Despite my efforts, undoubtedly a number of the "facts" I trust are
partly or wholly erroneous or have been given a misleading significance
because the requisite clarifying data have not yet been brought to light.

It does not follow, however, that these uncertainties foredoom any investigation of the appearance-reality relationship. In a real sense, all
studies must proceed with incomplete and imperfect data, and the
reader, like a plaintiff in a negligence suit, must live with the doctrine of
"assumption of risk." The truly relevant considerations, then, are: first,
are the questions asked in the study important enough to justify the assumption of risk; and second, are the available data so inadequate as to
make a reasonably empirical approach impossible, and an assumption of
risk merely a leap of faith. Let us examine these key considerations in
turn.

First, as to the substance of the inquiry, my interest in the appearance-
reality relationship is three-fold, reflecting the three portions of my
thesis:

(a) I am concerned with decision makers' perceptions of events, and in particular with such questions as these: what factors tend to distort these perceptions? How do decision makers attempt to counteract these distorting
factors? How successful are these attempts?

(b) I am concerned with how decision makers define crises. Are they viewed
mainly as threats to personal and national appearances or to substantive
national interests? Or are decision makers unable or unwilling either to
make the distinction or to grant it significance?

(c) I am concerned with decision makers' efforts, whether deliberate or not,
to lead mass or attentive publics to accept as reality appearances which,
from the decision makers' vantage and from hindsight, seem to have been
seriously inaccurate. What are the factors which tend to impel decision
makers toward candor or deception? What are the means they use to the
end of shaping mass and attentive public opinion? How effective are these
efforts?

These questions derive from my larger basic thesis, and may even be
characterized as components of it. Yet their significance is not mainly a
function of their being essential to this book; for on their answers may
hang the fate of democracy in America, if not of civilization itself. That
they are important enough to justify the aforementioned "assumption of
risk," then, is too self-evident to belabor. It is enough to invoke the wise
counsel of a distinguished statistician:

Far better an approximate answer to the *right* question which is often vague, than an *exact* answer to the wrong [or, I might add,] trivial question, which can always be made precise.... It would be a mistake not to face up to the fact, for by denying it, we would deny ourselves the use of a great body of approximate knowledge, as well as failing to maintain alertness to the possible importance in each particular instance of particular ways in which our knowledge is incomplete.[1]

Second, as to the availability of data from which the investigator can reconstruct reality and decision makers' and publics' perceptions, a vast literature exists.[2] Since the crises studied constitute some of the most spectacular and important of contemporary political events, accounts have proliferated almost beyond enumeration. In trying to reconstruct reality, I have attempted to exploit the various unearned advantages enjoyed by *post facto* analysts: freedom from time pressure and from responsibility for the actual implications of policy actions, and infallibility of hindsight. These advantages, however, are of only limited value in helping me to reconstruct decision makers' perceptions, and here I have relied most heavily upon contemporary accounts and memoirs.

Informing the entire investigatory enterprise was the recognition that from my point of view as well as from the decision makers', things are not always what they seem. And about government, especially, there is an odd and disturbing surrealistic quality: documents, statements, reports, all precise but incomplete, all clinging to form in lieu of life though focusing on life itself. To complicate matters further, ominous and vivid metaphors like "escalation," "overkill," and brinksmanship" are by now part of the familiar vocabulary of public awareness. Consequently, popular commentators on crises "prefer the automatic, the reflex, the cliché of velvet"; [3] and they prefer worn phrases not simply out of literary laziness, but in addition because these semantic practices reflect with great accuracy their unimaginative thinking patterns.

In an effort to compensate for these difficulties, I have analyzed every relevant document and commentary that I could find, searching books, newspapers, popular and learned periodicals, television interviews, mimeographed speeches, congressional hearings and reports, and government financed studies. Topically, the sources consulted centered not only on the specific crises on which this book concentrates, but also upon

---

[1] John W. Tukey, "The Future of Data Analysis," *Annals of Mathematical Statistics* 33 (February 1964): 13–14.

[2] For an overview of the literature, see the "Bibliographic Note" following chapter 7. In addition, the text contains numerous footnotes, which might provide "leads" for those wishing to pursue their own investigations into the topics under discussion.

[3] Louis Macneice, "Homage to Clichés," *Poems, 1925–1940* (New York: Random House, 1940 [1935]), p. 87.

crises in general, and on broader concerns of international relations and
the American political process. In addition, those areas of sociology and
social psychology dealing with small group behavior, leadership, and
perception were also combed for data bearing on the problems discussed.

Have all of these precautions insulated me from error? Almost surely
they have not. I can never be certain that I have not been so governed by
my own biases that, for example, I have implicitly operationalized "reality" in terms of facts reported by the *New York Times*. Moreover, there is
much information I have not seen: perceptions and conversations that
went unrecorded; documents lost, destroyed, or classified "secret"; data
made public but which eluded my efforts at discovery. Yet as P. W.
Bridgman has pointed out, "No analysis is self-terminating, but it can always be pushed indefinitely with continually accumulating refine-
ments." [4] And, he might have added, with continually diminishing re-
turns. I have tried to be reasonably exhaustive and objective, but the
drive for total knowledge is futile and for complete neutrality, deluding,
and probably bespeaks not so much thoroughness as self-indulgence. My
attempt to adhere to this recognition may explain the inevitable omission of some matters which the reader may deem important.

In dealing with the problems of appearance and reality—as faced by
decision maker and as created by decision maker—I have attempted to
construct the rough outlines of a theory from an examination of five specific and recent foreign policy crises. As Harry Howe Ransom observed
in a 1968 historical overview of the study of international relations, little
has been done in the way of extended case studies of major foreign policy decisions.[5] But, as I hope to make clear, it is not only the relative novelty of the case study approach that commends it to the researcher.

The five crises chosen are the Bay of Pigs invasion of 1961, The Cuban
missile crisis of 1962, the Gulf of Tonkin attacks of 1964, the Dominican
Republic intervention of 1965, and the Tet offensive of 1968. Why
choose these crises? For one thing, they share certain important similarities, permitting some fruitful comparison. All five, for example, were
recent and well-publicized. Together, they constitute, roughly speaking,
a sample of major international crises involving the United States during
the past decade. At the same time, however, there are important differ-

---

[4] P. W. Bridgman, *The Nature of Thermodynamics,* Harper Torchbooks (New York: Harper and Brothers, 1961), p. vii.
[5] Harry Howe Ransom, "International Relations," *Journal of Politics* 30 (May 1968): 352.
Related to this is Thomas Cronin's observation that "political science . . . has frequently
slighted the study of the presidency, so that important studies of presidential politics have
been noticeably few in the last decade . . ." Thomas E. Cronin, "New Perspectives on the
Presidency?" *Public Administration Review* 29 (November–December 1969): 670.

ences between the five crises, broadening the scope of the inquiry. The crises, for instance, did not all occur under the same President, did not all have international or domestic ramifications of the same magnitude, and were not all unexpected.

It is, of course, a commonplace to point out that case studies cannot "prove" anything. Yet this is not equivalent to assenting to bland *non sequiturs* of despair, like this from Richard Goodwin:

Almost every confrontation, particularly between the United States and the Soviet Union, is unique and unrepeatable. Thus, to generalize from one to another almost guarantees error. The Cuban missile crisis was not Berlin, nor is Vietnam another Korea.[6]

Certainly, in some respect, every event—not merely "almost every" event—is unique and unrepeatable. Even if a second event were an otherwise perfect duplicate of the first, the second version would differ in that it would have occurred at a different time. If uniqueness were to preclude generalization, then none could exist. Yet since this study's five crises are not, strictly, a representative sample of American foreign policy crises, the resulting generalizations are offered in a tentative, heuristic spirit. The data, necessarily, permit illustration of theory, but not verification or "proof."

The crises selected for study entail the consideration of two presidencies, those of Kennedy and Johnson. One crisis under each receives rather extended treatment, the Cuban missile crisis primarily because of its importance and the Dominican Republic intervention because of its complexity. The three other crises are considered somewhat more briefly. But in each of the five case histories, I have tried "to reconstruct the situation as defined by the decision maker"[7] in the hope that this will expose the decision-making process more clearly and thereby shed light on the areas of presidential perceptions and misperceptions, presidential definitions of "crisis," and presidential attempts to mislead the mass or attentive publics.

But, "a complex decision," as Herbert Simon has said, "is like a great river drawing from its many tributaries the innumerable component premises of which it is constituted."[8] And so, frequently, I have attempted to externalize for observation some of the more important

[6] Richard Goodwin, "The Unthinkable and the Unanalyzable: Book Review of *Arms and Influence* by Thomas C. Schelling," *New Yorker,* February 17, 1968, p. 127.
[7] Richard C. Snyder, "A Decision Making Approach to the Study of Political Phenomena," *Approaches to the Study of Politics,* ed. Roland Young (Evanston: Northwestern University Press, 1958), p. 17.
[8] Herbert A. Simon, *Administrative Behavior: A Study of Decision Making Processes in Administrative Organizations,* 2d ed. (New York: Macmillan, 1957), p. xii.

"component premises." In addition, I have tried to identify many smaller decisions related to the main ones, in the hope that in this way certain regularities—or "strategies" [9]—may be discerned.

At this point, it is necessary to define a key term, "decision making." By it, I mean "a process which results in the selection from a socially defined, limited number of problematic, alternative projects of one project intended to bring about the particular future state of affairs envisioned by the decision maker." [10] The essence of the task of deciding, then, is prediction, which, in turn, is subject to both conscious and unconscious controls. For this reason, presidential decision making must remain a mysterious and never wholly discoverable process. President Truman began his memoirs with these words:

The presidency of the United States carried with it a responsibility so personal as to be without parallel.... No one can make decisions for him. No one can know all the processes and stages of his thinking in making important decisions. Even those closest to him, even members of his immediate family, never know all the reasons why he does certain things and why he comes to certain conclusions.[11]

Another sobering fact which I have tried to keep in mind is that "not everything which gets decided gets decided by anybody's deciding." [12]

[9] Jerome S. Bruner, Jacqueline J. Goodnow, and George A. Austin, *A Study of Thinking,* Science Editions (New York: Wiley, 1962 [c. 1950]), p. 54. Whether a strategy is pursued consciously or unconsciously is immaterial.

[10] Richard C. Snyder, H. W. Bruck, and Burton Sapin, "Decision Making as an Approach to the Study of International Politics," *Foreign Policy Decision Making: An Approach to the Study of International Politics,* ed. Snyder, Bruck, and Sapin (New York: Free Press, 1962 [c. 1955]), p. 90. The decision-making approach itself has come under some criticism. One student of complex organizations has argued, for example, that decision making in the selection process by leaders of the organizations is less important than decision making concerning the retention of information carried out at the lower levels. Karl E. Weick, *The Social Psychology of Organizing* (Reading: Addison-Wesley, 1969), p. 101. Another authority has complained that "The decision making approach ... tends to hide the institutional bases of events, the structure of the situations within which decisions occur, and consequently the structural determinants of action." Victor A. Thompson, *Modern Organization* (New York: Knopf, 1961), p. 7. A third writer has charged that the approach "does not and indeed cannot take nonrational personality factors into account." Joseph E. Schwartz, "Strategic Thought: Methodology and Reality," in *Apolitical Politics: A Critique of Behavioralism,* ed. Charles A. McCoy and John Playford (New York: Crowell, 1967), p. 71. I do not believe, however, that these defects inhere in the decision-making approach as such, and in fact I have treated relevant organizational and personality factors at considerable length when I felt it was justified.

[11] Harry S Truman, *Memoirs, Vol. I: Year of Decisions* (New York: New American Library, 1965 [c. 1955]), p. ix.

[12] C. A. W. Manning, *The Nature of International Society* (New York: Wiley, 1962), p. 45. Cf., the distinction between "central decision" and "social choice" in Edward C. Banfield, *Political Influence: A New Theory of Urban Politics* (New York: Free Press, 1961), chap. xii.

Sometimes, in other words, processes already in operation do the "deciding." Thus a former British prime minister could declare:

I am not sure that there is such a thing as "power" or "decision." I would certainly find it very hard to give you an example of when I have ever exercised power or taken a decision . . . For one thing, there is just a build-up of big and small events, of big and small factors, and they may not be brought to your notice until the issue has already been decided; and, when you eventually have to decide, it may be in response to the smallest of them all. That is not "power" or "decision"; you are too much in the hands of events. For another thing, the in-tray is always full. That is what politics is: trying to empty the in-tray.[13]

Whether these general remarks apply with equal force to crisis situations must, of course, remain in question.

Acknowledgments

I cannot close this preface without acknowledging the assistance many persons have given me in the course of writing this book. My greatest debt is owed Professor Harry Howe Ransom of Vanderbilt University who first got me interested in the topic of foreign policy crisis decision making a lifetime ago, and has since provided me with numerous ideas for improving this study. Professors J. Leiper Freeman and George J. Graham, both also from Vanderbilt, added helpful suggestions. Additionally, portions of this work profited from criticism by Professors Margaret Haupt and Fred Willhoite of Coe College, and Professors Robert Robins and James Cochrane of Tulane University. For much of what may be valuable in this book's point of view, I am beholden to my dear friend, Kevin O'Brien, who died tragically before this work was begun. Had he lived to read the manuscript, he would certainly have improved it, but that is one of the more trivial losses from his passing.

Thanks are also due to the following authors and publishers who permitted me to quote passages from their works:

The Center for Strategic and International Studies, Georgetown University, for permission to quote from *Dominican Action—Intervention or Cooperation?* (Special Report Series, No. 2, July 1966).

Doubleday & Company, Inc., for permission to quote from *Interaction Ritual:*

---

[13] Unnamed prime minister quoted in Henry Fairlie, "Johnson and the Intellectuals: A British View," *Commentary*, October 1965, pp. 52–53. Fairlie has elaborated upon this view in *The Life of Politics* (New York: Basic Books, 1968), pp. 76–84.

Intimate Study of Crisis Diplomacy by Edward Weintal and Charles Bartlett copyright © 1967 by Edward Weintal and Charles Bartlett.

World Publishing Company, for permission to quote from *Lyndon B. Johnson: The Exercise of Power* by Rowland Evans and Robert Novak. An NAL book. Copyright © 1966 by Rowland Evans and Robert Novak.

Contents

1

The Broader Context

"Reality" is the one word which should always be enclosed in quotation marks.

Sir Richard Burton

This chapter deals with appearance and reality in foreign policy crisis decision making from a broad perspective. First, there is a discussion of the decision maker's obstacles to perceiving reality. Some of these are external—his reliance upon others for information, for example—and some are internal—such as the distorting psychological pressures accentuated by crisis conditions. Next, attention is paid to the citizens' obstacles to perceiving reality, including the misperceptions of decision makers who would educate the public, the frequent desire on the part of decision makers to mislead the public for national, personal, or partisan reasons, the inadequacies of the mass media as the public's "watchdog," and the pervasive apathy and ignorance of the mass public itself. Attentive publics, which may be important politically out of all proportion to their numbers, are more likely to have more reliable sources of information.[1] Finally, this introductory discussion raises competing value considerations concerning the advisability of political candor in crisis situations, which, in turn, raises the question of how decision makers make the critical determination that a crisis in fact exists.

---

[1] The term term "attentive public" was coined by Gabriel Almond in his pioneering *American People and Foreign Policy*, in which he described this group as "informed and interested in foreign policy problems, and . . . the audience for the foreign policy discussions among the elites." Gabriel A. Almond, *The American People and Foreign Policy* (New York: Harcourt, Brace, 1950), p. 138. The concept of "attentive public" is developed in greater detail in Donald J. Devine, *The Attentive Public: Polyarchal Democracy* (Chicago: Rand McNally, 1970), esp. chap. 3.

OBSTACLES TO PERCEIVING REALITY

We live in an age in which international crises are strung like shirts on a clothesline from one war to the next. Perhaps all ages have been like this, but today the backyard fences seem lower. The barriers of time and space, which used to conceal events from public view, cannot withstand the battering curiosity of the mass media. Yesterday's jungle skirmish in Vietnam becomes a televised diversion before dinner; a United Nations Middle East debate heard on a car radio breaks the monotony of a drive home from work. In peering over the backyard fences, in other words, we are likely to be standing atop a television set or at least a bloated issue of the Sunday *New York Times*. Yet we hardly pride ourselves merely on our accessibility to information. Certainly, Orwell's Ministry of Truth drenched the populace in news. What we are particularly pleased about is that fact is our language; the information available to the public on crisis events is not only voluminous, but also, by and large, accurate.

"By and large"—there, perhaps, is the rub. Few of us expect to hear the whole truth the whole time, and this healthy skepticism is not reserved solely for matters of international political crises. On an ordinary personal level, one friend rarely expects complete accuracy from the conversation of another nor are business associates much more demanding in their relations. Some degree of inaccuracy is taken for granted, and is commonly attributed to a gap in the speaker's knowledge of events or to his mistaking fantasy for fact. Political officials, too, often lack adequate information or are seduced by appearances masquerading as reality. The very word "appearance," appropriately enough, is in some sense deceptive. "Appearance" basically is a visual term; one sees an object which either is there or, if it is an hallucination, is not there. Determining its reality rarely raises practical problems. But political decision makers are confronted by events to be interpreted, and not by tangible objects to be seen.[2] Appearance, then, is not merely a matter of diligent solitary observation, but what is far more complex, a matter of judgment and selectivity. What criteria should be used to separate the relevant facts from the great mass of irrelevant facts? What meanings can be wrung from the relevant facts? Are enough relevant facts known to permit a decision? These questions—themselves lacking in final answers—are a few of many raised by the need for distinguishing appearance from reality. The task of the political decision maker is further complicated by the fact that, of necessity, he must rely heavily upon subordinates for the actual collection of information. In a real sense, therefore, he is a prisoner of *their*

---

[2] But cf., C. D. Broad, "Some Elementary Reflexions on Sense-Perception," *Philosophy* 27 (January 1952): 4.

values and efforts, and their standards of relevance may not coincide with his own.

Plainly, the difficulties of interpreting political events may be quite substantial, given the uncertainty concerning criteria of relevance and the practical necessity of a rough division of labor between data collection and policy decision. In times of crisis, these difficulties are likely to become even more formidable, for the sense of personal and social importance may itself constitute a pressure distorting appearances. Surprise, fear, frustration, anger—these and other reactions associated with crisis situations may impair the decision maker's ability to evaluate the nature of his difficulty and the alternative means of extrication. A disturbing conclusion emerges: the enormous significance of foreign policy crisis decisions in the nuclear age suggests that these distorting pressures may become most potent precisely when their possible consequences become most calamitous. This may yet prove to be the most significant fact of contemporary political life.

Much of this study focuses on the question of how the decision maker deals with the ever-present, ever-dangerous threat of serious misperception. In crises where the pressure for immediate action is very high, probably he can do little but hope that the past has provided adequately for the present contingency—that is, that the preexisting organization has done and is continuing to do a competent job of providing him with information. The case studies of the Dominican Republic intervention and the Tet offensive illustrate this kind of phenomenon, where the felt pressure on the President to respond quickly (with military action in the former and largely with rhetoric in the latter) was great, and his dependence upon subordinates decisive.

On other occasions where time pressures are less intense, the decision maker may take some precautions against misperceptions, chiefly listening to the counsel and opinions of advisers. The Cuban missile and Bay of Pigs crises are examples. These case studies, however, underline the proposition that national crises are apt to be personal crises, too. Thus, the criteria governing selection of advisers may be designed more to meet personal than informational or perceptual problems. Advisers, in other words, tend to be chosen mainly on the basis of the psychological support the decision maker believes they can offer, rather than the expertise they can bring to the subject, though the two qualitites, of course, sometimes overlap.

Generalizing from these case studies, we may hypothesize that the decision maker's attempts at countering serious misperceptions have generally not been strikingly successful, with the notable exception of the missile crisis. Nor, as will ultimately be suggested, is there much reason to believe that future technological, organizational, or other advances can insure the solution of the appearance problem for him. For the decision maker's problem derives from the inescapable facts that he and his assistants are not impersonal automatons, but merely men. As such, they cannot excape falling prey to normal human perceptual limitations—limited time, energy, intellect, and attention; and distorting factors—psychological needs and anxieties, prior beliefs, and opinions. Questions of degree, as a practical matter, may be crucial, developments may be expected to reduce somewhat the seriousness of misperceptions; but the problems, too, may be expected to endure.

POLITICIANS AND CANDOR

Citizens lack accurate information about important political events not only because leaders are unable to divulge it, but also because they are unwilling to do so. The recent torrent of criticism of the Johnson administration for its lack of candor should not mislead us into assuming that this type of behavior is only of recent origin. American Presidents, as Walter Lippmann wrote at the start of World War II,

announce, they proclaim, they declaim, they exhort, they appeal, and they argue. But they do not unbend and tell the story, and say why they did what they did, and what they think about it, and how they feel about it. Thus the general effect is secretive and standoffish, which certainly does not warm the heart in a time of trouble.[3]

And yet more today than in the past, we take for granted an official rhetoric less a language than a code. We are deluged with the daily categorical denials and assertions and, most vexing, with the elaborately qualified replies to simple questions—all revealing such linguistic cunning or gall that words themselves seem treacherous. Our ears are so accustomed to solemn official mumbling that we rarely notice revelation crackling like a snapped carrot. And when we do notice, most of us, with more tolerance than cynicism, accept the inevitability of the lie or the half-truth. It is the fault of the "system," not of individual venality, and we take it as just another fact of political life.[4] In ordinary times, only about one American in five blames his lack of understanding of public affairs upon political leaders: Americans are far more likely to blame

---

[3] Walter Lippmann, *New York Herald Tribune*, January 29, 1942, reprinted in *The Essential Walter Lippmann*, ed. Clinton Rossiter and James Lare (New York: Vintage Books, 1965 [c. 1963]), p. 470.

[4] See Robert E. Lane, *Political Ideology: Why the American Common Man Believes What He Does* (New York: Free Press, 1962), chap. 21.

their own apathy.[5] Yet this capacity for self-criticism has limits, and may be eroded by repeated and blatant failures of government propaganda.

Public reaction to these exposés falls within two extremes. At one pole is the Cynic, to whom

> a politician is an arse upon
> which everyone has sat except a man [6]

In this view, governments always lie when it suits their purposes; hence, popular expectations of simple honesty become naive. Instead, it is far more realistic to see politics as an obscene (and occasionally entertaining) farce, resigning oneself to the fact that "a good politician," as Mencken said, "is quite as unthinkable as an honest burglar." [7]

> "Politicians lie?"
> "Of course," answers the Cynic. "What do you expect?"

At the other pole is the Idealist. A politician's public acts, he believes, must be judged by the same ideals of conventional morality one applies to his own private acts. A leader's lack of frankness with the people, then, is as worthy of contempt as an ordinary citizen's lack of frankness with a friend. The politician's sin, in fact, may even be graver, for he has misled more people. This "privatization of politics" [8] quite neglects the

---

[5] In 1960, representative national samples of the populations of the United States, Germany, Italy, Mexico, and the United Kingdom were asked: "Many people we've interviewed have said that they have trouble understanding political and governmental affairs. Which of the reasons on this list best explains why this happens?" The answers distributed themselves in this fashion:

	U.S.	Germ.	It.	Mex.	U.K.
The problems are too complex	23%	29%	32%	13%	22%
People don't care and don't try	54	47	37	33	48
Those in power don't help people to understand	20	14	14	47	26
Other	1	2	2	1	1
Don't know	2	8	15	5	1

Percentages do not always total 100 due to rounding.
Source: National Opinion Research Center Study 427, "Citizenship Survey: Public Attitudes Toward Government and Political Affairs," February 1960. (Mimeographed.)
[6] e. e. cummings, "a politician is an arse upon," *100 Selected Poems* (New York: Grove Press, 1955 [c. 1944]), p. 87.
[7] H. L. Mencken, *Prejudices, Fourth Series* (New York: Knopf, 1924), p. 130. Often this belief is part of a larger social viewpoint, according to which "no man is worthy of unlimited reliance—his treason, at best, only waits for sufficient temptation." Mencken, "The Skeptic," *The Vintage Mencken,* ed. Alistair Cooke (New York: Vintage Books, 1955 [1919]), p. 73.
[8] Nelson W. Polsby and Aaron B. Wildavsky, *Presidential Elections: Strategies of Ameri-*

politician's essentially public role, and often produces villains of comic book purity. There have always been political purists with this outlook, but of late their number has swollen as the government has forced more and more people to conclude that it is deliberately misinforming them on a scale unequalled in United States history.[9] Hence, the notoriety of the "credibility gap": the inability of the government to sustain popular belief in the veracity of its statements.

Yet as Justice Holmes observed, "The minute a phrase becomes current it becomes an apology for not thinking accurately to the end of the sentence."[10] Without uttering "credibility gap" as if it were a sacred incantation, we must ask why politicians should choose to be candid and why citizens should value that candor.

In noncrisis times, the politician has little reason to be frank. Successful election campaigns, for example, are built upon the principles of generality, vagueness, and telling the people what they want to hear.[11] And if it is true that a candidate's interest in the electoral importance of his own reputation impels him to fulfill most of his promises,[12] it is also true that candidates try to make their promises as ambiguous as possible in order to appeal to the broadest swath of the electorate.[13] Politicians pursue these tactics not because of an innate deviousness, but rather because the political quality of the electorate forces them to do so. The electorate is extremely heterogeneous, and this places a premium upon broad and fuzzy appeals. At the same time, it neither knows nor cares a great deal about politics,[14] making it unlikely that large numbers of voters would be alienated by well-camouflaged vagueness and ambiguity.

---

can Electoral Politics, 2d ed. (New York: Scribner's, 1968), pp. 180–83.

[9] For example, at a time when American forces appeared to be making consistent and significant progress in the Vietnam War, pollsters concluded that "Seventy percent [of the American people] do not believe that they have been told the full story about the war." This was reported in a periodical which plainly supported the war. "The Mood in the Country as Poll Takers Find It," *U.S. News & World Report,* December 11, 1967, p. 92. Even a number of formerly "hawkish" politicians have come around to this view, as these remarks of Senator Stuart Symington to Deputy Assistant Secretary of State William H. Sullivan concerning American activities in Laos illustrate: "We incur hundreds of thousands of U.S. casualties because we are opposed to a closed society. We say we are an open society and the enemy is a closed society. . . . [Yet] here we are telling Americans they must fight and die to maintain an open society, but not telling our people what we are doing. That would seem the characteristic of a closed society." *Washington Post,* April 21, 1970.

[10] Letter from Oliver Wendell Holmes to Harold J. Laski, July 2, 1917, *Holmes-Laski Letters: The Correspondence of Mr. Justice Holmes and Harold J. Laski,* ed. Mark DeWolfe Howe, 2 vols. (Cambridge: Harvard University Press, 1953), 1:91.

[11] Lewis A. Froman, Jr., *People and Politics: An Analysis of the American Political System* (Englewood Cliffs: Prentice-Hall, 1962), pp. 96–97.

[12] Cf., Anthony Downs, *An Economic Theory of Democracy* (New York: Harper and Row, 1957), pp. 107–9.

[13] *Ibid.,* pp. 160–62.

[14] Angus Campbell, Philip E. Converse, Warren E. Miller, and Donald E. Stokes, *The*

In crisis situations, the public's interest rises sharply, but its knowledge remains at a fairly low level. Initially, then, crises are apt to make the public even more receptive to information emanating from a legitimate government because citizens demand news, and yet are unable to evaluate it adequately. But precisely because the public *does* tend to be more interested during crises, it becomes more alert to blatant discrepancies and inconsistencies contained in the official versions, particularly if these flaws are pointed out by a critical press or by well-known and respected political figures.

The fact that the fate of individual careers, if not that of the whole nation, may be involved in crisis decisions, however, leads the policy makers to attempt to maximize their control over events. Public knowledge and opinion have obvious relevance. In the first place, the decision makers try to create or maintain a "permissive consensus," leaving them "relatively free to work out a solution of the issue...." [15] They do not want their freedom of action unnecessarily limited by public attitudes or behavior.

Second, once the decisions have been made, public support or acquiescence may be necessary for their success. This may promote a tendency on the part of officials to attempt to manipulate attentive public opinion through the public dissemination of the "proper" information. The appearance of candor, however, is a very potent asset. This was illustrated by Winston Churchill's famous speeches to the British people during the Second World War. Writing at the time, Lippmann expressed the prevailing view:

Mr. Churchill seems to be the only statesman in the world who really believes that the people can and should be enabled to understand the war. Certainly he is the only one who goes to them whenever events have taken a new turn and tell them even in broad outline what has happened and why it has happened. Surely the willingness to explain what he has been doing is, even more than his great gifts of speech, the secret of his leadership. [16]

American Voter (New York: Wiley, 1960). That public apathy is consistent with the notion of a division of labor in society, and that extreme interest "might culminate in rigid fanaticism" or severely reduce the leaders' "maneuvering room for political shifts" necessary to cope with rapidly changing times, has been argued by Bernard R. Berelson, Paul F. Lazarsfeld, and William N. McPhee, *Voting* (Chicago: University of Chicago Press, 1954), pp. 196, 314–15. That apathetics tend to be less devoted to the democratic ground rules, making their self-exclusion a blessing for the system has been advanced by Herbert McClosky, "Consensus and Ideology in American Politics," *American Political Science Review* 58 (June 1964): 382.

[15] V. O. Key, Jr., *Public Opinion and American Democracy* (New York: Knopf, 1961), p. 35.

[16] Lippmann, *loc. cit.* See Ernst Kris and Nathan Leites, "Trends in Twentieth Century Propaganda," *Psychoanalysis and the Social Sciences: An Annual* (New York: International Universities Press, 1947), 1: 405–7. For an historical survey of war censorship and

The politician's recognition of the importance of appearing candid may actually force him to be fairly candid.

Third, politicians are interested not simply in the success of their policies, but also in the success of their careers. In this regard, the significance of the public's reaction to their handling of events is clear: if the politician is an elected official, public opinion will affect his chances for reelection; if he is an appointed official, public opinion will affect his chances of remaining in office or of being appointed or elected to other positions.

On balance, the politician's incentives for candor are not overwhelming. He will choose to be candid only if the facts are congenial with his argument or are necessary to preserve or create an honest public image.

If officials [17] are ready and willing to disseminate only "proper" information, are they able to do so? Can they effectively insure that the news media will follow the government's line during time of crisis? [18] Often the answer is "yes," though the officials' effectiveness is related to the resources they possess for public persuasion, especially their resources in three overlapping areas: prestige, roles, and skills.

No official, of course, exceeds the President in prestige. This not only means that he begins with a credibility advantage—which can, of course, be dissipated by abuse—but also that the media and the public pay him much more attention than anyone else.[19] In fact, at least since the First World War, succeeding Presidents have been getting ever-larger press coverage, even if they happened to be less dynamic than their predecessors.[20] This attention may not always be in the President's interest, it is true, but if he desires to propagate a particular view, the publicity may

---

official war news, see Joseph J. Mathews, *Reporting the Wars* (Minneapolis: University of Minnesota Press, 1957), chaps. 12 and 13.

[17] "Officials" here refers mainly to the President, his aides, and others in the executive branch, although occasionally a congressman or a private citizen acting in a public capacity may be included.

[18] It would be a mistake to overstate the media's political influence on their mass audience, for a number of substantial obstacles intervene (e.g., mass apathy and ignorance, preexisting opinions and beliefs, selective perception, competition among media). Still, the media *do* constitute the mass public's main source of information on contemporary political events. The emphasis in this study will be placed on the written media, not because the electronic media are insignificant but merely because of the presently insuperable practical problems concerning the availability of their work for analysis.

[19] For a history of Presidents' relations with the press through 1946, see James E. Pollard, *The Presidents and the Press* (New York: Macmillan, 1947).

[20] Elmer E. Cornwell, "Presidential News: The Expanding Public Image," *Journalism Quarterly* 36 (Summer 1959): 275-85. This supports the argument of a veteran British observer of American politics to the effect that the United States' politics is dominated by a "King-President." Louis Heren, *The New American Commonwealth* (New York: Harper and Row, 1968). Heren's view was easier to maintain before the election of President Nixon.

constitute a decisive edge; for he can be much more certain that his opinions will be reported by the media and noticed by the public than can any other figure. Today, especially with regard to television and radio, "the President has absolute control over the timing, format, and content of his presentation," and has been exploiting these advantages with increasing frequency. President Eisenhower, the first of the television age Presidents, lacked experience with the medium, but still made forty-nine live television appearances while in office. While he concentrated mainly on defending important and controversial decisions, his successor, President Kennedy, used it in order to publicize his "star" qualities, too, through such techniques as the live telecasting of numerous virtuoso press conference performances. President Johnson, though plainly far less effective, made almost one hundred appearances on live television during his tenure of five years and two months, and President Nixon may well surpass Johnson's appearance rate of roughly three telecasts every two months. Theodore Roosevelt spoke truer than he knew, when he termed the presidency a "bully pulpit." [21]

The President's aides may share a bit of the luster of his prestige, and others in the executive branch may rank high as well.[22] This usually is not due to any of their personal characteristics or accomplishments—most of the men are unknown to the public, and many of their statements are attributed to anonymous "informed sources" or "high officials," anyway—but instead to the fact that they speak for "the government."

"The average citizen," as a House subcommittee concluded:

assumes his Federal Government to be objective, impartial, and fair in its information services. He ordinarily accepts as authoritative that information which comes from government through official channels. Whereas the individual might reject propaganda coming to him from other sources, he is more likely to be receptive when it is offered in the guise of "information" which comes through official channels.[23]

As is customary, Congress has overstated the case somewhat. But, even granting this, one must concede that speaking in the name of "the government" imparts to officials an aura of disinterested, nonpartisan exper-

---

[21] Brief of Joseph Califano for the Democratic National Committee before the Federal Communications Commission, In the Matter of Obligations of Broadcast Licensees under the Fairness Doctrine—Docket No. 18859.

[22] M. Kent Jennings, Milton C. Cummings, Jr., and Franklin P. Kilpatrick, "Trusted Leaders: Perceptions of Appointed Federal Officials," *Public Opinion Quarterly* 30 (Fall 1966): 388; Kilpatrick, Cummings, and Jennings, *The Image of the Federal Service* (Washington: Brookings Institution, 1964).

[23] U. S., Congress, House, Committee on Expenditures in the Executive Department, *Twenty-third Intermediate Report*, 80th Cong., 2d Sess., 1948, H. Rept. 2474, p. 7.

tise which far better known congressmen or private citizens can only
envy.

The President's role in foreign affairs further reinforces his public persuasion advantage of prestige, for as one senator has acknowledged, "No
one denies that he is the initiator and the chief architect in this area." [24]
The public, in particular, wants and expects presidential leadership, and
is willing to give the President and his aides considerable latitude for action [25]—even to the extent that criticism sometimes is interpreted as obstructionist or, in extreme cases, actually unpatriotic.

Certain officials, too, in their roles as guardians of national security,
occupy advantageous influence positions. Occasionally, the influence
may take a crude form. At times, suggests a Pentagon reporter, officials
may try to silence other bureaucrats—perhaps by bugging offices, mon-
itoring interviews, threatening the use of lie detector tests, or talking of
possible job transfers. Officials have been known to invoke "national security" in an effort to suppress so unhazardous a story as one dealing
with proposed military pay raises.[26] Recently, two government agents
were even infiltrated into the Saigon press corps, apparently in an effort
"to uncover newsmen's sources of information." [27] And during South
Vietnam's February 1971, invasion of Laos, military authorities imposed
an "embargo" on news of the action, and an embargo on the fact that
there was an embargo. When asked whether this embargo on an embargo was also embargoed, a Pentagon spokesman replied straight-
facedly, "Yes it is."

By and large, however, officials avoid such meat-cleaver techniques,
and their relations with the press cannot be described in such sinister
terms. In fact, generally, there is not even much deep antagonism between the two,[28] for they seem to hold surprisingly similar views of the
obligations entailed by responsible journalism. Dan Nimmo's study of

---

[24] Frank Church, *Congressional Record,* 91st Cong., 1st Sess., June 20, 1969, p. S6884.
(Daily ed.)
[25] Roberta S. Sigel, "Image of the American Presidency—Part II of an Exploration into
Popular Views of Presidential Power," *Midwest Journal of Political Science* 10 (February
1966): 123.
[26] Richard Fryklund, "Covering the Defense Establishment," *The Press in Washington,*
ed. Ray Eldon Hibert (New York: Dodd, Mead, 1966), pp. 167–73, 168. Fryklund is the
Pentagon reporter for the *Washington Evening Star.* Though generally speaking, Presidents
tend to delegate the task of pressuring the press to subordinates, personal presidential intervention is by no means unknown. A Pulitzer Prize-winning *New York Times* reporter, for
example, has described an incident in which President Kennedy tried to persuade the
newspaper's publisher to transfer the correspondent from his Vietnam assignment because
his pessimistic dispatches constituted an embarrassment to the administration. David Halberstam, "Getting the Story in Vietnam," *Commentary,* January 1965, pp. 33–34.
[27] *New York Times,* January 29, 1970.
[28] Dan Nimmo, *Newsgathering in Washington: A Study of Political Communication* (New
York: Atherton Press, 1964), p. 211.

newsgathering in Washington makes this quite clear, particularly his survey of public information officers and newsmen on the question of the government's obligation to inform the public of activities.

TABLE 1

COMPARISON OF ATTITUDES OF INFORMATION
OFFICERS AND NEWSMEN TOWARD THE
OBLIGATION OF GOVERNMENTAL OFFICIALS
TO INFORM CITIZENS OF ACTIVITIES

Attitude	*PIO's* (N = 38)	*Newsmen* (N = 35)
Obligation to inform is complete (newsman retains right to decide what to print)	44%	36%
Obligation to inform is limited by necessities of decision making, national security, etc.	53	64
Obligation to inform is at official's discretion in all matters	3	—

If anything, newsmen appear to take a narrower view of their obligation to inform than do the very officials often vilified for "news management." Reporters seem to feel that media "watchdog" activity ought generally to be confined to matters less important than national crises, at which time the citizen role is apparently more salient than that of the newsman.[29] The press, in the words of one distinguished journalist, "has simply, out of a sense of patriotism, or 'responsibility,' silenced itself and supported the powers that be." [30] Sharing essentially the same views of national security and citizen obligations during time of calm, newsmen and officials can be expected to move even closer together under the pressure of crisis. Further fortifying the passivity of the press are its pre-

---

[29] By 1971, however, there were clear signs that years of official misstatements had taken their toll, leaving significant portions of the press corps far more restive than before. See William O. Chittick, "American Foreign Policy Elites: Attitudes toward Secrecy and Publicity," *Journalism Quarterly* 47 (Winter 1970): 689.

[30] Alan Barth, "Freedom and the Press," *Progressive*, June 1962, p. 32. Barth is an editorial writer for the *Washington Post.* James Reston of the *New York Times* agrees that "we have a very patriotic and even chauvinistic press on the whole. . . . The newspapers didn't help the country much, in my view, by taking a 'my country right or wrong' attitude when Presidents Kennedy and Johnson began slipping into the war in Vietnam. It is difficult to see how we can get a clear picture of the world as it is if we see it from our own side, like a football game, and do not challenge the national assumptions that we can do almost anything anywhere in the world." James Reston, *The Artillery of the Press: Its Influence on Foreign Relations* (New York: Harper and Row for the Council on Foreign Relations, 1967), p. 94. The charge that the press has not met its democratic obligations, due to insufficient diligence in the pursuit of news, has been voiced for years. See, e.g., Silas Bent, *Ballyhoo* (New York: Boni and Liveright, 1927), chap. 10, pp. 371–79; John Dewey, "Our Un-free Press," *Common Sense*, November 1935, pp. 6–7.

tentions to "objectivity," which most often take the form of uncritical repetitions of official versions of events.

Some members of the press, of course, do not fit this pattern. Partly, this may be due to the kind of audience they write for. If, like a number of columnists, they write with a reasonably sophisticated reader in mind, they may be more adventuresome in their speculation than an ordinary reporter. Or if their readership, while not sophisticated, is well-disposed to an attack on the administration, the writer may be emboldened. More probably, the writer's criticism reflects an orientation not toward his audience, but rather toward his publisher.[31] But in any case, critical newsmen rarely can penetrate the verbal effluvia surrounding the official version of the episode until quite some time has passed, and by then the mass public has lost interest as have even some portions of the attentive public. Furthermore, television—the mass public's most trusted source for news—is so oriented toward topicality that the tardy exposé may receive little or no coverage.

Typically, crises are unexpected, and characterized by very fast-moving events. Thus, even potentially critical reporters are likely to be unprepared for crises when they break out, and dependent largely on government for a working hypothesis to explain events until the later critical investigation can be undertaken. Moreover, in time of emergency, the

[31] Warren Breed, "Social Control in the Newsroom: A Functional Analysis," *Social Forces* 33 (May 1955): 326–27; Lewis Donohew, "Newspapers, Gatekeepers, and Forces in the News Channels," *Public Opinion Quarterly* 31 (Spring 1967): 68. But cf., William L. Rivers, "The Correspondents after 25 Years," *Columbia Journalism Review,* January 1962, p. 5. If the writer is not sufficiently attuned to his publisher's viewpoint, editors may attempt to impose the "proper" interpretation by rewriting the articles. For an example of a periodical's home office editing field dispatches in order to bring them into conformance with the magazine's position, see Halberstam's description of the schism within *Time* over its handling of Vietnam news in 1963. Halberstam, *op. cit.,* p. 34. With regard to the reporter's obligations in such a situation, the dean of the University of Illinois School of Journalism has commented: "On his [the reporter's] everyday assignments, he cannot dislodge an ethical decision on the grounds that the boss, not he, edits the paper; for that is a little as if Polly Adler's piano player should say that what goes on in the other rooms of the establishment doesn't concern him, that his dedication is to Bach." Theodore Peterson, "Social Responsibility—Theory and Practice," *Responsibilities of the Press,* ed. Gerald Gross (New York: Fleet, 1966), p. 49. Regarding the reporter's situation in television, Herbert Gans writes, "Network management remains aloof—at least as long as the ratings do not slip precipitously. Executive producers, however, like magazine and newspaper editors, also know what stories will displease management: principally those detrimental to the firm's business interests." Herbert J. Gans, "How Well *Does* TV Present the News?" *New York Times Magazine,* January 11, 1970, p. 38. Gans believes that selectivity in television news presentation is governed by media considerations (i.e., bias in favor of stories that can be filmed), professional judgments (i.e., bias in favor of stories of importance, topicality, interest, and drama), professional and personal values (i.e., bias in favor of "objective" treatment—political opinion biases generally are felt to be unimportant except to the extent that they reinforce dominant middle-class cultural values), and audience reaction (i.e., bias in favor of simply told stories that are unusual and dramatic). *Ibid.,* pp. 31–35. Outright censorship, Gans adds, "is usually limited to matters of 'taste.'" *Ibid.,* pp. 38–40.

pressure on informal governmental information sources to remain silent is apt to be much greater than normal, and may relax only after the urgency—and the public's interest—has faded. The confusion endemic to crisis reporting has been well described by a *New York Times* reporter, who covered the Dominican Republic intervention in 1965.

Snipers with rifles . . . are not the only danger in Santo Domingo. The propaganda-sniping from the military junta, from the rebels, and from the American Embassy is just as bad. It was impossible, much of the time, to check out what the embassy was telling us at briefings or what the rebels claimed at interviews or by telephone, and the job of accurate reporting became desperately difficult. Military briefings added to the confusion as the spokesmen frequently were unable to answer even the most elementary questions.[32]

If officials' roles as guardians of the national interest constitute a valuable resource in their efforts at public persuasion, another advantage lies in the executive branch's elaborately developed public relations skills, institutionalized over time and now largely in the hands of capable professional public information officers. Thirty years ago, an authority on government publicity noted:

The government publicist . . . is essential to even the minimum adequate coverage of events in Washington. The glut of occurrences each day in the vast and chaotic web of federal administration simply could not be followed by newspaper staffs unless they were enlarged by many times their present size.[33]

Intervening decades have served only to underscore the indispensability of the news release, the background briefing, and the press conference. When a Pentagon reporter writes of "handouts sift[ing] down onto our desks like snowflakes all day long," and his State Department counterpart speaks of their "vast number," [34] these correspondents are hinting, if only obliquely, at the symbiotic nature of the press-government relationship. For not only does the government need press collaboration for successful public persuasion, but the press needs government to provide much of the media's information.[35] Especially important in this regard

[32] Tad Szulc, "Dominican War Keeps Times Troops Hopping," *The Working Press: Special to the New York Times*, ed. Ruth Adler (New York: Putnam's, n.d. [1965]), p. 129.

[33] James L. McCamy, *Government Publicity: Its Practice in Federal Administration* (Chicago: University of Chicago Press, 1939), pp. 18–19.

[34] Fryklund, *op. cit.*, p. 177. Marvin Kalb, "Covering the State Department," *Ibid.*, p. 158. Herbert Klein, President Nixon's Communications Director, presumably noting the damage done to Johnson by the Washington press corps, devised a public information strategy stressing the briefing of the much less dangerous regional television executives and newspaper editors. *New York Times*, August 24, 1970.

[35] One veteran Washington correspondent and Pulitzer Prize winner has argued that

are the government's publicists, who answer reporters' questions, set up or themselves hold news conferences, and arrange interviews.[36] As one analyst has observed, wryly:

In a society in which a ladies' garden club, a church youth group, or an amateur choir will have a publicity committee, it is not strange that the great preponderance of news is deliberately released and the press has become more and more a handler of handouts.[37]

Public information officers, writes Nimmo, play three basic roles: the informer, aiding the newsman and expediting the flow of information; the educator, trying to create an atmosphere of understanding among the general public; and the promoter, attempting to develop a favorable public image for the agency, official, or policy.[38] In time of crisis, the promoter role dominates, as news becomes, in the words of a former Defense Department public relations chief, "part of . . . weaponry." [39] The public information officer and his staff, in addressing the public through

---

broadcast journalists are especially dependent upon government, particularly regarding their dealings with the Pentagon. "Broadcast journalism requires special access to the Defense Secretary, other high Defense officials, and White House personnel. Certainly everyone can cover the regular press conferences, but it is a coup to arrange one of those 'special' interviews on an exclusive basis. Such 'specials' go to a favorite network or even a favorite newsman, usually the apologists. Specials seldom are arranged for men who question the honesty, integrity or judgment of high officials of The Defense Department." This has "tended to keep the network newsmen and commentators from challenging The Defense Department bosses or the White House." Clark R. Mollenhoff, "Press Failure at the Pentagon," *Bulletin of the American Society of Newspaper Editors,* reprinted in U.S., *Congressional Record,* 91st Cong., 1st Sess., July 15, 1969, p. E5916. (Daily ed.) Ironically, Mollenhoff later became an official within the Nixon administration, dealing with its press relations. As such, he had to maintain that broadcasters and the press generally have been insufficiently attentive to the administration's point of view. A leading newscaster agrees with Mollenhoff's earlier assessment. "Television news requires more cooperation from its subjects than any other reporting medium," writes Walter Cronkite. "In other types of journalism, it is possible to compile a rather round report without the cooperation of the central individual." Cronkite, "Television and the News," in *The Eighth Art* (New York: Holt, Rinehart, and Winston, 1962), p. 236.

[36] Nimmo, *op. cit.,* chap. 6. Nimmo is careful to note that the publicist does not take complete and sole responsibility for performing these services.

[37] James L. McCamy, *The Administration of American Foreign Affairs* (New York: Knopf, 1950), p. 322.

[38] Nimmo *op. cit.,* pp. 54–55.

[39] Assistant Secretary of Defense for Public Affairs Arthur Sylvester, *New York Times,* October 31, 1962. Sylvester was referring to his attitude during the Cuban missile crisis. In a more general context, Sylvester later argued that "today in the cold war . . . determination of releasing, withholding [information concerning national security] . . . has to be geared into what the man who goes before the people every four years to submit his stewardship, no matter who he may be, must be in line with what he and his top advisers are doing." Quoted in Ted Lewis, *Boston Sunday Herald,* February 3, 1963. That, as a result of this withheld information, the electorate might lack an adequate basis for judging the President's "stewardship" was a prospect Sylvester did not consider.

the media, try to direct their attention to some information, while deemphasizing or withholding other portions of the news.[40] So potent are the government's resources and so favorable is the foreign affairs-national defense setting that

[t]here is real reason for concern as to whether this system of countervailing power operates with anything like the same effectiveness in the field of foreign policy and national defense—area where official doctrine carries impressive weight and where official error may bring awesome catastrophe.[41]

These words appear even more ominous, when one notices that they were written before the tremendous impetus given governmental public relations by the Kennedy administration, and before the great crises of the last decade.[42] But even earlier, of course, Orwell had devised "Newspeak" and "Doublethink," modeling them not after Nazi or Soviet propaganda but instead the gray product of the BBC.

A good deal of this study is concerned with the decision maker's activities in relation to the mass and attentive publics. Efforts to create a permissive consensus once the decision has begun to be implemented are il-

---

[40] Well aware of the profound influence of language upon thought, government publicists and their opponents often concentrate much of their efforts on telling key words or phrases to the public. Advocates of reduced defense spending, for example, spoke repeatedly of "cost overruns," a term which soon took on connotations of waste, excessive industry profits, and inadequate government management and fiscal control. Deputy Defense Secretary David Packard countered by ordering the Defense Department to drop the use of "cost overrun," and replace it with the more "workable" phrase, "cost growth." Similarly, the *New York Times* reported that the United States Command in Vietnam directed military press officers to ban "search and destroy" in favor of "search and clear," "mercenary" in favor of "Civilian-Irregular Defense Group soldier" or "volunteer," "Vietcong deserter/defector" in favor of "rallier or returnee," "Hamburger Hill" in favor of "Hill 937," etc. *New York Times,* January 11, 1970. At about the same time, the U.S. Command denied that unfavorable news reports were censored by the Armed Forces Vietnam Network. What was practiced, officials said, was not censorship, but rather "editorial selection" based on "prudent exercise of judgment." *Des Moines Register,* January 29, 1970. Linguistic manipulation is also illustrated in the currently popular terms "Vietnamization," "pacification," and "reconstruction"—all "words that Aldous Huxley or George Orwell would have relished." Robert Shaplen, "Letter from Saigon," *New Yorker,* January 31, 1970, p. 47.

[41] Francis E. Rourke, *Secrecy and Publicity: Dilemmas of Democracy* (Baltimore: Johns Hopkins Press, 1961), p. 207. Rourke, a restrained and sober analyst, voices this ominous judgment soon after deemphasizing the importance of internal propaganda in ordinary domestic affairs.

[42] Senator Stephen Young of Ohio has reported, for example, that Defense Department expenditures on public information and public relations rose over 1,500 percent from fiscal 1959 to fiscal 1969 (i.e., from $2,755,000 to $44,062,000), U.S., *Congressional Record,* 91st Cong., 2nd Sess., August 21, 1970, p. S13912. (Daily ed.) Additionally, of course, Defense Department public relations expenditures constitute only a portion of the government's total efforts in the area of propagandizing on behalf of its foreign policy. The President and the State Department are active, too, as is the Central Intelligence Agency, which on several occasions has actually sought to hide the government origin of its propaganda.

lustrated by these studies of the Dominican Republic intervention, the Gulf of Tonkin attacks, and the Cuban missile crisis. The Bay of Pigs invasion provides an example of an attempt to reinforce the prevailing and "proper" opinion before the key decision was acted on. As for the Tet offensive, inter propaganda itself constituted the government's main nonmilitary response to the crisis, at least in the short run.

These efforts varied considerably in their effectiveness. The missile crisis saw the most successful venture in opinion shaping, as both mass and attentive publics were joined in an enduring permissive consensus. The Tonkin Gulf attacks at first saw an impressive permissive consensus, but gradually a portion of the attentive public became increasingly critical, and eventually a congressional exposé destroyed the value of the propaganda. The Dominican Republic intervention, while being opposed from the outset by a segment of the attentive public, was accompanied by mass support which, presumably, has lasted to the present. With the Bay of Pigs invasion, a permissive consensus developed on behalf of excising the Castro regime from the hemisphere; but the obvious and disastrous failure of the means employed to that end won no backing. Finally, the Tet offensive illustrates a propaganda campaign whose failure among the attentive public—and among portions of the mass public as well—was indisputable. Media reports from the scene diverged too far from evaluations from Washington.

The decision maker's informational relations with the public, however, are not directed solely at publicity, for officials may sometimes see greater advantage in concealment than exposure. Information, as in the case of the missile crisis, may be kept from public view mainly for tactical reasons. But as Weber pointed out in his classic discussion of bureaucracy, secrecy may also be sought for the personal benefit of those in positions of authority.[43] The case studies suggest that actions from this motive may not be unusual. Hidden facts, for example, helped to camouflage the ill-prepared nature of American officialdom in the Dominican Republic, in addition to providing a basis for more persuasive public arguments in favor of intervention. During and after the Tet offensive, too, information was suppressed, apparently so as not to make the relevant governmental structures seem poorly informed and outmaneuvered.

Bureaucrats may seek secrecy, however, not merely from personal interests, but out of policy convictions. Data surrounding the Tonkin Gulf attacks, for instance, seem to have been kept from public and congressional view at least partly because decision makers believed exposure

---

[43] Max Weber, "Bureaucracy," *From Max Weber: Essays in Sociology,* trans. and ed. H. H. Gerth and C. Wright Mills (New York: Oxford University Press, 1958), p. 233.

would jeopardize a policy decision to prop up the South Vietnamese government with greater American military activity after the coming elections. The Bay of Pigs invasion was characterized more by a mixed policy-personal secrecy rationale than the other crises studied: tactically, secrecy seemed necessary for a successful invasion; moreover, key officials were able to use the tactical claims for secrecy to shield the plan from potential opponents who might threaten the policy decision.

The case studies indicate that secrecy efforts, like publicity efforts, may meet varying degrees of success. The missile crisis was most successful, and the Bay of Pigs and Tet offensive least. The enemy was kept completely in the dark as to the American response to the missiles in Cuba; but invasion preparations were almost common knowledge months before the Bay of Pigs landing, and official attempts to hush up the extent of the Tet setback were notably ineffective. Suppression of information relating to the Tonkin Gulf Resolution produced an effective policy instrument in the short run, though a congressional exposé ultimately destroyed its utility. The hiding of facts concerning actual events during the Dominican revolt and American reasons for intervention, while met with skepticism and hostility by portions of the attentive public, has remained quite successful for the mass.

CITIZENS AND CANDOR

Now to ask why nonpoliticians should value candor so highly. Such a view, of course, has not always prevailed. Twenty-three centuries ago, Plato defended the philosopher kings' duty to deceive their subjects, and a number of renowned political philosophers, including Machiavelli, Rousseau, and Hegel, have since elaborated upon this theme. More recently, a former Assistant Secretary of Defense for Public Affairs has asserted that crises bestow upon governments the "right to lie." [44] In fairness, none of these writers suggests that official lying itself is a positive good. They contend merely that deception sometimes is a permissible means to certain ends. On this point, perhaps, even political purists must agree: to maintain that a government ought always to be candid for its own sake is to indulge in a myopic, quixotic, and possibly disastrous kind of pedantry.

The critical question becomes, then, what are the circumstances that justify deliberate departures from the truth? The most obvious answer is the "national interest," [45] but, historically, such a vague, patriotic ratio-

---

[44] Arthur Sylvester, "Speaking Out," *Saturday Evening Post*, November 18, 1967, p. 10. Sylvester served in the Kennedy administration.

[45] As President Kennedy put it when talking to a group of newspaper publishers after the

nale has had a way of serving very personal and narrow interests. As Arnold Wolfers has pointed out:

> To say that something is in the interest of the state is like saying that a good roof is in the interest of the house, when what one really means is that a good roof is considered vital by the house's inhabitants. . . .[46]

With the "national interest" thus a matter of subjective definition, it is difficult for leaders even with the best of intentions to disentangle their own advantage from that of their country. Plainly, a clearer and more objective criterion would be desirable; yet probably it is impossible to develop or enforce a satisfactory standard to justify official deception.

Those giving the benefit of the doubt to the government tend to argue that the mass of the people simply know too little about politics to profit much from official frankness. Thus, after examining the polls, a political scientist concluded in 1949 that only a quarter of the electorate "consistently shows knowledge of foreign problems."[47] Today, after nearly two decades of the Cold War and the amazing development of the mass media, the problem of ignorance persists like a winter cold. A study by the University of Michigan's Survey Research Center conducted in the summer of the presidential election year of 1964, for example, disclosed that twenty-eight percent of the adult population was unaware of a Communist government in China, over half had not heard of Nationalist China, and, most disturbing, a fourth did not know of any fighting in Vietnam.[48] A March 1966, National Opinion Research Center nationwide survey revealed that only "68% knew we were bombing targets in the North at the time of the survey, 47% could name the capital of South Vietnam, and 41% could name the capital of North Vietnam."[49] None of

abortive Bay of Pigs invasion, "Every newspaper now asks itself, with respect to every story, 'Is it news?' All I suggest is that you add the question, 'Is it in the national interest?' " *New York Times,* April 28, 1961.

[46] Arnold Wolfers, "The Actors in International Politics," *Theoretical Aspects of International Relations,* ed. William T. R. Fox (Notre Dame: University of Notre Dame Press, 1959), p. 86. Cf., the famous "goal displacement" theory of Robert Michels in his classic *Political Parties* (Glencoe: Free Press, 1949 [1915]).

[47] Martin Kriesberg, "Dark Areas of Ignorance," *Public Opinion and Foreign Policy,* ed. Lester Markel (New York: Harper and Bros. for the Council on Foreign Relations, 1949), p. 51. Nor did the ignorance problem lend itself to obvious solutions. A six-month information campaign of very high intensity aimed at informing Greater Cincinnati adults of the United Nations, for example, produced very meager results. Shirley A. Star and Helen MacGill Hughes, "Report on an Educational Campaign: The Cincinnati Plan for the United Nations," *American Journal of Sociology* 55 (January 1950): 389.

[48] A. T. Steele, *The American People and China* (New York: McGraw-Hill for the Council on Foreign Relations, 1966), pp. 257, 262, 294.

[49] Sidney Verba *et al.,* "Public Opinion and the War in Vietnam," *American Political Science Review* 61 (June 1967): 319 n. 9. The authors concluded that these meager results con-

these examples of ignorance can be blamed upon government. In fact, they suggest that the passage of forty-five years has not yet overturned an American diplomat's judgment that "the problem of the modern foreign minister, seeking legislative and popular support, is often how to get the people to absorb more information rather than to keep information from them." [50]

Ignorance of this magnitude—in the face of enormous governmental and private efforts to inform the public—is sobering, indeed. And the realization becomes even more disheartening when one notes that much of the knowledge that the public does possess is out of date due to the slowness of its learning and absorption processes. In the quicksilver world of international politics, this time lag means that the public often is concerned about situations which have ceased to exist or have at least been significantly altered. Information, once accurate, becomes obsolete, and consequently, erroneous. And the results of public misinformation may be even more deleterious than those of no information at all.

Yet it is not only the public's ignorance that mocks its demands for official candor. In addition, it is argued, most Americans are too emotional and irrational to be able to analyze properly the remote and abstract international situation. As one exponent of *Realpolitik* put it, "The kind of thinking required for the successful conduct of foreign policy must at times be diametrically opposed to the kind of consideration by which the masses and their representatives are likely to be moved." [51] Popular beliefs about foreign affairs tend to reflect not factual knowledge, but merely moods fluctuating from one emotional pole to another.[52] Mundane policy justifications of expediency attract few followers, as warlike

---

stituted "relatively high levels of information on the issue" (p. 319), implying that information levels on other foreign policy issues are even lower.

   That public ignorance can lead to odd and inconsistent opinion patterns has long been recognized. A recent illustration is provided by a Gallup poll taken the day after President Nixon's televised announcement that American troops had entered Cambodia. They would remain there only a short time, the President emphasized, and represented an effort not to widen the war but to shorten it. Of the ninety-five percent of Gallup's sample who said they had heard or read about the fighting in Cambodia, fifty-eight percent opposed sending troops there and fifty-five percent felt that the United States would be unable "to avoid a major involvement of our troops in Cambodia." Nonetheless, fifty-one percent said that they *approved* "of the way President Nixon is handling the Cambodia situation." *Washington Post*, May 5, 1970.

   [50] DeWitt C. Poole, *The Conduct of Foreign Relations under Modern Democratic Conditions* (New Haven: Yale University Press, 1924), p. 156.

   [51] Hans J. Morgenthau, *In Defense of the National Interest* (New York: Knopf, 1951), p. 223.

   [52] Almond, *op. cit.*, pp. 53–68. But cf., William R. Caspary, "The 'Mood Theory': A Study of Public Opinion and Foreign Policy," *American Political Science Review* 64 (June 1970): 536. Caspary, by arguing that "American public opinion is characterized by a *strong* and *stable* 'permissive mood' toward international involvements" (p. 546), leads the reader to the inference that the traditional debate between advocates of popular control and elite

sentiment approaches the zeal of "crusades" and the desire for peace isolationism.[53] The emotional momentum thus created, it is said, cripples the development of a pragmatic foreign policy, sensitive to change and flexible as to means.

To the advocates of greater official candor, these arguments are simply those of the snob, indulging himself in sentimental reveries over a romanticized past. Louis J. Halle, for instance, laments the

decline in the standards of international conduct which is the price that has been paid for the shift of political power from a cosmopolitan elite to the nationalistic and often xenophobic masses of people. It is dangerous because it impairs the civility on which human relations must depend, and also because the verbal excesses to which it leads may go to a point at which there is no longer any possibility of avoiding their implementation by deeds.[54]

The tone is that of an aged member of a formerly exclusive men's club remembering the good old days before the *nouveau riche* were admitted. Xenophobic masses are recalled, but not xenophobic leaders; cosmopolitan elites are recalled, but not parochial ones; civility among policy makers is recalled, but not the deceit or cowardice it frequently masked. This is a very selective reading of history, ancient or modern.

In the century of Freud, moreover, it is a bit late to speak simplistically of "rational" leaders and "irrational" people. Officials, of course, have greater expertise, but this hardly immunizes them to the subtle and myriad unconscious needs and anxieties to which all men are prone.

Moreover, if most of the public is indifferent and ignorant,[55] a significant minority—the "attentive public—is not. And these individuals, who know and care a good deal more about foreign affairs than their fellow

control over foreign policy may be a disagreement in search of a problem; for the overwhelming majority of the people favor elite control.

[53] Yet while problems of the Vietnamese war seem to have contributed to a significant growth in isolationist sentiment, it would hardly be accurate to view this movement as a great opinion "fluctuation." The Gallup poll, for example, asked representative national samples of the adult population: "Would it be better for the United States to keep independent in world affairs—or would it be better for the United States to work closely with other nations?"

	Keep Independent	Work Closely	No Opinion
1969	22%	72%	6%
1967 (Pre-Tet offensive)	16	79	5
1963 (Pre-escalation)	10	82	8

Source: *New York Times*, February 23, 1969.

[54] Louis J. Halle, *Dream and Reality: Aspects of American Foreign Policy* (New York: Harper and Bros., 1959), p. 155.

[55] One writer has gone so far as to say, "The people's right to obtain information does not, of course, depend on any assured ability to understand its significance or use it wisely.

citizens, are likely to have a disproportionate influence upon foreign policy, partly by dint of the very intensity of their opinions.

Although authorities may disagree as to where to draw the line demarcating justifiable deception, they are at least united on this: that a democracy should be as little encumbered with misinformation as possible. If the essence of democracy is the people's power to select its leaders through regular, competitive free elections,[56] the voters' decisions probably will be more in accord with their perceived self-interest if their information is accurate. The candor of the government, of course, will significantly affect the quality and quantity of their political knowledge. Furthermore, a widespread belief that the government is being unnecessarily deceptive may reduce public confidence in its leaders and institutions. In this way, the entire legitimacy of the system may be called into question for large numbers of people. Democracies are particularly vulnerable to the destabilizing effects of a crisis in legitimacy because they rely less on coercion and more on voluntary compliance and confidence than do other forms of government.[57] As the *New York Times* editorialized:

> A democracy . . . our democracy . . . cannot be lied to. This is one of the factors that makes it more precious, more delicate, more difficult, and yet essentially stronger than any other form of government in the world. The basic principle involved is that of confidence. A dictatorship can get along without an informed public opinion. A democracy cannot. Not only is it unethical to deceive one's public as part of a system of deceiving an adversary government; it is also foolish. Our executive officials and our national legislature are elected on stated days, but actually they must be re-elected day by day by popular understanding and support. This is what is signified by a government by consent.[58]

Ordinary citizens in democracies, in short, should value candor because it helps to make voting more rational and the democratic system itself more stable.

And yet—and here is the problem—in certain crises candor may prove disastrous by foredooming the proper formulation and execution of policies. Governments cannot tell their own people the truth without also sharing it with their enemies, and ignorance or uncertainty among one's

---

Facts belong to the people simply because they relate to interests that are theirs, government that is theirs, and votes that they may desire to cast, for they are entitled to an active role in shaping every fundamental decision of state." Edmond Cahn, *The Predicament of Democratic Man* (New York: Delta, 1962 [c. 1961]), p. 180.

[56] See Joseph A. Schumpeter, *Capitalism, Socialism and Democracy*, 3d ed. (New York: Harper and Bros., 1950), chap. 22, esp. p. 269.

[57] Cf., Seymour Martin Lipset, *Political Man: The Social Bases of Politics* (Garden City: Doubleday, 1960), chap. 3.

[58] Editorial, *New York Times*, May 10, 1961.

foes may be of decisive tactical value. Moreover, since public opinion itself is an element of national power, when governments inform their
people of unpleasant truths, they may lower morale or promote divisive-
ness, and thereby weaken the national capacity to overcome the immediate challenge. Plainly, though candor is generally valuable, frankness is
not government's first obligation nor political education its primary task.

If crises are viewed by the decision maker as giving him license to lie,
it becomes important to be able to identify them—which is to ask: what
are the characteristics of a "crisis"? Basic to this book's approach to this
question is the position that what makes an event a "crisis" is that decision makers, not *post hoc* analysts, perceive it as such. The event, of
course, may be falsely perceived, in which case the danger it poses may
be seriously exaggerated or neglected, but the starting point of this study
is an acceptance of crisis as decision maker defined. How, then *do* decision makers define crisis? Different experts, naturally, offer different answers. Anthony Wiener and Herman Kahn, for example, emphasize the
decision makers' perception of a "crisis" as a situation which is both
turning point and threat,[59] while Charles Hermann writes of decision
makers' perceptions of "high threat" to "high priority goals," short decision time, and surprise or "the absence of awareness on the part of policy
makers that the situation is likely to occur." [60]

The book stresses the significance of decison makers' perceptions of
high threat to high priority goals and short decision time.[61] These "high
priority goals," however, as the case studies will suggest, may be the en-
hancement and maintenance of certain desirable appearances, namely
the national and presidential images or self-images of strength, competence, and resolve. With "crisis" so subjective a concept, so much a
creation of the decision makers themselves, the requirement that one exist before official deception can be justified can hardly operate as an effective limitation on presidential discretion.[62]

---

[59] They enumerate ten other criteria for determining the existence of crises. Anthony J.
Wiener and Herman Kahn, *Crises and Arms Control* (Hudson Institute, 1962), pp. 8–11.

[60] Charles F. Hermann, *Crises in Foreign Policy: A Simulation Analysis* (Indianapolis:
Bobbs-Merrill, 1969), pp. 30–31. For a helpful review of the literature on the concept of
"crisis," see pp. 21–35. The question of how "high" the threat or the goals' priority must be,
remains, of course, elusive.

[61] The element of surprise is present in most crises (such as the Missile Crisis, Dominican
Republic intervention, and Tet offensive), but is not itself a necessary attribute. A sense of
being "trapped," of being "compelled" by earlier decisions and events to choose a dangerous path may be an adequate substitute for the unexpected (as the Bay of Pigs affair illustrates).

[62] It is important to realize that the large element of subjectivity in a crisis definition does
not necessarily imply that Presidents cynically term a nonthreatening situation a "crisis"
because it may be to their advantage to do so. This seems to have occurred with respect to
the Gulf of Tonkin crisis discussed in chapter 4, but more often Presidents are quite sincere
in labeling a threat to their own or their nation's image a threat to substantive national in-

SUMMARY

At the outset, the decision makers' obstacles to perceiving reality were discussed, including their dependence upon subordinates for data collection, their vulnerability to psychological pressures arising from crisis situations, their normal processes of selective attention and perception, and their proclivity for choosing advisers mainly on the basis of their capacity to supply support and security in time of stress. Next, the citizens' obstacles to perceiving reality were treated. Among these were the decision makers' misperceptions which may doom honest efforts at public education, and the decision makers' frequent desire to purvey inaccurate appearances as reality for self-defined personal, partisan, or national interests. The mass media—often thought of as the mass public's "watchdog" concerning such government actions—are generally ineffective in this role, due to their emphasis on objectivity, topicality, and responsibility, and the mass public's own impressive indifference and ignorance. Sectors of the media with attentive publics as audiences, however, may be significant in enlightening and activating these aware and disproportionately important groups. Finally, a question of competing value claims was raised. On the one hand, candor from politicians is said to be valuable because its absence trivializes the citizens' voting decisions with misinformation, and, if conspicuous and significant enough, may even cause numbers of citizens to question their system's legitimacy. Yet, on the other hand, such candor sometimes may be obtained only at a very high cost—a crucial tactical disadvantage vis-à-vis a foreign power, perhaps, or domestic political divisions too great to permit adequate policy execution. Aggravating the difficulty of finding a solution to this dilemma is the apparent fact that crises themselves are defined by decision makers mainly in terms of the threat a given set of circumstances seems to present to national and presidential images and self-images of strength, competence, and resolve.

---

terests. Probably, this is due less to the fact that these images may importantly affect key international power relationships than to the fact that the situations do constitute, from the President's vantage, true crises; that they may be more personal than national is a distinction easily lost in the pressure and hurly-burly of events. For more on this general problem, see section 1 of chapter 7.

2

Cuba: The Bay of Pigs

The best laid schemes o'mice and men
Gang aft a-gley;
An' lea'e us nought but grief and pain,
For promis'd joy.

Robert Burns, "To a Mouse"

President Kennedy's first important encounter with seductively inaccurate appearances began, two weeks after his election triumph in November 1960. It culminated five months later in the disastrous attempt by American-backed Cuban emigrés to invade Cuba at the Bay of Pigs, and overthrow the regime of Premier Fidel Castro. In examining this episode, this chapter will undertake to explore the relationship of appearance and reality in three basic aspects. First, the President's own attempts at penetrating appearances are considered, with special emphasis placed upon the importance of preexisting governmental structures and plans, and upon the influence of advisers. Second, the government's actions regarding public opinion (at home and abroad) are discussed—principally, the government's failures to secure adequate secrecy for the operation in the preparatory phase, or to absolve the United States of blame for the invasion itself. Third, the question of why the President defined the situation in Cuba as a crisis demanding immediate action is considered.

I

In his campaign against Richard Nixon, Kennedy had repeatedly attacked Castro, blaming the Republicans for a "dangerous and malignant . . . enemy on our very doorstep only eight minutes by jet from Florida." [1] Speaking of Nixon, Kennedy asked rhetorically, "If you can't stand up to Castro, how can you be expected to stand up to Khrushchev." [2] Later, he advocated strengthening "the non-Batista democratic anti-Castro forces in exile, and in Cuba itself, who offer eventual hope of overthrowing Castro," [3] and in a televised debate charged that "Castro's influence is growing mostly because the Administration has ignored Latin America." [4] Kennedy, in short, used Cuba "as a symbol of the administration's alleged tendency to drift," [5] and as two chroniclers of the events have written, "regarding Cuba his essential policy was one that ultraconservatives could applaud." [6] All of this had the effect of committing the newly elected President to a "hard-line" on Cuba—at least in a verbal sense—even before he formally took office.[7]

Meanwhile, in the closing months of the Eisenhower administration, important developments were proceeding apace. Relations with Cuba were deteriorating rapidly, as Castro nationalized American-owned banks and corporations, made overtures toward the Soviet Union and China, and accused the United States of planning aggression against his regime. The Eisenhower administration declared that Castro had betrayed his revolution by creating a dictatorship, and that Communists were assuming increasing influence in the government. Just two weeks before the November election, Eisenhower announced an embargo on all exports to Cuba, except medical supplies and food. Soon afterward, Castro reacted to the atmosphere of heightened tension by mobilizing his

---

[1] *New York Times,* October 7, 1960.

[2] *New York Times,* October 16, 1960.

[3] *New York Times,* October 21, 1960. Nixon, although aware of the CIA's plans for Cuba, attacked this proposal as "recklessly dangerous." *New York Times,* October 24, 1960. He opposed supporting invading exile forces, he said on a televised debate, because the United States was legally committed not to intervene in Latin America, and "we would probably be condemned in the United Nations, and we would not accomplish our objective." *New York Times,* October 22, 1960. Later, Nixon charged that Kennedy had been briefed on the CIA operation and had known that the Vice President would not disclose the plan *before* Kennedy had advocated strengthening the exiles. This, Nixon said, left him angry and shocked. Richard M. Nixon, *Six Crises* (Garden City: Doubleday, 1962), pp.352–54.

[4] *New York Times,* October 22, 1960.

[5] Stanley Kelley, Jr., "The Presidential Campaign," *The Presidential Election and Transition 1960–61,* ed. Paul T. David (Washington: Brookings Institution, 1961), p. 82.

[6] Karl E. Meyer and Tad Szulc, *The Cuban Invasion: The Chronicle of a Disaster* (New York: Praeger, 1962), p. 71. Thus, right-wing columnist George Sokolsky cheered on Kennedy (Sokolosky quoted in Victor Lasky, *J.F.K.: The Man and the Myth* [New York: Macmillan, 1963], p. 755) while James Reston and C. L. Sulzberger supported Nixon *(New York Times,* October 22 and October 24, 1960, respectively). In this regard, Joseph Kraft has argued, "Politically, he [Kennedy] tended to court the opposition and ignore his friends. . . . His motto might have been: no enemies to the right." Joseph Kraft, *Profiles in Power: A Washington Insight* (New York: New American Library, 1966), p. 6.

[7] Prior to the campaign, Kennedy had shown little interest in Cuba. Thus, his hard-line stand on Cuba probably did not spring from a long-standing conviction, and, presumably, could still be changed by rational argument.

militia, and charging the United States with harassment, intrigues, and a planned invasion. Washington, however, declared its unwillingness to play Goliath to Castro's David, and denied these plots vigorously and unequivocally. When presidential press secretary James C. Hagerty replied, "Nuts," to a Cuban charge of planned aggression,[8] most Americans agreed that the notion was so unfounded as to seem ridiculous. Castro nonetheless again accused the United States of plotting an invasion against him, and warned:

To invade Cuba, the United States will have to mobilize huge forces. . . . The judgment of the United States military forces is erroneous if they think Cuba can be taken in a week-end or a few hours operation.[9]

On January 2, Castro declared that eighty percent of the officials at the American embassy were spies, and demanded that the size of the staff be reduced from eighty-seven persons to eleven.[10] Apart from the humiliation acceding to this demand would have entailed, on a practical level it would have been nearly impossible for the embassy to have functioned with such a skeleton crew. Many observers concluded, therefore, that this gambit actually represented an attempt by Castro to provoke the United States into breaking off relations with Cuba completely. If so, it certainly succeeded; for President Eisenhower declared that the demand exceeded the "limit to what the United States can in self-respect endure," and with only seventeen days of his term remaining, severed diplomatic relations with Cuba.[11] Kennedy, the President-elect, was not even consulted.[12] The effect of all these well-publicized surface events was to make it even more difficult for Kennedy to retreat from his fairly belligerent posture toward Cuba. Public opinion was growing more virulent, and official actions had been taken which could not easily or painlessly be undone.

The most important developments, however, were those which had been going on beneath the surface. On March 17, 1960, President Eisenhower ordered the CIA, in his words, "to begin to organize the training

---

[8] *New York Times*, January 2, 1961.

[9] *New York Times*, January 2, 1961.

[10] *New York Times*, January 3, 1961. The embassy said American personnel totaled eighty-seven, but Castro estimated the number at three hundred.

[11] *New York Times*, January 4, 1961.

[12] James Reston, *New York Times*, January 4, 1961. Another example of Eisenhower—the supposedly indecisive President—attempting to compel his successor to follow a preset Cuban policy also occurred in January, when Kennedy was elected but had not yet taken office. In the early part of the month, Eisenhower told his staff that he wanted the Cuban exiles to set up a government in exile. "I'd like to see recognition accorded promptly," he said, "If possible, before January 20." This was the date on which Kennedy was to be inaugurated. Dwight D. Eisenhower, *Waging Peace, 1956–1961* (Garden City: Doubleday, 1965), p. 614.

of Cuban exiles, mainly in Guatemala, against a possible future day when they might return to their homeland." [13] Small bands of trained guerrilla leaders and organizers were to be secreted into Cuba, where they could form the core of a resistance movement. With each successful ambush or act of sabotage, it was felt, their ranks would grow, as peasants and members of the military and the government would defect to the rebels. Ultimately, the Castro regime would fall, with no overt American participation in the military action in Cuba having been necessary. Buttressing the plan was the knowledge that a similar approach had worked in German and Japanese occupied territories during World War II, and that Castro himself had never commanded a large army in his struggle against the government of dictator Fulgencio Batista. The analogies, however, proved to be quite imperfect, for, unlike the others, Castro was not lacking in mass support.

In the weeks following the President's order, exiles were recruited for the operation, many of them being given military training in Guatemala. As this proceeded, the Movimiento Revolucionesio del Pueblo—a progressive exile faction with the best developed underground contacts on Cuba—increasingly came to be thought of by the CIA as too radical politically and economically, and insufficiently obedient to the agency's orders. As this faction with the widest actual and potential following in Cuba was being effectively excluded from much of the policy-making operations, unpopular conservative or pro-Batista elements were rising to prominence. A couple of days before Kennedy's inauguration, the purge of social reformers from positions of power was made virtually complete. [14]

II

By the time the new President took office, the tentative plan of ten months before, as if it had contracted a kind of strategic elephantiasis, had grown to impressive proportions. Talk was no longer in terms of special small landing parties or of guerrilla infiltration, for the "optimistic forecasts of the development of an anti-Castro underground did not materialize." [15] The plan now involved invasion. [16] Castro's response to

---

[13] *Ibid.,* p. 533. Lyman B. Kirkpatrick, Jr., a prominent CIA official at the time, has offered the most convincing treatment of the operation's original rationale, and his version is followed here. Kirkpatrick, *The Real CIA* (New York: Macmillan, 1968), pp. 191–92.

[14] Meyer and Szulc, *op. cit.,* p. 92. Kennedy's later efforts to purge the forces of Batista "met with only token compliance by the CIA operational personnel at the working level in the training camps. . . ." Paul W. Blackstock, *The Strategy of Subversion: Manipulating the Politics of Other Nations* (Chicago: Quadrangle Books, 1964), p. 269.

[15] Kirkpatrick, *op. cit.,* p. 192.

[16] Sorensen, a close adviser of Kennedy, suggests that Eisenhower apparently was not in-

Kennedy's inauguration, however, was almost conciliatory. Partly, this may have been due to Kennedy's having been a Democrat, for his party was known to have been more solicitous historically of Latin American interests than had been the Republican. Partly, Castro's change in attitude may have been related to Kennedy's numerous anti-Batista references during the campaign. Mostly, however, it was probably an emotional let-down following Eisenhower's departure, for Castro apparently had been convinced that Eisenhower had planned an invasion to take place before he stepped down. As a result, throughout the summer, Cuba had been filled with tension. "From Fidel Castro to the humblest *quajire* toiling in the fields," as Haynes Johnson has observed, "everyone talked about it [the invasion], prepared for it, and waited for it." [17] When the expected invasion failed to materialize and Kennedy was sworn in, Castro's immediate reaction was to order a demobilization of the militia, tone down his anti-American propaganda, and generally adopt a wait-and-see attitude.

Kennedy, meanwhile, found the invasion preparations in full swing, with their "own self-contained dynamics." [18] The CIA leadership—particularly, its respected chief and second in command, Allen W. Dulles and Richard M. Bissell, Jr., respectively—was committed to the project, personally and organizationally. Perhaps remembering the ease with which their agency had toppled the Arbenz government in Guatemala seven years earlier, they became confident salesmen of the invasion. As they presented the plan to the President, they seemed, in Arthur Schlesinger's words, "less analysts than . . . advocates. . . ." [19] Or as another official recalls, "Allen and Dick didn't just brief us on the Cuban question, they sold us on it." [20]

During this period, Kennedy seems to have made no serious effort to reduce the plan's growing momentum, and even his official rhetoric showed no signs of softening. "Communist domination in this hemisphere can never be negotiated," he declared in his March State of the Union message.[21] At the same time, his chief Latin American adviser, Adolf A. Berle, an old New Dealer and a hard-line Castro opponent, announced the administration's rejection of an Argentine offer to mediate

formed of the decision "to arm the exile army." Theodore C. Sorensen, *Kennedy* (New York: Harper and Row, 1965), p. 295.

[17] Haynes Johnson, *The Bay of Pigs: The Leaders' Story of Brigade 2506* (New York: Norton, 1964), p. 18.

[18] Louis J. Halle, "Lessons of the Cuban Blunder," *New Republic*, June 5, 1961, p. 13.

[19] Arthur M. Schlesinger, Jr., *A Thousand Days: John F. Kennedy in the White House* (Boston: Houghton Mifflin, 1965), p. 241.

[20] Unnamed White House adviser, quoted in Stewart Alsop, "The Lesson of the Cuban Disaster," *Saturday Evening Post*, June 24, 1961, p. 68.

[21] *New York Times*, March 7, 1961.

Cuban-American differences. A few weeks later, an official White Paper was made public that termed the Castro regime "a clear and present danger to the authentic and autonomous revolution of the Americas," comparable to "the invasion of the hemisphere and the seizure of American states by the Nazi movements serving the interests of the German Reich." [22] In retrospect it seems that these hardening words represented an attempt to prepare the public—or, more precisely, the attentive public—for the invasion to come; for they emphasized the dual themes of the Cuban danger and the American resolve.

The President and his top advisers held a number of meetings to discuss the invasion plan, but the decisive conference seems to have taken place on April 4. Present from the State Department were Secretary Dean Rusk and Assistant Secretary for Latin American Affairs Thomas C. Mann;[23] from the Pentagon were Secretary of Defense Robert S. McNamara, Assistant Secretary of Defense for International Security Affairs Paul Nitze, Army General and Chairman of the Joint Chiefs of Staff Lyman L. Lemnitzer, Air Force General Thomas D. White, and Admiral Arleigh Burke, Chief of Naval Operations; Treasury Secretary C. Douglas Dillon, a former undersecretary of state in the Eisenhower administration; Arkansas Senator J. William Fulbright, Chairman of the Senate Foreign Relations Committee; three presidential advisers with some knowledge of Latin America, Berle, Schlesinger, and Richard Goodwin;[24] and, of course, from the CIA, Dulles and Bissell.

Bissell, the possessor of "an unsurpassed talent for lucid analysis and fluent exposition," set down the case for the invasion.[25] The refugee force, he said, would land at the Bay of Pigs and control the territory until the exiles' civilian political organization, the Cuban Revolutionary Council, proclaimed itself a "government in arms." This declaration would cause the internal resistance to join with the exiles.[26] By that time,

---

[22] *New York Times,* April 4, 1961.

[23] Mann had been on the staff of John Peurifoy, who, as ambassador to Guatemala, had been a key figure in the CIA-directed overthrow of the leftist Arbenz government. Peurifoy had earlier been significant in securing American help for the right-wing government of Greece.

[24] On Goodwin's rather limited acquaintance with Latin America, see Patrick Anderson, *The Presidents' Men* (Garden City: Doubleday, 1968), pp. 221–23. A liberal known for "his advocacy of radical departures in Latin American policy" (p. 222) and for his aggressively outspoken personality, Goodwin apparently voiced no opposition to the invasion plan at the April 4 meeting or at any other time.

[25] Schlesinger, *loc. cit.* This follows Johnson's version of the argument, *op. cit.,* p. 68.

[26] Yet as a former Pentagon defense analyst has pointed out, it was "not known that there was any long-term preparation of a base of support within the population in advance of military operations; it simply appeared to be assumed, on the basis of intelligence estimates, that such support would exist. To have gained it with high probability would have required the training of cadres and their infiltration in small groups over a long period of time so that they could organize a guerrilla attack from within. For such a move to succeed,

Casto's ineffective air force would have been destroyed by exile planes in attacks prior to the invasion, insuring the refugees the critical control of the skies.

Even if events did not proceed according to plan, Bissell argues, the invasion would not be a complete failure. If the exiles could not hold the beach, they would simply move inland to the Escambray Mountains. There, as guerrillas, they would provide a force for internal resistance, and work to overthrow Castro.[27] After Bissell's presentation, Dulles spoke briefly and optimistically of the plan.

More important than CIA salesmanship in convincing the President, however, seems to have been a number of negative factors. First of these was a lack of opposition from his advisers that amounted to what Robert Kennedy was to term "virtual unanimity."[28] Schlesinger dissented, but as one participant put it, "he was mighty quiet about it."[29] The Joint Chiefs of Staff at one point raised doubts about the military feasibility of the operation; and Senator Fulbright opposed it with a force that left the President "visably shaken."[30] But these few, and for the most part soft and rarely heard, voices were not enough to reinforce Kennedy's own doubts to the point where he would feel sufficient confidence in them to act on them, and halt the operation.

The loose personalized nature of the President's relations with his advisers seems to have helped the project along. The National Security Council, in particular, "was sharply reduced as an advisory body"[31]—so much so that Bundy might have been giving it too much credit when he called it, deprecatingly, "one instrument among many."[32] In its place,

---

the men would, ideally, have had to be of the population with which they would have had to work. These men were not. They would have had to work with peasantry and laborers where Castro's main support exists; but they came from the middle class that was excluded from the revolution. They could not in any case have been assured of support by the peasant and labor classes had they claimed it." Seymour J. Deitchman, *Limited War and American Defense Policy: Building and Using Military Power in a World at War,* 2d ed. (Cambridge: M.I.T. Press, 1969), pp. 239–40.

[27] Actually, swamps near the Bay of Pigs made the possibility of escaping inland quite remote, and the mountains were distant.

[28] Robert F. Kennedy, "Thirteen Days: The Story About How the World Almost Ended," *McCall's,* November 1968, p. 171.

[29] Johnson, *loc. cit.*

[30] Alsop, *op. cit.,* p. 69. But cf., Schlesinger, *op. cit.,* p. 252. Edward R. Murrow, Director of the United States Information Agency, heard of the coming invasion indirectly from a reporter, and "strongly opposed the scheme in his conversations with [McGeorge] Bundy and [USIA Deputy Director Donald] Wilson, but otherwise suffered in loyal silence." Thomas C. Sorensen, *The Word War: The Story of American Propaganda* (New York: Harper and Row, 1968), p. 139.

[31] Edward A. Kolodziej, "The National Security Council: Innovations and Implications," *Public Administration Review* 29 (November-December 1969): 573.

[32] McGeorge Bundy, the President's Special Assistant for National Security Affairs. U.S., Senate, Committee on Government Operations, Subcommittee on National Security Staff

the President relied on "small, informal groups . . ." [33] This, a former CIA
official has charged, was simply inadequate, for, lacking "any staff organization to review the operation," the President was at the mercy of
"briefers [who] came in, talked to him and his principal advisers, answered questions, and then left." [34] Kennedy's "System," as a close student of White House affairs noted later, "favors people who know
exactly what they want to do. It is tough on people who have dim misgivings—even if these misgivings happen to be very important." [35] And
even if the person having them was the President. [36]

Kennedy, however, had not made a serious effort to encourage criticism of the plan. Even his inclusion of Fulbright at the meeting—the President's only significant move in this direction—was almost half-hearted. [37]
In March Kennedy had offered the senator a ride to Florida in the presidential plane, and Fulbright, who had read of the preinvasion activities,
saw the trip as an opportunity to discuss the situation with the President.
Fulbright and an aide drew up a memorandum, arguing that whether
the invasion succeeded or failed, the United States would be the loser,
and would be denounced throughout the hemisphere. [38] The key assumption that the exiles would arouse mass popular support was also questioned. Fulbright showed the memorandum to the President on their
March 30 flight, where it seemed to have had no impact.

Three days later, however, Kennedy asked Fulbright to "a meeting to
discuss the subject of your memorandum." [39] This turned out to be no
mere "meeting," but rather the full-scale April 4 conference. Fulbright
was "[e]xcited, unprepared for such an occasion, and faced with over-

---

ing and Operations, *Administration of National Security, Selected Papers,* 87th Cong., 2d
Sess., 1962, p. 6.

[33] Kolodziej, *op. cit.,* p. 574.

[34] Kirkpatrick, *op. cit.,* pp. 261, 203.

[35] Unnamed close student of White House affairs, quoted in Joseph Kraft, "Kennedy's
Working Staff," *Harper's,* December 1962, p. 36.

[36] That he entertained doubts all observers seem agreed. E.g., Alsop, *op. cit.,* p. 68; Sorensen, *op. cit.,* p. 140; Sorensen, *Kennedy,* p. 295; Schlesinger, *op. cit.,* p. 238.

[37] The Fulbright episode is discussed in Sidney Hyman, "Fulbright: The Wedding of Arkansas and the World," *New Republic,* May 14, 1962, p. 42. Nor did Kennedy solicit further
comments from J. Kenneth Galbraith, the newly appointed ambassador to India, who, in a
farewell letter to the President, expressed "my concern over the surviving adventurism in
the government." As Galbraith recalled later, "I put it very strongly to the President—we
have had an unparalleled series of disasters, Yalu River, Guatemala, U-2, where we have
failed to measure the overall consequences of failure or (as in Guatemala) even success of
military operations or intervention." J. Kenneth Galbraith, *Ambassador's Journal* (Boston:
Houghton Mifflin, 1969).

[38] The memorandum is reproduced in J. William Fulbright, *Fulbright of Arkansas: The
Public Positions of a Private Thinker,* ed. Karl E. Meyer (Washington: Robert B. Luce,
1963), pp. 195–205.

[39] John F. Kennedy, quoted in Haynes Johnson and Bernard M. Gwertzman, *Fulbright:
The Dissenter* (Garden City: Doubleday, 1968), p. 175.

whelming contrary views from the experts,"[40] though he managed to reiterate the substance of his memorandum ably.

What is instructive about the Fulbright episode is not simply that a dissenter was invited to give his opinion, but that the original initiative had been taken by the senator not the President, and that the method of invitation put Fulbright at a disadvantage as compared with the supporters. Moreover, others who might have voiced criticism—such as UN Ambassador Adlai Stevenson[41]—were simply not included at all, giving Fulbright the difficult and futile task of uttering his opposition alone.[42] It may even have been that Fulbright was included not to challenge the plan, but rather to legitimate it further by helping to make it seem that "both sides" had received a hearing.[43]

The second important negative factor contributing to the plan's adoption—in addition to the lack of an effective opposition at the highest decision-making level—was the apparent plethora of disadvantages connected with a refusal to act. The Soviets were strengthening Castro militarily, it was said, making this the last opportunity a clandestine effort would have for success. Once he became truly fortified, only an overt American invasion could dislodge him, and Kennedy was clear in ruling this out. Moreover, the exiles were anxious to fight, and Guatemala was pressuring the United States to close down its training camps.

Additionally, there was the question of how to "dispose" of the exiles, should the invasion be cancelled. If their hopes were dashed, they could hardly be expected to remain quiet about their preparations. Their reve-

---

[40] *Ibid.,* p. 177.

[41] That Stevenson was misled by the CIA is contended by his deputy at the UN Mission, Francis T. P. Plimpton, in Richard J. Walton, *The Remnants of Power: The Tragic Last Years of Adlai Stevenson* (New York: Coward-McCann, 1968), p. 30. That Stevenson would have viewed the invasion as "a kind of mistake that truly honorable and intelligent men never make" is argued by Kenneth S. Davis, *The Politics of Honor: A Biography of Adlai E. Stevenson* (New York: Putnam, 1967), p. 158. The *Times'* military analyst, Hanson Baldwin, has tried to explain Stevenson's omission from the decision-making process in these words: "It was bureaucracy at its worst, with the right hand sometimes not knowing (as in the case of Adlai E. Stevenson at the United Nations) what the left hand was doing." *New York Times,* August 1, 1961. Yet it is difficult to agree with Baldwin's implicit assumption that Stevenson's exclusion was inadvertent.

[42] It is also true, however, that Fulbright's efforts at influencing the President were remarkably restrained for one so convinced of the folly of the mission. Had it not been for the accident of a presidential invitation, the senator might never have voiced his criticism at all. And, of course, he failed to follow up on his criticism when it had not persuaded the President on his first hearing, not seeking out Kennedy for a reargument. This was a Fulbright with a very limited view of Congress's role in foreign policy, hardly exceeding discreet private memoranda and public expressions of support. Following the Dominican Republic intervention, a more activist Fulbright was to begin to emerge.

[43] That dissenters are invited to the White House for this purpose is suggested by President Johnson's former press secretary, George E. Reedy, *The Twilight of the Presidency* (New York: World, 1970), p. 11.

lations would make the United States and its President seem both devious and indecisive, for the government had made an enormous rhetorical investment in "opposition to Castro Communism" and "devotion to freedom." [44]

> Words subjected to prolonged abuse
> Take their revenge upon the oppressor, strike.
> A phrase outraged by vulgar repetition
> Returns at last to haunt its ravishers. [45]

The exiles' revelations, the facts biting through words like a lion through its keeper's hand, had to be suppressed. For the revelations would have constituted not only an immense propaganda coup for the Communists, but also a serious personal defeat for the President. As his close friend and assistant, Theodore Sorensen, has written, Kennedy "did feel that his disapproval of the plan would be a show of weakness inconsistent with his general stance." [46] This show of weakness, aside from reducing his own popularity and dirtying his image, might also be of partisan value to Republicans. If he turned down the project, his administration would be "plastered with a label of 'weakness' and would never get off the ground in the great enterprises he had set for it." [47] This, in any case, was the fear, although the label of "failure" at the Bay of Pigs did not, of course, doom his "great enterprises," if, indeed, the President had at that point any specific "great enterprises" in mind.

All of this suggests that the Cuban problem, from Kennedy's view, may have been one more of appearance than of reality. For action seemed required not because Castro threatened the United States nor because he was on the verge of extending his influence in the hemisphere through the "exporting of revolution." Instead, for a nation bent on keeping up appearances he was an affront—an accusation regarding America's imperialistic past and impotent presence concerning Cuba. Furthermore, for reasons already mentioned, halting the invasion plans

---

[44] This was neither the first nor the last time that a client entirely dependent upon the United States ended up exerting decisive influence upon its "master." Syngman Rhee, during the Korean conflict, and Ngo Dinh Diem and Nguyen Van Thieu, during the Vietnamese war, each partially succeeded in using American propaganda about his nation's independence in order to justify his opposition to American policies. American rhetoric constituted a weakness, which could easily be exploited by those with the skill and inclination to do so.

[45] Daryl Hine, "Life and Letters," *New Republic*, December 21, 1968, p. 38.

[46] Sorensen, *op. cit.*, p. 297.

[47] Hilsman, *To Move a Nation*, p. 32. It is also possible to argue, however, that the earlier an administration produces a public relations or policy gaffe, the longer the electorate has to forgive and forget. This is one reason why the political costs of obvious presidential errors tend to increase with the President's tenure in office.

or doing nothing about Castro would have entailed personal damage to Kennedy's own appearance, especially in the eyes of the domestic electorate.

But if the problem were suffused with appearances, so was the suggested solution.

III

Probably Kennedy would never have initiated the invasion plan, but he was nonetheless willing to approve it. In ratifying the invasion recommendation, he seems to have confused two appearances for the realities of the situation. In the first place, the President accepted a seriously distorted view of the situation in Cuba. Kennedy apparently discounted Castro's charisma to the extent of denying that he "ruled with popular support. . . ." [48] A number of published reports by recent visitors had disputed this contention—including a series in the *New York Herald Tribune,* which Schlesinger brought to Kennedy's attention[49]—but they could not overturn it in his mind.

The influence of the confident Dulles and Bissell was of particular importance in this regard. In his April 4 presentation, for example, Bissell had described Cuban history in terms of smaller forces conquering larger ones with the help of the general populace. Yet despite their influence, neither Dulles nor Bissell was especially knowledgeable concerning Latin America, each having concentrated upon Europe for most of his career. Top agency officials are not expected to be expert specialists, but rather generalists, with administrative abilities and a sense of perspective. Thus, there was nothing surprising or damaging about Dulles and Bissell's lack of expertise in Latin American affairs. What was surprising—and fatal to the operation—was the utter inadequacy of their efforts to discover the Cuban reality behind the propagandistic appearances. Not experts themselves, they were at least obligated to consult and work with experts, if only those in their own agency. This they failed adequately to do. For the crucial position of the Miami manager of the operation, for example, they selected a man known as "Frank Bender." A German refugee, he was not even fluent in Spanish, and compounded his ignorance of Cuba by surrounding himself with yes-men. The men chosen to train the exiles in Guatemala for their invasion were so poorly

---

[48] Sorensen, *loc. cit.* On Castro's charisma, see Ward M. Morton, *Castro as Charismatic Hero* (University of Kansas, Center of Latin American Studies: Occasional Publications, No. 4; Lawrence, Kansas: University of Kansas, 1965); Richard R. Fagen, "Charismatic Authority and the Leadership of Fidel Castro," *Western Political Quarterly* 93 (June 1965): 275.

[49] Schlesinger, *op. cit.,* p. 247. The President had not yet cancelled his subscription to the *Herald Tribune* for what he felt to be its unfairly critical treatment of him and his party.

acquainted with Cuban topography and guerrilla tactics that most of the
training was in largely irrelevant conventional combat techniques. This
is not to say that the CIA was without persons knowledgeable about
Cuba or that information had not been gathered on Cuban attitudes toward Castro. But Dulles and Bissell were unwilling to consult estimates
of their agency which differed from their own, and did not even inform
the CIA's own Deputy Director in charge of intelligence (research) of the
project, let alone ask him to investigate the accuracy of its assumptions.

If they made this kind of use of their own organization, it is hardly surprising that they refused to check their estimates against independent
evaluations from abroad or from other agencies or private sources in this
country. In July of 1960, for example, the Institute for International Social Research published and sent to the White House and State Department an extensive survey of the political attitudes of the urban and semi-
urban population of Cuba.[50] The survey, taken about three months
earlier, revealed widespread support for the regime, with about eighty-
six percent of the sample speaking of it favorably.[51] The most commonly
mentioned fear expressed concerning the future of Cuba was that it
would return to Batista-day conditions or that Castro would be displaced
by counterrevolutionaries. These major findings, which completely con-
travened the CIA's estimates and spelled disaster for the mission, were
even published in the *New York Times.*[52] There is no evidence that the
administration even noticed the report.[53] By the same token, the CIA dismissed a series of warnings from members of the anti-Castro Cuban underground that effective popular uprisings required considerable preliminary work, including a sizable sabotage campaign.

This suggests that the CIA was able to convince other top-level decision makers that the agency's estimates were not a fit subject for investigation. Roger Hilsman, then Director of Intelligence and Research
for the State Department, recalls that he was not even informed of the
invasion plan until, as he says:

---

[50] Lloyd A. Free, *Attitudes of the Cuban People toward the Castro Regime* (Princeton: Institute for International Social Research, 1960). This incident is recounted by Free's associate, Hadley Cantril, *The Human Dimension: Experiences in Policy Research* (New Bruns-
wick: Rutgers University Press, 1967), chap. 1.

[51] Support for Castro was lowest among upper and upper-middle income classes from
Havana. This class of individuals was especially prevalent among the exiles. Thus, the class
whose opinion of Castro was most out of phase with the rest of Cuba was the class which
the CIA relied upon most for its information on his general popularity.

[52] *New York Times,* August 2, 1960.

[53] Thomas Sorensen states that the "study was made available to USIA, which presumably sent it to the State Department and CIA (though it may not have reached those in
charge of the secret Cuban project). Not knowing of the invasion plan, USIA did not send
the . . . study to the White House after Kennedy became President. . . ." Sorensen, *The
Word War*, pp. 140–41.

One day Allen Dulles let drop a remark that made me realize something was up. I went straight to Secretary of State Rusk and told him what I had learned. I reminded him that . . . an invasion of a hostile shore was probably the most difficult of all military operations, and that if the CIA expected the brigade of a thousand Cuban refugees to win against Castro's two-hundred-thousand man militia, the assumption must be that the Cuban people would rise. I was no expert on Cuba, but there were plenty of people in the Bureau of Intelligence and Research who were, and I asked the Secretary for permission to put them to work on the question. "I'm sorry," he replied, "but I can't let you. This is being too tightly held." [54]

That this refusal on grounds of secrecy could be offered despite the facts that (a) Hilsman's specialists had top secret clearance; (b) rumors about the camps in Guatemala and Florida were already circulating freely in Miami and throughout the Caribbean, [55] and had even been reported in the national press; [56] (c) numerous reporters who had visited Cuba disputed the assumption of intense and widespread opposition there to Castro; and (d) review by the State Department's Director of Intelligence and Research had been standard procedure when important military operations had been contemplated. That in the face of all this Rusk could address Hilsman like a butler denying entrance to a party-crasher reveals the extent to which the Secretary had been cowed by the CIA and the Joint Chiefs. "There was so deep a commitment," Hilsman says, "that there was an unconscious effort to confine consideration of the proposed operation to as small a number of people as possible, so as to avoid too harsh or thorough a scrutiny of the plan." [57] In other words: we've made up our minds; don't bother us with facts.

Presumably, the rationale behind this exaggerated concern with secrecy within government was the extreme desirability of a tactical surprise. That is, it may have been general knowledge that the United States planned to launch or supply an invasion of Cuba, but the critical questions of where, when, and how were much more closely guarded. In fact,

---

[54] Hilsman, *loc. cit.*

[55] Invasion preparations had been made public at least as early as October 30, 1960, by a Guatemala City newspaper, *La Hora.* Schlesinger, *op. cit.,* p. 235.

[56] E.g., *New York Times,* January 10, 1961, and January 20, 1961; Ronald Hilton, "Are We Training Cuban Guerrillas?" *Nation,* November 19, 1960, pp. 378–79; "Asylum or Staging Ground? Cubans in Florida," *ibid.,* January 7, 1961, p. 1; *Miami Herald,* January 11, 1961. A top CIA official later conceded that despite "the necessity for absolute and complete security in any such operation, the leaks about the operation, from its very inception were horrendous. In fact, these leaks alone were sufficient to have justified dropping the entire project." Kirkpatrick, *op. cit.,* p. 188. Kirkpatrick went so far as to admit that the CIA itself contributed to the breakdown of secrecy, in the sense that its increasing involvement in the preparations stimulated an already rampant factionalism among the emigrés; resentful Cubans were the main source of the leaks. *Ibid.,* p. 189.

[57] Hilsman, *loc. cit.*

the very lack of strategic surprise served to add to the importance of tactical surprise. And yet the effect of this kind of emphasis, as an intelligence analyst had written a dozen years before in words ringing like an eerie prophecy, is to leave the agency "free to steer its own course behind the fog of its own security regulations." [58] The CIA's course was to lead to disaster.

Underlying its exaggerated concern with secrecy, perhaps, was the belief that the President would not let the mission fail, despite his stated opposition to the overt commitment of American forces. The CIA leadership, in other words, may have felt that Kennedy would bail out the landings in the event that the necessary indigenous uprisings did not materialize. Pepé San Roman, an exile leader, recalls, for example, that the exiles had not been instructed to move inland as guerrillas if the invasion should fail. "What we were told" by the CIA, he says, "was, 'If you fail *we* will go in.' " [59] After the invasion, it became known that although Dulles had informed the President that the exiles had been trained in guerrilla warfare, no such training had been offered since November 4, when the force consisted of only three hundred refugees. This belief that Kennedy would save the mission—if Dulles and Bissell held it—bespeaks a devotion to policy over the President the CIA leadership was to serve. It also suggests an ignorance of Kennedy rivaling its ignorance of Cuba.

Yet if the CIA failed in its intelligence function, the failure was not the agency's alone, for the President took few precautions to insure its reliability. Agency specialization, as Harold Wilensky has pointed out, may be a major source of misinformation because it encourages interagency rivalries and a preoccupation with the organization's narrow point of view. Centralization compounds the danger by eliminating some possible competing sources of information in the name of efficiency. [60] The CIA—the *central* intelligence agency with a *specialized* operations branch—met both danger criteria, and constituted what might be termed

---

[58] Sherman Kent, *Strategic Intelligence* (Princeton: Princeton University Press, 1949), p. 168.

[59] Quoted in Johnson, *loc. cit.* Kirkpatrick notes that "The Americans who participated have . . . strongly maintained that they never made such a commitment." Yet he admits that the exiles "were certain that if they started to falter, United States forces would come to their assistance," and concludes lamely that "while the Americans didn't go so far as to say that United States forces would actually land in Cuba, it is only fair to expect that in the excitement and emotional heat just before the landing they must certainly have been as encouraging as possible." Kirkpatrick, *op. cit.,* p. 196. Such prevarications inevitably conjure up images of a lawyer trying to win an acquittal for an unsavory client charged with misleading advertising in the sale of a used car.

[60] Harold L. Wilensky, *Organizational Intelligence: Knowledge and Power in Government and Industry* (New York: Basic Books, 1967), pp. 48, 58.

an "internal interest-group" [61] within the national security establishment. Yet Kennedy was ineffective in meeting the informational challenge posed by the organizational situation, making insufficient use of such standard leadership techniques as stimulating competition among information sources or engaging the advice of experts with a hostile point of view. Thus, what is surprising is perhaps less the failure of the CIA—which was seen at the time as purveying a particular plan of action—than the failure of the President to take this into account, and act on it in the interest of more accurate information. [62]

Thus misled, the President approved an invasion plan, which assumed, in Schlesinger's words, that "the successful occupation of a large beachhead area would rather soon incite uprisings by armed members of the Cuban resistance." [63] This was essential in saving the planned invasion of only 1,400 men from being dismissed as quixotic; but the assumption was, as Castro had said, "erroneous."

Events, of course, quickly overwhelmed the administration's wishful thinking. Ten weeks earlier, a returning reporter had said that "the small Cuban forces training so ostentatiously" under CIA direction "seem to me to be heading for slaughter," [64] and he was right. The invasion did not embolden Castro's opponents, but rather emphasized their impotence. Whatever internal resistance organizations that did exist on the island apparently were not informed of the plan. Castro, in short, was a much more imposing enemy than Kennedy and his optimistic advisers had supposed. Appearances deceived.

If Kennedy were unable to penetrate the myth of Castro's unpopularity, he evidently believed that the rest of the world would be unable to penetrate America's claims of noninvolvement in the invasion. If American assistance were covert and no Americans were among the landing party, [65] so the argument went, the nation would be safely insulated from the public responsibility for the action. This naive contention did not go unchallenged by the President's advisers, [66] but it survived the attacks rather easily, and emerged as an important decisional premise.

---

[61] Philip Selznick, *Leadership in Administration: A Sociological Interpretation* (New York: Harper and Row, 1957), p. 93.

[62] The standard explanation, of course, is that Kennedy was new at his job. Yet this explanation merely provokes the further question: why, if he were so new to the exercise of power, did he choose to embark thus handicapped on such a risky enterprise? The answer given above—essentially elaborations on a theme of inertia—belies the administration's glib talk of "new directions" and departures from the past.

[63] Schlesinger, *op. cit.,* p. 247; Sorensen, *op. cit.,* p. 303.

[64] Samuel Shapiro, "Castro's Cuba Revisited," *New Republic,* February 6, 1961, p. 16.

[65] Even this condition was not met. Schlesinger reports that "the first frogman on each beach was, in spite of Kennedy's order, an American." Schlesinger, *op. cit.,* p. 274.

[66] Kennedy's desire to dissociate the United States from the invasion may have stemmed from his wish to avoid alienating domestic liberal opinion and foreign opinion, especially

The insistence that the United States not be blatantly involved in the invasion was one reason that the invasion force was as militarily weak as it was—certainly, far too weak to accomplish its purposes. Moreover, once the invasion began, the gossamer appearance of a wholly Cuban action was easily destroyed, leaving American involvement and deceit embarassingly exposed. Kennedy himself shortly admitted this involvement. His admirers then and since have applauded the magnanimity of his willingness to assume full responsibility.[67] Yet, as President, what other options did he have? Had he blamed other officials, not only would he have appeared cowardly, but in addition, he would have been admitting that he had been unable to control the important policies of his own administration. As President, of course, Kennedy deserved full responsibility; the buck, in Harry Truman's words, stops here. And yet as the revelations concerning the invasion emerged, it was plain that the Eisenhower administration was deeply implicated.[68] By confessing, then, as opposed to remaining silent, Kennedy effectively depoliticized the invasion by showing that the Republicans were not free of blame. This astuteness, however, was confined to the admission of guilt, and did not extend to the planning or execution of the crime.

It proved easier for the President and his advisers to mislead themselves than to mislead the world.[69]

The Bay of Pigs episode is an example of presidential failure to dis-

---

in Latin America. Given the preexisting permissive consensus in the United States (involving both mass and attentive publics), outright American involvement almost certainly would have been widely supported, provided that the invasion succeeded. And with all-out American participation, the invasion could hardly have failed to oust Castro.

[67] E.g., "T.R.B. from Washington," *New Republic*, May 1, 1961, p. 2; Sorensen, *op. cit.,* p. 309; Charles Lam Markmann and Mark Sherwin, *John F. Kennedy: A Sense of Purpose* (New York: St. Martin's Press, 1961), p. 176. So smitten with Kennedy was the press that a militant speech of his made after the fiasco hinting at the possibility of future interventions received almost unanimous editorial praise, a straw vote put to the editors on whether they considered the President to be "doing a good job" produced a favorable response of 120 to 10, and a long speech by the Senate's leading authority on Latin America attacking the premise that Cuba posed a military threat went virtually unreported. Neal D. Houghton, "The Cuban Invasion of 1961 and the U.S. Press, in Retrospect," *Journalism Quarterly* 42 (Summer 1965): 426. Further, the press had for months willingly joined the administration in convincing the public that "Cuban charges . . . of impending invasions from the States were utterly without foundation." *Ibid.,* p. 427.

[68] The roles of the CIA and Joint Chiefs also surfaced, causing them to share much of the blame, thereby making their prospects of increasing their influence over policy at the President's expense rather dim. That the White House staff was instrumental in helping to place blame upon them is persuasively argued by *Life's* White House correspondent, Hugh Sidey, *John F. Kennedy, President* (New York: Atheneum, 1963), p. 141.

[69] An interesting postscript to the crisis concerns the President's future use of those advisers whose instincts had been right on the Bay of Pigs. Neither Schlesinger nor Fulbright was consulted during deliberations preceding the Cuban missile crisis; and Chester Bowles, who had written a lengthy memorandum opposing the invasion plan, was eased out of his position as undersecretary of state a few months after the failure, although apparently for

tinguish appearances from reality. Although there was plenty of time to take precautions, few actually were utilized. Inordinate confidence was placed in the recommendations of an agency with a vested interest in the invasion. Attempts at correcting this one-sided interpretation of events were feeble and ineffective.

Decision makers faced no problems regarding the creation of a permissive consensus; for months of propaganda had convinced most Americans, whether of the mass or attentive publics, that the Castro regime threatened American security and was, in addition, unacceptably inhumane.

Thus, the government's public relations were less concerned with publicity than with secrecy, and its interest in this regard served two purposes. Ostensibly, secrecy was necessary in order to insure the tactical surprise of the invasion. Even more important, perhaps, secrecy provided a rationale for saving the plan from critical review by potentially skeptical segments of the bureaucracy. The failure to hide the invasion preparations from the outside world made it impossible to persuade American or foreign publics that the United States had not been involved. At this point, Kennedy shrewdly confessed to America's role, ironically contributing to his reputation for honesty and forthrightness.

That the Cuban situation was deemed in the first place to constitute a "crisis" requiring American action was difficult to justify from a substantive point of view. For it could not convincingly be shown that Castro—either independently of as an ally of the Soviet Union—presented a serious and immediate threat to the United States. His continuance in power, however, plainly did pose a perceived threat to the President's image. Kennedy had campaigned on a tough anti-Castro stand, and, upon taking office and finding invasion preparations in full swing, could abandon them only at the cost of appearing weak-willed and irresolute; for clearly the groups affected by such abandonment would not suffer in silence. In order to avoid onerous labels, then, Kennedy agreed—perhaps against his own better judgment—to the action, remaining too cautious and unenthusiastic to favor an all-out invasion.

---

other reasons. Rusk, McNamara, Dillon, and Nitze, on the other hand, all of whom assented to the invasion plan, retained their influence in policy making in general, and in crises decisions in particular.

3

The Dominican Republic: Revolution and Intervention

April is the cruellest month . . .

T. S. Eliot

The problem of appearances and reality in foreign policy decision making is far too fundamental to have bothered only the Kennedy administration. Appearances—in the same twin sense of decision makers mistaking appearances for reality and also trying to convince the world that American-oriented appearances *were* reality, and defining the situation as a crisis because it threatened certain presidential and national appearances—also plagued President Johnson. To say this, however, is not to point out shortcomings in particular administrations, but rather to indicate a problem which seems to inhere in the very process of foreign policy decision making itself.

In considering the Dominican Republic crisis, an effort will be made to discern how the President attempted to brush away appearances, and discover the real nature of events. The press of time, the influence of advisers, and the behavior of subordinates will be stressed. This chapter will also be concerned with the government's actions relating to public opinion on the home front, especially the techniques used to try to create a permissive consensus and their success, and the nature of and possible motivations for the suppression of information.

I

The Dominican Republic is a tiny, impoverished nation comprising the western portion of the island of Hispaniola in the Caribbean. The facts concerning its revolution and the subsequent American intervention are quite complex, and some are not yet free of dispute.

43

About the initial incident at least there is no doubt. This was the assassination that ended the incredibly brutal thirty-one-year-old dictatorship of Rafael Trujillo on May 31, 1961. His son, Ramfis, attempted to carry on—for a while with the support of American diplomats, who looked to him for "stability," but later with their hostility—yet lasted less than a year. By the end of 1962, Dominicans were holding free parliamentary elections. Juan D. Bosch, honest, well-meaning but tempermental and ineffectual, was elected by a large margin. But Trujillo and his predecessors as despots had not left the nation well-prepared for democracy, and the problems simply overwhelmed Bosch. To make matters worse, his relations with the right-wing senior military officers, never good, deteriorated rapidly. Finally, in September, 1963, after seven months in office, he was ousted in a military coup led by Brigadier General Elias Wessin y Wessin.[1] Bosch was accused of "allowing Communists and followers of Premier Castro to infiltrate his government,"[2] but among Dominicans, popular resentment and frustration concerning the coup was common. Freedom—the opportunity to participate in politics and the absence of police-state fears—had quickly come to be prized highly. Now, a return to the dreaded Trujillo days seemed likely.[3]

President Kennedy—a popular figure in the Dominican Republic because he was widely thought to have been partially responsible for Ramfis Trujillo's exit—publicly expressed his opposition to the coup.[4] Immediately, he suspended diplomatic relations with the Dominican Republic, and cut off American economic assistance. Anti-Bosch feeling was prevalent in Washington, however, and the new Dominican military regime

---

[1] The role of the United States in this coup apparently was characterized by considerable ambivalence. On the one hand, Ambassador John Bartlow Martin spared no effort in trying to keep Bosch in power. This is described in Martin's *Overtaken by Events: The Dominican Republic from the Fall of Trujillo to the Civil War* (Garden City: Doubleday, 1968), Part II. On the other hand, Sam Halper, the former chief to *Time* magazine's Caribbean bureau, alleges that the Defense Department's Military Assistance and Advisory Group mission was involved in Bosch's overthrow. Sam Halper, "The Dominican Upheaval: A Revolution Delayed," *New Leader,* May 10, 1965, pp. 3–4. A correspondent of the *Washington Post,* who was present in the Dominican Republic before and after the coup, also feels that "Martin's efforts appear to have been undercut most seriously of all by some U.S. military attachés. . . ." Dan Kurzman, *Santo Domingo: Revolt of the Damned* (New York: Putnam, 1965), p. 103.

[2] *New York Times,* April 26, 1965.

[3] Kurzman, *op. cit.,* pp. 109–11.

[4] See, e.g., President Kennedy's news conference of October 9, of which a transcript is printed in the *New York Times,* October 10, 1963. Yet Rafael Trujillo had been viewed by the Kennedy administration as only "a peripheral distraction," and when he seemed to be in trouble near the end of his rule, a Caribbean meeting to shore him up was almost arranged between the two leaders. During this period, Kennedy apparently was significantly influenced by his father and by Hearst society gossip columnist Igor Cassini, an unregistered foreign agent of Trujillo. Robert D. Crassweller, *Trujillo: The Life and Times of a Dominican Dictator* (New York: Macmillan, 1966), pp. 430–31.

argued ominously that American policy was encouraging subversive elements on the island, and playing into the hands of those working for a Cuba-type upheaval. As a result, in December after less than a month in office, President Johnson restored full diplomatic relations with the Dominican Republic, in exchange for promises that elections would be held by the end of 1965. When J. Donald Reid Cabral, a Dominican businessman favorably disposed to the United States, was named head of the provisional government, American aid followed shortly.[5] Over a sixteen-month period, the United States gave Reid sixty-one million dollars in economic aid, two million dollars in military aid, and permitted the CIA to help him build a police force of eight thousand men and warn him of plots against his regime. All this proceeded despite the fact that the United States knew from its own public opinion polls that the regime had virtually no popular support, and even intended to cancel the promised elections.[6]

Although a man of some ability,[7] in a matter of months Reid became increasingly isolated politically. Workers and politicians of the left were alienated by his program of financial austerity—instituted at the insistence of his nation's creditors, the United States and the International Monetary Fund—and hurt deeply by a surging unemployment brought on by a drop in the world market prices of sugar, bananas, and coffee, and by a decline in tourism. The seriousness of the political implications of this economic crisis were presaged in the results of a poll taken of Dominicans prior to the elections in 1962 by the Institute for International Social Research, and distributed to the White House and the State Department.[8] Dominicans, the survey revealed, saw their living standard as abysmally low, and had as their chief aspiration—both as a personal and

---

[5] It has been alleged that in the recognition and resumption of aid Johnson "carried out plans laid in the Kennedy administration . . ." Georgetown University, The Center for Strategic Studies. *Dominican Action—1965: Intervention of Cooperation?* (Special Report Series, No. 2, July 1966), p. 2. The most careful analyst of the intervention concurs. Jerome Slater, *Intervention and Negotiation: The United States and the Dominican Revolution* (New York: Harper and Row, 1970), pp. 16–17.

[6] *New York Times*, November 14, 1965. Slater contends, however, that Reid was to receive but forty-five million dollars from the U.S. and other sources, and spent only 18.4 million dollars of that. Slater, *op. cit.*, p. 17n.

[7] Undersecretary of State Thomas C. Mann, for example, called Reid "the first honest President" of the Dominican Republic "in a long time." Quoted in Max Frankel. *New York Times*, November 14, 1965. Almost every writer, whether critic or supporter of American actions in the Dominican Republic, seems to find some kind words for Reid. E.g., Kurzman, *op. cit.*, p. 121; Tad Szulc, *Dominican Diary* (New York: Delacorte Press, 1965), pp. 4, 66; Philip Geyelin, *Lyndon B. Johnson and the World* (New York: Praeger, 1966), p. 242; and Rowland Evans and Robert Novak, *Lyndon B. Johnson: The Exercise of Power*, Signet Book (New York: New American Library, 1968), p. 536.

[8] Lloyd A. Free, *The Attitudes, Hopes and Fears of the Dominican People* (Princeton: Institute for International Social Research, 1965).

as a national aim—the elevation of their economic condition. Not only did they desire economic gain; they also expected it. When it failed to materialize under Reid, their dissatisfaction was intense, inflaming what had been merely "a deep sense of malaise. . . ." [9] That Reid owed his position to an unpopular coup and the support of corrupt military officers strengthened neither his personal prestige nor his regime's legitimacy.

Reid's response to this emotional tidal wave was to postpone elections until September. This, however, served only to anger further a "people who [had] longed . . . ardently for democratic political rule." [10] At the same time, rumors spread to the effect that Reid planned to cancel the elections or at least to insure his own victory at the polls by excluding his two main opponents from the contest, Bosch and Trujillo's last puppet president, Joaquin Balaguer. [11] This infuriated a number of middle-grade and junior military officers, who favored Bosch's return, and were dissatisfied with Reid's inability to root out corruption among the senior officers and dismiss those who had served under Trujillo. Convinced that Reid would block their efforts if he remained in power, the younger officers began to plot his ouster. Even nature seems to have conspired against him, as Santo Domingo was struck with the most severe water shortage in fourteen years, helping to "fray tempers and put the population on edge." [12] When, after proddings from the United States, Reid began in earnest to attack graft, smuggling, and other privileges of the military, the senior officers became progressively hostile. Following talk of slicing the military's generous budget allotment, Reid "discovered he did not have a friend in court." [13]

During these tense days, Santo Domingo was buzzing with rumors of military conspiracies, a few of them having even been reported on the front pages of *El Caribe*, one of the city's two leading newspapers. Earlier in the spring, American Ambassador W. Tapley Bennett, Jr., had warned Washington of the unstable situation, saying, "We are almost on the ropes in the Dominican Republic," [14] and the CIA uncovered four plots in March and early April. [15] On April 22, Reid, sensing a conspiracy, removed several officers from active duty. [16]

---

[9] Szulc, *op. cit.*, p. 4.

[10] Kurzman, *op. cit.*, p. 39.

[11] Reid denied this. Kurzman, *op. cit.*, p. 124. But the *New York Times* reported a February address of Reid to the Puerto Rican Broadcasters Association, in which he said that "if political agitation continued, the return of [exiled] Juan D. Bosch and Joaquin Balaguer would be ruled out." The *Times* added that Reid was "expected to be a candidate." *New York Times*, February 28, 1965.

[12] Szulc, *op. cit.*, p. 5.

[13] Geyelin, *loc. cit.*

[14] Message of W. Tapley Bennett, Jr., to Thomas C. Mann, quoted in Kurzman, *loc. cit.*

[15] *New York Times*, November 15, 1965.

[16] Szulc, *op. cit.*, p. 7. This account conflicts with that reported by Georgetown Univer-

Despite all these warning signals—which, of course, are far more audible in retrospect than they were at the time—the American Embassy "was denuded of its top personnel." [17] This misreading of the seriousness of the situation may be partially attributed to the senior American officers' having been fairly new to their posts. When full diplomatic relations had been restored sixteen months before, a whole new set of high-level officials had been assigned to the embassy. Although Bennett, for example, was a Foreign Service veteran of the Caribbean, he had been in the Dominican Republic only thirteen months. Benjamin Ruyle, the First Secretary of the embassy, had been there barely a year. The chief CIA representative, Edwin N. Terrell, however, had been in Santo Domingo for a considerably longer time, and this may help to account for his organization's disproportionate influence in the coming crisis. The other officials, perhaps, were to become victims of their inexperience.

In any event, Bennett left Santo Domingo on April 23 to visit his sick mother in Georgia, and to consult with his superiors in Washington. In addition, eleven of the thirteen members of the Military Assistance and Advisory Group were in Panama for a routine military conference, one of the three military attachés was dove hunting with a Dominican general who had helped to assassinate Trujillo, and the Director of the Economics Mission was in Washington. As a result, the embassy in Santo Domingo was headed by its chargé d'affaires, William B. Connett, Jr., who had been in the country less than half a year.

The situation in Washington was also less than ideal. Jack Hood Vaughn, the ex-boxer and Marine who had risen to Assistant Secretary of State for Inter-American Affairs, was at a conference in Mexico, and the CIA was in the midst of a change of command. Admiral William Raborn had been named on April 11 to replace John McCone as CIA chief, and was slated to be sworn in formally on April 28. The last week of April, in short, found the official apparatus for gathering and analyzing information relating to the Dominican Republic in disrepair.

The limitations of the apparatus, however, went far beyond the fact of key personnel happening to be out of town or new at their jobs. Even had everyone been present, the American staff would have been severely handicapped, for in the preceding months they had not become adequately acquainted with the forces at work in the little country. The senior members of the staff had apparently restricted their personal contacts to Dominican businessmen, senior military officers, larger landowners,

---

sity's Center for Strategic Studies, which alleges that on "April 22, Reid told Ambassador Bennett that he saw no indications that there would be any attempt against his government in the near future." *Op. cit.,* p. 8.

[17] Szulc, *loc. cit.*

and moderate rightist politicians.[18] Keeping in touch with Reid's opponents and with middle grade military officers was a function delegated to the embassy's junior members. Speaking of the Ambassador, for example, a Washington official later remarked, "Tap didn't seem to know anyone who was to the left of the Rotary Club."[19] Though he traveled widely in the Dominican Republic, Bennett appears to have been incapable of empathizing with the lower classes, who comprised the overwhelming majority of the population. As a colleague of his at the embassy observed, "Tap seemed ill at ease with people who were not well dressed and to whom he had not been properly introduced."[20] Perhaps this lack of familiarity helps to account for Bennett's failure to appreciate the significance of many developments flowing from the Trujillos' downfall. For the mass of Dominicans, at least the residents of Santo Domingo, inert, fatalistic acceptance of life had given way to a profound desire for improvement and self-rule.

The embassy's practice of limiting its contacts largely to the conservative portion of Dominican society did not represent an innovation on the part of local officials. Far from it. The State Department in general and specifically Assistant Secretary of State Thomas C. Mann, the President's chief Latin American adviser, were often criticized for precisely this policy. Analysts frequently suggested, for example, that Mann was insufficiently aware of popular aspirations and the growing forces for change, and even an admirer conceded that "he does not warm to the new."[21] The embassy's practices, in other words, whether deliberately or not, reflected general attitudes prevalent within the parent organization, the State Department.

It was not only that the embassy and the State Department were most familiar with the conservative forces in society. In addition, the officials were most favorably disposed toward these forces. How else could American officials advocate instituting an austerity program in a country already faced with mass unemployment and an annual per capita income of two hundred dollars? When the conservative forces were threatened—

---

[18] That this practice did not end with the April revolution was suggested by two members of the House Foreign Affairs Committee, who visited the Dominican Republic in November. Edward R. Roybal of California and Donald M. Fraser of Minnesota concluded: ". . . we got the distinct impression that the United States lacked adequate communication with the various groups and forces in that country. . . . It will be essential that our diplomatic contacts not be limited to the elite. . . ." U.S., Congress, House, Committee on Foreign Affairs, *Report of the Special Study Mission to Chile, Peru, and the Dominican Republic*, 89th Cong., 2d Sess., 1966, H. Rept. 1746, p. 9.

[19] Unnamed high administration official in Washington, quoted in Szulc, *op. cit.*, p. 67.

[20] Unnamed embassy associate of Bennett, quoted in *loc. cit.* Much the same was said of Connett. Marcel Niedergang, *La Révolution de St. Dominique* (Paris: Libairie Plon), p. 39.

[21] Leonard Gross, "The Man Behind Our Latin American Actions," *Look*, June 15, 1965, p. 37.

the individuals whose values, attitudes, and ways of life were most like those of the embassy officers—American officials were not without clues in deciding on which side to bestow their favors.

So long as the narrow portion of the population with whom the top embassy officials were familiar remained in power, the disadvantages of this approach could be hidden behind a curtain of stability. Behind this curtain, however, was an intense and widespread frustration, and a corresponding demand for better times. But the embassy, it appears, was inadequately aware of these attitudes, and this was to prove a serious impediment to its attempts to evaluate the nature and speed of change, once it began.

II

April 24 was a Saturday, and the already depleted embassy staff was even smaller on the weekend. Early that afternoon, a "rather mixed bag" of military officers moved against Reid.[22] Many were democratic supporters of Bosch, advocating "greater participation of all classes in the cultural, economic and political life of the country."[23] Others, however, were "pro-Balaguer Trujillistas" or outright opportunists.[24] Almost as if reinforcing its prior implicit prediction that trouble was not imminent, the American embassy reacted by telling the State Department in Washington that "the rebellion did not seem to amount to much."[25] But it did. The rebels, after a brief setback, quickly won the upper hand. Realizing this, the "loyal"[26] military commanders met with the rebels, and all decided that Reid should be replaced by an interim military junta. Free elections were to be held within three to six months. His situation clearly hopeless, Reid resigned on April 25, the second day of the revolt.[27]

---

[22] Slater, *op. cit.,* p. 19.

[23] Jose Antonio Moreno, "Sociological Aspects of the Dominican Revolution" (unpublished Ph.D. dissertation, Cornell University, Department of Sociology, 1967), p. 258. This fascinating work was written by a participant-observer on the rebel side, who was living in Santo Domingo working on his dissertation when the revolution erupted.

[24] Slater, *op. cit.,* p. 20.

[25] Szulc, *op. cit.,* p. 6.

[26] "Loyalist" was the term applied to the forces opposed to the pro-Bosch rebels, although it seems that the forces' "loyalty" was only to themselves. As a result of this terminological confusion, self-contradictory statements abound, of which the following is an example: ". . . it had become clear that the loyal Dominican military commanders were not going to support Reid, no matter what else they might decide to do." Georgetown University, *op. cit.,* p. 15. That the United States was willing to label military commanders refusing to support their own leader "loyal" indicates where American sentiments lay, despite protestations of neutrality.

[27] Reid had asked Connett for American armed assistance, but had been turned down on the grounds that the ships were too far away, and that the United States had refused to help Bosch in a similar situation a year and a half earlier. Kurzman, *op. cit.,* p. 132. Georgetown

Bosch's backers, however, were gaining greater and greater influence, and soon the rebels seized the Presidential Palace, and announced their support for his return. All the "loyalist" commanders, seeing a fight as futile, capitulated—all, that is, except General Wessin,[28] and his forces were so small that after sending a company to occupy the end of a bridge he was left with only two hundred men. Santo Domingo, meanwhile, "went wild," as "mobs roamed the streets . . . chanting 'Viva Bosch!' and linking arms with rebel troops." [29] There was some violence, but Dominican newspapers reported only about ten deaths on April 25.

That afternoon, however, Dominican air force planes strafed the Presidential Palace, and began machine gunning and bombing various portions of Santo Domingo. Why did the air force chief of staff, whom Wessin reports had earlier urged him to surrender,[30] now take up what had hitherto been considered a lost cause? An answer will be suggested shortly. The air attacks seemed to the rebels to be a prelude to more thorough-going actions, specifically, tank and infantry attacks. In response to these threats, the rebels began to distribute guns, rifles, and machine guns to civilians,[31] and service stations began to supply free gasoline for gasoline-bottle bombs.[32] Major acts of violence were about to begin.

The events of these two days, in short, involved swift, sweeping, spectacular change. The American officials on the scene constituted the critical link between Washington and developments on the island. How, then, did these officials react? It is, of course, impossible to answer with certainty, but the question obviously is too important to ignore, and merits at least some speculation. Although the officials had not been enthusiastic about Reid's government, they had learned how to deal with it and what to expect from it. This familiarity seems to have bred security and confidence. But with the revolt, all of this vanished literally overnight, and since the rebels were the cause of the change, they quickly be-

University's Center for Strategic Studies contends, unconvincingly, that Reid's sole motive was to prevent bloodshed and not to retain his power. *Op. cit.*, p. 17.

[28] U.S., Congress, Senate, Committee on the Judiciary, Subcommittee to Investigate the Administration of the Internal Security Act and Other Internal Security Laws, *Hearing, Testimony of General Elias Wessin y Wessin*, 89th Cong., 1st Sess., 1965, pp. 156–57. Hereinafter cited as *Wessin Testimony*.

[29] Kurzman, *op. cit.*, p. 133. *New York Herald Tribune*, April 26, 1965.

[30] *Wessin Testimony*, p. 156.

[31] Szulc estimated that 20,000 weapons may have been distributed (*op. cit.*, p. 18), but the Associated Press maintained that only about 3,000 civilians received guns (*New York Times*, April 27, 1965), and Kurzman believes the number was between 3,000 and 5,000. *Op. cit.*

[32] Georgetown's Center for Strategic Studies attributes this to the Maoist Popluar Democratic Party (*op. cit.*, p. 16), but there is no other report of this.

came the focus of official hostility. This reaction appears to have been accentuated by the fact that the existence and nature of the revolt itself constituted brazen and irrefutable evidence of the American officials' failure. Part of their job, after all, had been to advise Washington of impending revolutions or at least to predict their outcome with accuracy; but in neither duty had the embassy staff succeeded.

In this situation of flux and uncertainty, the staff members clung to the one value of which they and their superiors in Washington were sure: there must be no Communist takeover in the Dominican Republic. A corollary of this was that Bosch's return must be prevented, for it was felt that this would mean "Communism in the Dominican Republic in six months." [33] Whether this conclusion stemmed from a belief that Bosch was unable or unwilling to fight off the Communists is not clear, for while some American officials were content to describe him contemptuously as a "poet-professor" or a "do-gooder," Mann did not stress this kind of well-meaning ineptitude. Bosch, said the undersecretary in testimony before the Senate Foreign Relations Committee, was an ambitious schemer, who "would make an alliance with the devil himself if he thought it would get him into office." Nor was this hypothetical. Mann charged that Bosch, "according to intelligence information," had "reportedly told" a representative of a pro-Castro organization in the spring of 1964 that he wanted and needed its help. Thus, at the time of the revolution, officials may have been convinced that Bosch had made an "effective alliance" with Dominican Communists. [34] Mann's charge, however, is so hedged with qualifications that suspicions arise that it may have been concocted after the revolution to justify American behavior during it.

Whatever the reason, all American officials in Santo Domingo apparently believed that with Bosch in power, communism could not be far behind. And by confining their personal contacts largely to individuals holding this view, the officials' beliefs were reinforced and strengthened. The fact that the staff knew little about the rebels also made them seem more ominous for being unknown. In none of their interpretations of events were the officials likely to encounter opposition from Washington. Certainly, that Mann was known as a "hard-liner" on communism in the hemisphere gave small incentive to place a non-Communist interpretation upon events in their reports. All of this meant that following Reid's ouster, officials who earlier had underestimated the likelihood of trouble and the seriousness of this revolt, made it plain that they would

---

[33] Szulc, *op. cit.,* p. 19.
[34] *New York Times*, November 14, 1965.

not compound this error by underestimating the seriousness of the Communist danger.[35]

The implication clearly was that the United States should aid the forces opposing the rebels, and the embassy wasted no time in making this explicit. As early as April 25, the Second Secretary of the embassy refered to the rebels as part of a "Communist movement," [36] and Connett told Washington that all the senior officials "feel Bosch's return and resumption of control of the government is against U.S. interests, in view of the extremists in the coup and Communist advocacy of Bosch's return." [37] Already, Connett added, he had agreed to help Wessin "fight to block return of Bosch . . . even though it could mean more bloodshed." [38] The embassy's military attachês, by this time, "had given 'loyalist' leaders a go-ahead to prevent what was described as the danger of a 'Communist take-over.' "[39] It was this "go-ahead," of course, that caused the Dominican air force chief to change his mind about surrendering to the rebels, and agree to help transform a virtually bloodless coup into a civil-war by attacking Santo Domingo.[40]

At this early stage, no American military intervention was proposed, though as Max Frankel of the *New York Times* has concluded, the United States "was prepared to use its own troops if the rebels gained the upper hand." [41] Six ships of Task Force 44.9 in the Caribbean had already been alerted for the possible evacuation of 1,200 American nationals. The ships, as their commander admitted, had "a capability of three times the expected evacuation need," and were sent in anticipation of military contingencies "covering the spectrum from positive civic action, to show of force, to assault." [42] Included in this alert was a Marine task force of 1,500 men. The State Department publicly described the action as a "routine precautionary move," and emphasized that the United States had no intention of using the Marines to intervene.[43]

---

[35] The proverbial Foreign Service caution apparently reinforced this unanimity by silencing those harboring doubts as to the wisdom of American intervention. William A. Bell, "The Cost of Cowardice: Silence in the Foreign Service," *Washington Monthly*, July 1969, p. 23.

[36] Arthur E. Breisky, quoted in Szulc, *op. cit.,* p. 21.

[37] Actually, Cuba did not begin to support Bosch as the "constitutional" leader until April 26. *New York Times,* April 27, 1965. The following day, Cuban broadcasts accurately predicted that American forces were preparing to land in the Dominican Republic "on the pretext of rescuing American citizens." *New York Times,* April 28, 1965.

[38] Quoted in Geyelin *op. cit.,* p. 246.

[39] Philip Geyelin, *Wall Street Journal,* June 25, 1965.

[40] Slater, however, seems to believe that the key factor leading to armed loyalist action was their belief that the rebels would return Bosch to power, and that he "would probably seek to destroy [the regular military's] power and position. . . ." Slater, *op. cit.,* p. 24.

[41] *New York Times,* November 14, 1965.

[42] Captain James A. Dare, "Dominican Diary," *United States Naval Institute Proceedings* 91 (December 1965): 38.

[43] *New York Times,* April 27, 1965.

The following morning, on April 26, Connett informed Washington that he believed that there was a serious threat of a Communist takeover and that there was little time to stave off such an eventuality.[44] The embassy remained committed to Wessin, dispatching its military attachés to his headquarters, where they relayed "to the embassy battle reports and requests for assistance."[45] Ambassador Bennett seems fully to have shared these views on the imminence of a Communist victory and the necessity of helping Wessin. Three days later, reporters en route to Santo Domingo overheard him speaking on the radio to a new "loyalist" chief. "Do you need more aid?" asked Bennett. "Believe that with determination your plans will succeed."[46] Later, he referred to the rebels as "Castro forces,"[47] and in private, called them "Communist scum."[48]

By April 27 it appeared that Wessin's forces were on the verge of victory, and "administration officials were expressing relief over the apparent collapse of the insurrection. . . ."[49] Ambassador Bennett, who had returned from Washington several hours earlier, met with rebel leaders who asked him to arrange a cease-fire. Bennett refused, and while what he actually said remains in dispute,[50] the reason for his action seems clear: Washington favored Wessin's side, and was unwilling to interfere with events moving his way. "I went to bed that night," one embassy staff member recalled later, "thinking it was all over."[51] Mainly "at the insistence of the CIA,"[52] General Wessin, "the symbol of a returning dictatorship,"[53] was replaced by a three-man military junta headed by an obscure air force colonel, Pedro Bartolome Benoit. The United States then could appear to be dealing with a government—albeit "a government on paper only"[54]—instead of merely supporting a faction.

---

[44] Georgetown University, *op. cit.*, p. 23.

[45] Szulc, *op. cit.*, p. 25.

[46] *Ibid.*, p. 57; Kurzman, *op. cit.*, p. 178.

[47] Szulc, *op. cit.*, p. 58; Kurzman, *loc. cit.*

[48] Szulc, *op. cit.*, p. 92.

[49] *New York Times*, April 28, 1965.

[50] According to Bennett, his refusal simply reflected "the U.S. view . . . that the matter should be settled by Dominicans talking with Dominicans." Georgetown University, *op. cit.*, p. 28. Colonel Francisco Caamaño Deño, a leader of the rebel delegation, had a different version. He says that when the rebels allegedly offered to accept a junta government in order to end the bloodshed, Bennett replied: "You should have realized before you started the trouble that you couldn't hold out. Now it's too late. . . . Go and see Wessin yourself. You are finished." Quoted in Kurzman, *op. cit.*, p. 152. This haughty treatment infuriated Caamaño, he recalls. Since the rebels seemed on the brink of defeat, negotiating with them may have appeared senseless to an embassy already committed to Wessin's forces. See Geyelin, *Johnson and the World*, p. 248.

[51] Ruyle, quoted by Geyelin, *Wall Street Journal*, June 25, 1965.

[52] Senator Joseph Clark, a Democrat from Pennsylvania, U.S., *Congressional Record*, 89th Cong., 1st Sess., 1965, 3, pt. 18: 24241.

[53] Szulc, *op. cit.*, p. 42.

[54] *Ibid.*, p. 43.

III

By early afternoon of the following day, the military situation had been dramatically reversed. Now it was the junta's forces who were "on the verge of collapse," and an American official noted "an atmosphere of despair in [their] military headquarters." [55] Their communications problems were especially serious, severely hampering coordination efforts and lowering morale as well. Desperate, Benoit appealed to Bennett for help, and at 1:48 P.M. the Ambassador cabled the State Department. "[T]hese people are facing leftist forces," he said, adding, "What would be the effect on the morale of the air force and others" if their pleas were denied? [56]

After a brief interval, Bennett cabled Washington again.

... the issue [he said] is really between those who want a Castro-type solution and those who oppose it. I don't want to over dramatize, but if we deny the communications equipment, and if the opposition to the leftists lose heart, we may be asking for a landing of Marines to protect U.S. interests and for other purposes. [57]

Walkie-talkies were provided for the junta, but Washington was unwilling to intervene militarily unless absolutely necessary to forestall a rebel victory.

The junta's situation continued to deteriorate, and Benoit asked Bennett for 1,200 Marines to salvage the junta cause. "You had better send American troops in," Benoit said in effect, "because a Communist takeover threatens." [58] Ambassador Bennett passed the request along to Washington, but added, "I do not believe the situation justifies it." [59] Uneasy over recent developments, however, he did not advocate excluding a Marine landing from future consideration, and recommended "contingency planning in case situation should break apart." [60]

Later that afternoon, Benoit made a similar request, maintaining that the "present revolt is directed by Communists," whose victory would create "another Cuba." [61] At 4:54 Bennett relayed the appeal to Washington.

Perhaps the Ambassador had finally become wholly convinced. In any case, at 5:14 he cabled Washington. The junta, he said, was rapidly falling into despair and defeat. In order to forestall its collapse and, secondarily, to safeguard "American lives ... in danger," [62] he recommended

[55] Georgetown University, *op. cit.*, p. 33.
[56] Szulc, *loc. cit.*
[57] *Ibid.*, p. 44. A slightly different version is reported in Geyelin, *op. cit.*, p. 249.
[58] Senator Clark, U.S., *Congressional Record,* 89th Cong., 1st Sess., 1965, 3, pt. 18: 24242.
[59] Quoted in Geyelin, *Johnson and the World,* p. 250.
[60] Evans and Novak, *op. cit.*, p. 538.
[61] Quoted in Geyelin, *loc. cit.*
[62] Quoted in Evans and Novak, *op. cit.*, p. 534.

the landing. It could, he suggested, be hidden behind official talk of protecting the evacuation of American citizens.

President Johnson received the message while meeting with his advisers. They included Secretaries Rusk and McNamara, Undersecretary of State George W. Ball, Special Presidential Assistant for National Security Affairs McGeorge Bundy, CIA Director Raborn, and Special Assistant Bill Moyers. It may be significant that all the advisers except Raborn and Moyers were veterans of the Cuban missile crisis. This experience may have reinforced their belief that crises could be managed boldly and successfully, if Washington would only take the initiative—and this, of course, was in perfect line with Bennett's recommendation. Certainly, Raborn with his "damn the torpedoes" reputation was unlikely to advocate timidity, and there is no evidence to suggest that Moyers dissented. Johnson thus surpassed even Kennedy at the Bay of Pigs in his refusal to solicit hostile or differing opinions.

Partly, this may have reflected a concern for speed, since the position seemed to be deteriorating rapidly—though from the point of view of safeguarding American lives no dire emergency yet existed.[63] More importantly, probably, the President had already made up his mind, and seems to have viewed additional affirmation or opposition as superfluous. Then at the apogee of his presidential success—highly popular with the public, and enormously influential with Congress—he had great and exaggerated confidence in his own political judgment. Furthermore, suggests his former press secretary, George Reedy, Johnson's extraordinary capacity for give-and-take which had contributed so much to his success as Senate Majority Leader had been seriously eroded by the isolation and primacy of the presidency. "He had become accustomed to substituting command for persuasion," writes Reedy. "And he was not comfortable having around him people who would argue against an impulse, even though the same people would not reveal their disagreement in public." [64] The President's initial circle of advisers, then, was extremely narrow.

The influence of the advisers in support of firm and quick action, in any case, appears to have been exercised before the Ambassador even sent his cable—if it were exercised at all. For the President's immediate reaction was not to discuss the matter with them, but to instruct McNamara to prepare for the landings. Bennett's message, in other words, apparently triggered a preexisting presidential decision: American forces would be committed if the rebels seemed about to overwhelm

---

[63] As Senator Fulbright pointed out, "No American citizen was killed or injured until *after* the Marines were landed and the Marines had exchanged shots with the revolutionists." U.S., *Congressional Record,* 89th Cong., 1st Sess., 1965, 3, pt. 18: 23864. (Emphasis added.)

[64] George E. Reedy, "Does the U.S. Need a King?" *Look,* March 10, 1970, p. 33.

the junta. By 6:53 the naval commander, waiting off Santo Domingo, had been ordered to send five hundred Marines ashore. Congressmen, Latin American leaders and ambassadors, and Organization of American States officials [65]—each was informed and none was consulted.[66]

Having made the basic decision to intervene, Johnson was then faced with the decision of how to present the intervention to the world. Since the importance of the intervention consisted not only in its substance but also in its appearance, the question of presentation can hardly be exaggerated. The President, in short, was aware that beyond its immediate impact upon a revolution in a tiny Caribbean country, his decision would affect his own stature and that of his nation as well.

Time was short. If he withheld a public statement too long, the delay itself would arouse criticism. A brief televised speech for that night was planned. The original draft of the speech, according to columnists Rowland Evans and Robert Novak, stressed the goal of protecting American lives, but also at Rusk's urging hinted obliquely at a second goal of preventing a Communist take-over. This approach was in line with Rusk's earlier advice to the President to the effect that the revolt was "yet another test of U.S. resolve" with worldwide repercussions—especially in Vietnam—if this country did not meet the test.[67] United Nations Ambassador Adlai Stevenson, however, argued that the second—and in fact overriding—goal be omitted. Stevenson suggested that "until the Presi-

---

[65] Actually, the OAS was not even formally notified until *after* the President informed the nation of his decision on television that night. Evans and Novak report the Secretary-General of the OAS, José Mora, learned of the landing through a chance viewing of Johnson's speech on television. The State Department had not even informed him. *Op. cit.,* p. 242. This is not very surprising, given the contempt with which Johnson held the OAS. "The OAS couldn't pour——out of a boot if the instructions were on the heel," he had said on one occasion. Geyelin, *op. cit.,* p. 254. The OAS, American officials long had felt, acts too slowly in crisis decisions. Actually, of course, these officials desired not simply speedy decisions but speedy pro-American decisions. Yet "Latin Americans do not regard the inter-American system as an instrument for furnishing swift endorsement of United States policies. Rather they look to it to impose a measure of restraint upon their powerful neighbour: to maintain the principle of non-intervention." Gordon Connell-Smith, *The Inter-American System* (London: Oxford University Press, 1966), pp. 341–42. Yet as Ronald Steel has pointed out, "the United States has tended to treat nonintervention as a concession to Latin American sensibilities rather than as a principle of diplomacy—and as a fairly expendable concession at that, to be ignored or pushed aside whenever the demands of the cold war seem to dictate." Ronald Steel, *Pax Americana* (New York: Viking Press, 1967), p. 205. See Jerome Slater, "The Limits of Legitimization in International Organizations: The Organization of American States and the Dominican Crisis," *International Organization* 23 (Winter 1969): 48.

[66] Nonetheless, Secretary McNamara in his unintentionally satirical *Essence of Security* counts the OAS's role in the Dominican Republic as one of "the first attempts to substitute multinational for unilateral policing of violence." Another instance cited is the allied effort in South Vietnam. Robert S. McNamara, *The Essence of Security: Reflections in Office* (New York: Harper and Row, 1968), p. 154.

[67] Geyelin, *loc. cit.*

dent could make a compelling case—that is, until the CIA and the United States Embassy in Santo Domingo could complete their investigation on the scene—it would be a mistake to drop in the Communist angle by indirection." [68] Moyers and Richard Goodwin, both reputedly knowledgeable about public opinion, seconded Stevenson's suggestion, and Johnson adopted the single goal "humanitarian" [69] strategy that night. Implicit in this nonpolitical pose was the assumption that the United States would maintain strict neutrality, showing no favoritism toward any faction. Washington, in fact, pointedly stressed this in its releases to the press, and as late as May 3 Senate Majority Leader Mike Mansfield repeated three times in a Senate speech that "we can accept the word of the President of the United States that we will not take sides with any individual or group, and that includes General Wessin y Wessin. . . ." [70]

The humanitarian strategy had the important advantage of assuring virtually unanimous domestic support at the vital initial phase; for what American could oppose his government's safeguarding the lives of his fellow citizens endangered by a Caribbean revolution? This strategy also temporarily blunted the edge of diatribes against American "gunboat diplomacy." Events were soon to reveal, however, how shortsighted such a strategy was; for all interested persons were not willing to await (or even to trust) a CIA and embassy investigation before uttering in public the views circulating in private on the island. [71]

Meanwhile, the State Department was attempting to cover its tracks by obtaining a request from Benoit which made no reference to a Communist threat. As Mann told the Senate Foreign Relations Committee:

So we . . . said to our Ambassador, "See if Benoit would be willing to give us an additional message which places the request squarely on the need to save

---

[68] Evans and Novak, *op. cit.*, p. 542. Stevenson's argument, then, was that the President should have adequate evidence before he told the people of the alleged Communist threat; no suggestion was made that he should have adequate evidence before acting on that basis. According to Kurzman, Stevenson had contended "that an indirect charge would inflame controversy even more than a direct one" (*op. cit.*, p. 185), but this raises the question of why he did not therefore advocate a direct charge instead of omission.

[69] The term "humanitarian" recurs in approving contemporary descriptions of the President's actions. See, e.g., the remarks of Senators Mike Mansfield, Leverett Saltonstall, and Frank Church, U.S., *Congressional Record,* 89th Cong., 1st Sess., 1965, 2, pt. 7: 9218, 9220, 9221, 9451.

[70] U.S., *Congressional Record,* 89th Cong., 1st Sess., 1965, 2, pt. 7: 9220-21.

[71] An old friend of Stevenson's has argued that the Ambassador had not been informed that the administration's prime concern was the threat of a Communist take-over, and in fact was genuinely surprised to hear Johnson mention that threat in his April 30 televised speech. Eric Sevareid, "The Final Troubled Hours of Adlai Stevenson," *Look,* November 30, 1965, p. 84. If this be true, it hardly speaks well for Stevenson's political acumen, for Rusk's sentence and the common talk in the administration that Bosch was "soft" on communism should have raised doubts as to the explanatory satisfactoriness of a humanitarian

American lives" . . . and Benoit said "I will be happy to make this as a second request." [72]

Later, a helicopter was dispatched to pick up this "skimmed-down version" [73] of Benoit's earlier request.

In the President's brief televised statement, he declared that he had sent four hundred Marines "in order to give protection to hundreds of Americans who are still in the Dominican Republic and to escort them safely back to this country." [74] No mention was made of a threatened Communist take-over. Nor was this possibility raised the next day, when 1,200 more Marines landed and 2,500 airborne troops began arriving at the junta's headquarters. As the size of the American contingent increased, the rationale of protecting American lives seemed less and less satisfactory. Ultimately, it was called into question by elements as diverse as the antijunta *New York Times* and the former Trujillo supporter, Senator Allen J. Ellender of Louisiana. [75] At a closed meeting of the OAS, Latin American diplomats "passionately spoke of 'U.S. intervention,' charging the action was reminiscent of U.S. gunboat diplomacy of a bygone era." [76] In the United States, a number of liberals, individually and through the press, began to echo these views.

These critics were clearly in the minority. The vast majority of congressmen, the press, and the general public supported the President, who was "still following the public opinion polls as if it were the week before election." [77] Johnson, nonetheless, "became inordinately concerned with criticism of his action." [78] Partly, this may have reflected his general tendency to take adverse comments on his public role as personal attacks. Apparently an ingredient in his personality, this tendency seems to have been heightened by his accession to the presidency, which appears to have made him painfully aware of his lack of personal public appeal—a lack made all the more obvious by his following Kennedy, a supreme stylist, into office. [79] Perhaps as a means of compensating for this lack,

goal for the landing. Stevenson later disapproved of the intervention, calling it a "massive blunder." Stevenson to broadcaster David Schoenbrun, quoted in Walton, *op. cit.,* p. 171.

[72] Quoted by Frankel, *New York Times,* November 14, 1965.

[73] Geyelin, *Wall Street Journal,* June 25, 1965.

[74] Lyndon B. Johnson, "Statement by President Johnson, April 28," *Department of State Bulletin* 52 (May 17, 1965): 738. Although Johnson said that "military authorities" had requested the landing to protect American lives, he did not specify whether "military authorities" referred to the rebels or the junta.

[75] Editorial, *New York Times,* May 2, 1965. U.S., *Congressional Record,* 89th Cong., 1st Sess., 1965, 2, pt. 7: 9222.

[76] *New York Herald Tribune,* April 30, 1965.

[77] James Reston, *New York Times,* May 7, 1965.

[78] Evans and Novak, *op. cit.,* p. 540.

[79] On this, see Eric F. Goldman, *The Tragedy of Lyndon Johnson* (New York: Knopf, 1969).

Johnson appears to have been determined to outperform Kennedy, and in the process of competition became, as Evans and Novak put it, "rather thin-skinned." [80] One long-time Washington columnist called Johnson "the most sensitive President I have ever known or read about. He spots everything critical that is written about him and pounces on it like a hawk." [81] Another correspondent observed that "Johnson wants not criticism but loyalty. When he doesn't get it he becomes hostile." [82]

The President's concern with criticism may also have stemmed from a desire to retain the support of liberal intellectuals, a desire which was later expressed by his dispatching a respected liberal and former ambassador to the Dominican Republic, John Bartlow Martin, to the island. This support was desired not only because Kennedy had it, but also because it was necessary for the success of Johnson's own policies.[83] The liberals' active backing for his domestic programs was essential, and their acquiescence in the Vietnam war was obviously preferred. By April 30, as two supporters of the Dominican intervention have written, "the President's obsession with criticism had embarked him on the most blatant personal campaign to sell the intervention to the country through the White House press corps that any President in history had ever undertaken." [84]

During this time, an escalation of atrocity revelations began to appear in the press, with the effect of buttressing the "humanitarian" strategy. This, of course, was not the first time in American history that such tales had been used in support of military actions. In the late 1890s, William Randolph Hearst, Joseph Pulitzer, and other "yellow journalists" had publicized brutal concentration camps set up in Cuba by General Valeriano "Butcher" Weyler as part of Spain's effort to suppress a revolution. These and other exposés of misery and exploitation in Cuba had been mainly responsible for the growth of widespread popular feeling against Spain. When in 1898 the American battleship *Maine* was sunk in Havana harbor with heavy loss of life, the "yellow press" had attributed the

---

[80] Evans and Novak, quoted in Richard B. Stolley, " 'Presidents Are Awful with the Press; Johnson Is Worse,' " *Life*, May 17, 1965, p. 37.

[81] Roscoe Drummond, "Point of View: The President and the Press," *Christian Science Monitor*, May 5, 1965. At this writing, Johnson had not yet been subjected to the torrent of bitterness, invective, wit, and downright hate, which his later major escalation of the war in Vietnam was to bring on.

[82] James Reston, quoted in John K. Jessup, "Two Most Eminent and Strikingly Different Columnists," *Life*, May 17, 1965, p. 38. As John Molloy put it, "Johnson's conception of the press was as that of a cheerleader." John D. Molloy, "Nixon and the Press," paper delivered at the meeting of the Midwest Political Science Association, Chicago, May 1, 1970.

[83] The relations of Kennedy and Johnson with the intellectuals is perceptively analyzed by the British journalist Henry Fairlie, "Johnson and the Intellectuals," *Commentary*, October 1965, pp. 49–55, esp. pp. 49–52.

[84] Evans and Novak, *op. cit.*, pp. 544–45.

disaster to Spanish agents, and had demanded United States intervention in Cuba. Although Spain acceded to almost all American demands, "public opinion [had] frenziedly demanded war," [85] and so had Congress. The result was that President McKinley, who had pursued an antiwar policy, had submitted to the pressure, and the Spanish-American War was fought.[86] Less than twenty years later, reports of German barbarities in Belgium, and the horrors of submarine warfare as practiced against the *Lusitania*, the *Sussex*, and the *Housatonic* had helped to prepare the way for the American entry into World War I.

In neither of these instances, however, had the administrations exaggerated the atrocity stories in order to create a more warlike public opinion. Quite the contrary, both Presidents McKinley and Wilson had sought to *avoid* American involvement in war. McKinley, for instance, had attempted to convince the public to withhold blame for the *Maine* disaster until an official inquiry could be completed, and Wilson had successfully resisted pleas to break off diplomatic relations with Germany for nearly a year until the *Housatonic* was sunk.[87]

In the Dominican revolution, atrocity stories seem clearly to have been planted by the American government in order to gain public support for its opposition to the rebels, and ultimately, for its military intervention. The atrocity escalation began at a low level. For the first three days of the revolt, the United States confined itself to "deplor[ing] the violence and disorder in the Dominican Republic," [88] and even conceded that there was no damage to American lives or property. Blanket condemnations of violence, however, do not convey a sense of fear, of revulsion, of anger. For this, concrete illustrations are needed. The earliest illustration of any importance was provided on April 27 by the first returning American evacuees, who described four hours of terror they had experienced at the Hotel Embajador in Santo Domingo.[89] The hotel had been filled with over a thousand Americans awaiting evacuation, when a pack of young rebels burst into the lobby, saying that they were search-

---

[85] Ernest R. May, "Emergence to World Power," *The Reconstruction of American History,* ed. John Higham (New York: Harper and Bros., 1962), p. 183.

[86] Marcus Manley Wilkerson, *Public Opinion and the Spanish-American War: A Study in War Propaganda* (Baton Rouge: Louisiana State University Press, 1932), p. 132. But cf., Mark M. Welter, "The 1895–98 Cuban Crisis in Minnesota Newspapers: Testing the 'Yellow Journalism Theory,' " *Journalism Quarterly* 47 (Winter 1970): 719.

[87] After the United States' entry into World War I, Wilson created a Committee on Public Information headed by George Creel which was so chauvinistic in spirit and misleading in its picture of postwar life that it aroused long-term popular hostility to national security propaganda that influenced President Roosevelt a quarter century later. Richard W. Steele, "Preparing the Public for War: Efforts to Establish a National Propaganda Agency, 1940–41," *American Historical Review* 75 (October 1970): 1640ff.

[88] Lyndon B. Johnson, quoted in the *New York Times,* April 28, 1965.

[89] Szulc, *op. cit.,* pp. 33–34.

ing for "counterrevolutionaries." Their main target seems to have been Rafael Bonilla Aybar, who had been the "nerve center of the civilian campaign to paint Bosch as a Communist" [90] in 1963, and whom they feared would leave the country with the American evacuees. In their search, the rebels lined the Americans against the lobby wall. Several shots were fired at the upper windows and balconies of the hotel, and a few submachine gun bursts were fired into the lobby's ceiling. After a while, the rebels left. No one was injured, and the evacuation itself proceeded uneventfully. The Americans naturally were frightened, and their statements to the press upon their return reflected this terror. United States officials could have attempted to put the event in perspective by noting that this kind of incident is endemic to revolutions, by emphasizing that no one had been harmed, and by pointing out that the rebels had not been motivated by anti-Americanism but by factional animosity. None of these things was done. No attempt was made to minimize the spectacular nature of the event. Instead, the President later was to refer to armed rebels dashing through the hotel's hallways firing into rooms and closets, and Secretary Rusk was to speak of "people running around the hotel, shooting it up with tommyguns and so forth." [91] The incident was used as part of the rationalization for intervention.

The next day, April 28, found the embassy dealing in gorier affairs, as it told Reuters of "a pretty savage drumhead kind of justice" practiced by the rebels. With shouts of the Castorite cry "Al Paredon!" (to the wall!), twelve persons allegedly had been shot. [92]

The following afternoon, Ambassador Bennett held a press conference to brief American correspondents, who had just arrived. Unfamiliar with the situation and having no reason to doubt the Ambassador's word, they relied heavily upon his accounts in their first stories. [93] They were told of several "Al Paredon!" incidents; rebels had slain their opponents in mass executions; they had killed Wessin's soldiers and policemen, cut off their heads, and paraded them on spikes in downtown Santo Domingo like gigantic, grotesque hors d'oeuvres; rebel leader Colonel Caamaño's mind had snapped, and he had shot in cold blood Colonel Juan Calderón, a friend of the Ambassador and a former aide-de-camp to Reid.

In telegrams to the State Department, Bennett repeated these and sim-

---

[90] Kurzman, *op. cit.*, p. 93.

[91] "Secretary Rusk's News Conference of May 26," *Department of State Bulletin* 52 (June 14, 1965): 942.

[92] *New York Times*, April 29, 1965.

[93] See e.g., *New York Times*, April 30, 1965; "Dominican Republic: The Coup that Became a War," *Time*, May 7, 1965, p. 28; "Full Story of Caribbean War: How Reds Plotted a Take-Over," *U.S. News and World Report*, May 3, 1965, p. 34. *Time* was so taken by the administration's version of events that it made General Wessin its cover figure.

ilar stories, and they began to be incorporated into the President's speech. In his May 4 remarks to congressional committees, for example, he referred to Bennett's report that the rebels "had threatened to line a hundred up to a wall and turn a machine gun loose on them," and spoke, of "six or eight embassies [having] been torn up. There has been almost constant firing on our American Embassy [and] from 1,000 to 1,500 bodies . . . are dead in the street. . . ." [94] The next day, correspondents were told that "eyewitnesses" had seen rebels machine gun Bonilla Aybar to death. Similar statements from the President were heard as late as June 17.[95]

Certainly atrocities occur in civil wars, and this was no exception. But when reporters later examined these stories they were found to be either dubious or false. No incidents of "Al Paredon!" no incidents of mass executions, no incidents of spiked severed heads—for none of these tales could any substantiating evidence be found. As for the other stories, Colonel Calderón and Bonilla Aybar turned up alive, one embassy was entered by a mob in search of individuals seeking political asylum there but no embassy was torn up, the American embassy was fired on a few times but did not even show bullet marks, and "no more than six or ten bodies were found in the streets at one time." [96]

It is impossible to say whether Bennett deliberately misled Washington with his scare stories in order to increase support there for his recommendation before and after it was implemented. Perhaps he was acting on orders from above; perhaps he sincerely believed some of the stories he purveyed. Officials admitted some of the inaccuracies when the crisis was safely past, blaming them on naive reporters who had confused the embassy's self-admitted untested "rumors" with verified facts.[97] It is significant, however, that no real or imagined atrocities seem to have been attributed to the junta, although the loyalists had attacked Santo Domingo with planes and engaged in mass executions of rebels.

While the atrocity stories were useful in supporting the "humanitarian" rationale for intervention, public attention could not so easily be limited. Both supporters and critics of the action instead came to justify or attack it in terms of a threatened Communist take-over of the Dominican Republic. One reason for this was Bennett's April 29 press confer-

---

[94] Lyndon B. Johnson, "Remarks by President Johnson, May 4," *Department of State Bulletin* 52 (May 24, 1965): 822.

[95] Kurzman, *op. cit.,* p. 197. Lyndon B. Johnson, "Assessment of the Situation in the Dominican Republic," *Department of State Bulletin* 53 (July 5, 1965): 20.

[96] *New York Herald Tribune,* May 5, 1965.

[97] Portions of the press embraced this explanation in a paroxysm of masochism. See, e.g., Seldon Rodman, "Close View of Santo Domingo," *Reporter,* July 15, 1965, pp. 20–27. Draper has assembled evidence suggesting persuasively that Bennett had not presented all the atrocity tales as untested rumors. Draper, *Dominican Revolt,* p. 94n.

ence stressing the importance of Communists in the rebellion. This interpretation was widely reported by the news media, and the administration's single-goal rationale was becoming overwhelmed by such talk. The embassy, which "was even more desirous than Washington to push the charge of 'Communist control,'" [98] was impelling the administration to alter its public rhetoric in order to salvage its image of candor. The President, therefore, decided to speak to the nation again, and in a second televised address on April 30 referred to "signs that people trained outside the Dominican Republic are seeking to gain control." [99] This was "the first public indication by the administration that Castro-controlled Communists may be playing a role in the revolt," [100] and it marked the acceptance of a double-goal strategy: saving American lives *and* preventing a Communist take-over. Since the clear majority of the public, the press, and the politicians approved both goals, the President maintained his popular support. Domestic liberal critics, however, became louder and more strident after the second goal was officially announced. And the London *Observer* noted an "unprecedented ... unanimous condemnation of U.S. intervention by the Governments of Latin America, whatever their political complexion. . . ." [101]

In response to all this added criticism, the President decided to make still another televised address, and on the evening of May 2 delivered a lengthy and rather disorganized speech. The dual goals of American policy now emerged in full bloom:

We are there to save the lives of our citizens and to save the lives of all people. Our goal, in keeping with the great principles of the inter-American system, is to help prevent another Communist state in this hemisphere. [102]

The most interesting part of the speech, however, was the portion in which the President elaborated on his earlier allusion to "people trained outside the Dominican Republic." Now he offered this interpretation of events:

---

[98] Kurzman, *op. cit.,* p. 186.

[99] Lyndon B. Johnson, "Statement by President Johnson, April 30," *Department of State Bulletin* 52 (May 17, 1965): 742. Had he been referring to himself and other American officials, he could hardly have been disputed.

[100] *New York Herald Tribune,* May 1, 1965.

[101] London *Observer,* May 2, 1965. "Notable among the complainants," the *Observer* added, "is Venezuela, whose Foreign Minister summoned the U.S. Ambassador to receive an official protest." Venezuela, which had itself been faced with Communist guerrillas, was hardly likely to underestimate the likelihood of a Communist threat elsewhere in the hemisphere.

[102] Lyndon B. Johnson, "Statement by President Johnson, May 2," *Department of State Bulletin* 52 (May 17, 1965): 745.

The revolutionary movement took a tragic turn. Communist leaders, many of them trained in Cuba, seeing a chance to increase disorder, to gain a foothold, joined the revolution. They took increasing control. And what began as a popular democratic revolution, committed to democracy and social justice, very shortly moved and was taken over and really seized and placed into the hands of a band of Communist conspirators.[103]

The revolutionary movement was thus seen as passing through three stages: non-Communist, Communist-influenced, and Communist-controlled. By implication, the crucial point from the American vantage occurred when influence became control. As Mann later explained to a *Times* journalist, "there really is no problem, as far as our policy is concerned, unless and until the Communists succeed in actually capturing and controlling a movement." [104] Actually, of course, this does not seem to have been a very accurate description of the administration's attitude: Communist influence was sufficient to create a "problem" for the United States because it might lead to Communist control; in fact, the non-Communist stage created a "problem," since it might lead to the Communist influence stage. Almost as soon as the revolution began, as was pointed out earlier, it appears to have been perceived as creating a Communist "problem," on the theory that even if the Communists proved unable to win direct control, they could later dominate a Bosch government or take over after a period of chaos.

It is hardly surprising, then, that before long, unidentified "American sources" began to leak stories to the press concerning Communist leaders identified among the rebels. On April 29, Secretary McNamara told several senators that "an element" of the rebel forces was Communist, but that they had not yet been dominated by them. On the same day, however, "American sources" reported at least fifty "known left extremists or Castro-Communist sympathizers," who were involved in the revolt and had "wrested control" of it.[105] The press and the public, in short, were well prepared for the two-goal strategy, when it finally emerged formally in the President's speech the following evening. The primary importance of the speech, in fact, seems to have been to provide an opportunity for politicians and the press to laud openly the President's decision on anti-Communist grounds. And this they did, whether they had generally been thought of as sympathetic to his administration or not.[106]

---

[103] *Ibid.,* p. 744.

[104] Quoted in Max Frankel, *New York Times,* May 9, 1965.

[105] *New York Times,* April 29, 30, 1965.

[106] See, e.g., the remarks of such traditional supporters as Senators Russell Long of Louisiana, Frank Church of Idaho, and Edward Long of Missouri. U.S., *Congressional Record,* 89th Cong., 1st Sess., 1965, 2, pt. 7: 9222, 9450–51, 9820; and among the press, Charles Bar-

One result of all of this praise was that the American public strongly endorsed the President's action. A Gallup poll, for example, asked a nationwide sample of adults, "How do you feel about President Johnson's sending troops into the Dominican Republic?" Seventy-six percent answered "favorable," while only seventeen percent answered "unfavorable." This endorsement, however, was accompanied by an unusually large confession of ignorance; for when asked whether the troops would remain for a vear or two or leave shortly, nearly a third of the respondents offered no opinion at all.[107]

IV

The praise from the press, politicians, and public never wholly doused the doubts about the President's decision. For many Americans, a question remained concerning the degree to which the view of a Communist-dominated pro-Bosch faction—the administration's private, and, ultimately, public view as well—conformed to reality. To begin with, there had never been any doubt regarding Bosch's own sympathies. Far from being a Communist, his administration in 1963 was criticized by former ambassador Martin for concentrating on saving money and balancing the budget "to the neglect of party and people. . . . He was running the government like an old lady saving string in a country store." Bosch, in fact, described himself as a "classical economist," who honored not Karl Marx but Adam Smith.[108] In line with this, Theodore Draper has demonstrated "Bosch's refusal to collaborate with the Communists." [109]

In response to charges that he failed to suppress the Communists while in office, Bosch noted the "strong sentiment" opposing this practice due to Trujillo's habit of persecuting his enemies on this ground. If he would have joined with the army and police to combat Communists, he said, "I would have ended up as their prisoner, and they, for their part, would

---

tlett, "The Case for Dominican Action," *Washington Evening Star,* May 4, 1965; Ray Cromley, "United States Action Is Boost for Vietnamese," *Washington Daily News,* May 12, 1965, and editorials in the *Christian Science Monitor,* May 3 and May 5, 1965. See, e.g., the remarks of such opponents as former President Eisenhower and former Republican presidential candidates Barry Goldwater and Richard Nixon, *New York Times,* May 3, 1965; and among the press, the *St. Louis Globe-Democrat,* May 4, 1965, and the *Casper* (Wyo.) *Star Tribune,* May 2, 1965.

[107] "U.S.A.," *Polls* 1 (Spring 1966). Yet Thomas Sorensen, in his superficial study of American propaganda, contends, "Evidence of Communist control of the revolution was so thin, and the 'protection' rationale so reminiscent of the era of 'gunboat diplomacy,' that neither the President at home nor USIA abroad had much success in getting people to believe it." Sorensen, *The Word War,* p. 265. Though the official version may not have been salable abroad, it certainly did not lack for consumers at home.

[108] Martin, *op. cit.,* p. 351.

[109] Theodore Draper, "A Case of Defamation: United States Intelligence versus Juan Bosch," *New Republic,* February 19, 1966, p. 19. Communists, for their part, held Bosch in contempt as a tool of American imperialism.

have completely destroyed the Dominican democratic forces." Persecution of Communists was, in any case, unnecessary, he contended, for they were too few and too divided to constitute a threat.[110]

Since Bosch himself was in exile in Puerto Rico during the entire uprising, these facts should not be overemphasized. He may have been anti-Communist, and his refusal to suppress Communists may have constituted evidence of good sense and not "softness"; but he was not present. The question, then, becomes whether the Communists had become so prominent among the pro-Bosch rebel forces as to have been able successfully to infiltrate his government upon his return, if, indeed, they would have permitted a non-Communist government to be established and to function at all.

There is no entirely satisfactory answer to this question, but one approach might be to ask how many Communists attached themselves to the pro-Bosch forces. At the critical time following the President's April 28 decision to intervene, CIA Director Raborn told Fulbright that three had been identified.[111] This figure appears even punier when one recalls that the pressures on Raborn were solely in the direction of *over*-estimation. Later, official public estimates varied widely in number and reliability, as one list followed another. Initially, names were taken from the signers of an anti-Wessin propaganda leaflet. There were eight signers, and Ambassador Bennett told the press and Washington that at least two and possibly all of the names belonged to men associated with extremist groups.[112] Soon afterward, lists of fifty-three, fifty-four and fifty-eight names began to appear, none of these containing any of the first eight. Dan Kurzman, the *Washington Post*'s correspondent covering the revolution, reported that an official told him that the lists "had been in CIA desk drawers long before the revolt broke out—simply names of Communists or suspected Communists as are gathered in every country."[113] After a two-week investigation of the names on the list of fifty-three—the longer lists turned out to have contained duplicate names—James Goodsell of the *Christian Science Monitor* concluded that between sixteen and eighteen of the persons mentioned had not even been available for participation in the revolution.[114]

---

[110] Juan Bosch, "Communism and Democracy in the Dominican Republic," *Saturday Review,* August 7, 1965, p. 12.

[111] Johnson and Gwertzman, *op. cit.,* p. 209.

[112] Szulc, *op. cit.,* pp. 70–71. This estimate was reported in the *New York Times,* May 1, 1965.

[113] Kurzman, *op. cit.,* p. 194. Bosch, however, had estimated that there were between 700–800 Communists and 3,000–3,500 Communist sympathizers in the nation while he was in office. Bosch, *loc. cit.* That the CIA's list was less than one-thirteenth of Bosch's estimate—and he was hardly likely to *overstate* their number—speaks poorly for the agents' diligence.

[114] *Christian Science Monitor,* May 19, 1965. Two were in prison; six were out of the

At the same time these lists were given to the press, the embassy told reporters that three men with Communist ties had been given important jobs by Caamaño, and that he had made a deal with the Communists to give them a "decisive voice" in his government in exchange for their support.[115] These were the most impressive revelations made thus far of Communist penetration into the high circles of rebel policy makers, but both tales proved inaccurate.[116] Undeterred by this, the administration persevered, and by the middle of June released its final expanded list of seventy-seven Communists. Ten of the previous fifty-three names had been removed.[117]

The lists were so skimpy and their errors so frequent that they quickly became an embarrassment to the administration. Instead of shoring up the intervention, they seemed to cast doubt upon the informational basis of the decision. Finally, the administration began to counterattack. On a CBS television program, Ambassador Bennett replied to these attacks:

I don't think it's so important the actual number when one recalls that Fidel Castro began with twelve men. I think it's a question of training, of determined objectives and of being able to influence others who, for very legitimate reasons, may be in the fight.[118]

It was left to Secretary Rusk in his May 26 press conference to carry this type of argument a step further:

...I am not impressed by the remark that there were several dozen known Communist leaders and that therefore this was not a very serious matter. There was a time when Hitler sat in a beer hall with seven people.[119]

What neither Bennett nor Rusk mentioned, of course, was that when Castro and Hitler commanded very few supporters, they did *not* con-

---

country during the revolt; four were caught and jailed by the Dominican police by April 26; and four to six were not in Santo Domingo at the time.

[115] This latter story was given extensive coverage in "After the Battle in the Caribbean—," *U.S. News and World Report*, May 10, 1965, p. 35.

[116] Kurzman, *op. cit.*, pp. 197–99.

[117] This list is reprinted in *Wessin Testimony*, pp. 215–20.

[118] Quoted in Theodore Draper, "The Dominican Crisis: A Case Study in American Policy," *Commentary*, December 1965, p. 58. Undersecretary Mann echoed this analysis in his interview with Leonard Gross, *op. cit.*, p. 35.

[119] Dean Rusk, "Secretary Rusk's News Conference of May 26," *Department of State Bulletin* 52 (June 14, 1965): 940. The implication that Castro and the Dominican Communists belong in the same category with Hitler—concerning either their brutality or their constituting a threat to the United States—is too ridiculous to bear refutation. In fact, in terms of brutal tyranny, as Draper has observed, "It is not too far-fetched to put Trujillo in the same class as Hitler. . . ." Theodore Draper, Review of *Trujillo: The Life and Times of a Dominican Dictator*, by Robert D. Crassweller, *New York Times Book Review*, August 7, 1966. And for the first twenty-nine of his thirty-one years in power, Trujillo enjoyed the active or tacit support of the United States.

stitute a threat to the existing order. Only when social, economic, and political conditions—partly through the fault of the governments themselves—developed in such a way as to permit Hitler's and Castro's
support to grow did they become significant. The answer, then, would
not have been simply to suppress Hitler or Castro. Social forces are not
usually so feeble that they wither with the death or imprisonment of a
great man. Probably, other revolutionaries would have emerged to take
their place and topple the system. The answer, instead, would have been
to prevent the system's degenerating to a point where it became vulnerable to extremists' attacks and could be overthrown. But, critics argued,
by intervening in the Dominican revolt against the rebels, the United
States was quashing the very reformist elements who alone could save
the system and prevent an eventual extremist take-over.[120]

Ultimately, administration supporters simply labeled attempts to determine the number of Communists active in the revolt as "irrelevant." [121]
Certainly, this was true, in the sense that the lists had not been available
to the President and his advisers when they had made their key decisions. But in judging the extent to which their intuitive feelings of a
Communist threat was warranted by the facts, the lists plainly were very
relevant.

Even if the administration's longest list of seventy-seven names had
been completely accurate, it is highly doubtful that such a small number
of persons could have gained control of the country. One reason for this
was that "all the Communist groups . . . did not agree in policy among
themselves." [122] There were, in fact, no less than three separate Communist or Communist-influenced parties in existence at the time. The only
real advantage of small size to a group is the opportunity it affords for
greater cohesion and unity of purpose. When this is lacking, its chances
for success become very dim, indeed. Thus, it is hardly surprising that
most of the loose talk about the Communists having plotted the anti-

---

[120] It is also possible to argue, however, that what Dominicans really wanted was modernization and raised living standards, and that these could be achieved only through an au-
tocratic system, which alone could overcome the cultural conservatism of the people and
force them to make the short-run sacrifices necessary for long-run economic development.
This kind of argument has been advanced by David E. Apter, *The Politics of Modernization*
(Chicago: University of Chicago Press, 1965). But, Apter is careful to point out, the au-
tocratic elite must be willing and able to modernize, and there is little evidence suggesting
that the Dominican junta met these requirements.

[121] See, e.g., Evans and Novak, *op. cit.,* p. 549. Raymond Moley, "Perspective: LBJ and
His Critics," *Newsweek,* June 7, 1965, p. 88. Mann's reply to criticism was that "the kind of
proof the public demands involves breaking up your intelligence sources." Quoted in
Gross, *op. cit.,* p. 36. This explanation, of course, completely fails to deal with the series of
absurdly inaccurate lists.

[122] Theodore Draper, "A Case of Defamation: United States Intelligence versus Juan
Bosch," *New Republic,* February 19, 1966, p. 19.

Reid coup or the revolution that followed seems to have had little basis in fact. At one point in the revolution when the embassy was making exaggerated claims, the *Times* reported that the only evidence supporting Communist planning was that "in recent weeks a small number of Dominican Communists trained in Cuba and Czechoslovakia began returning to their homeland." [123] After the revolution, the Central Committee of the Dominican Communist Party criticized Communists for having "not been capable of appreciating the imminence of the armed insurrection that was in gestation as a product of the national situation. Consequently, our party was NOT prepared for the armed insurrection; and, therefore, it was not capable of directing it." [124]

An even more serious obstacle to a Communist take-over than division within the movement was the fact that the mass of Dominicans had been anti-Communist, anti-Castro, and pro-American. This was made irrefutably clear in the 1962 survey taken by the Institute for International Social Research. [125] When polled on whether their nation should side with the United States, the Soviet Union, or neither in the cold war, eighty-three percent of Dominicans chose America, one percent Russia, and five percent neither. Another question asked which country "has a political system and way of life that you admire and would like to see followed here in the Dominican Republic?" Sixty-five percent mentioned the United States, less than one half percent named the Soviet Union, and none at all named Cuba. On ten-point scales of popularity, the average score for the United States was 9.1 and for President Kennedy 9.4; the average score for the Soviet Union was 1.0 and for Chairman Khrushchev 1.0; and the average score for Cuba was 0.6 and for Premier Castro 0.3. The Cuban score was the lowest ever given to a foreign country in any of the Institute's surveys. Finally, Dominicans were asked whether Dominican Communists would serve their nation's interests if they gained power. Only three percent said that they would, while eighty-six percent thought that the Communists would work for the best interests of the Soviet Union.

These findings were reflected in a 1964 State Department intelligence report, which concluded that "Pro-Communist influence has been found among some university and secondary students, in a small segment of organized labor and, to a limited degree, among young professionals." [126]

---

[123] *New York Times*, April 30, 1965. This conclusion was reached after Bennett's misleading April 29 news conference, at which he told newly arrived reporters of fantastic rebel atrocities and of Communist involvement—much of which was inaccurate.

[124] Central Committee of the Dominican Communist Party, "Auto-criticism Document," *El Popular*, August 16, 1965, quoted in Szulc, *op. cit.*, pp. 296–97.

[125] Free, *op. cit.*

[126] U.S., Department of State, "World Strength of the Communist Party Organizations," quoted in Kurzman, *op. cit.*, p. 194.

During the revolt itself, eyewitness witness correspondents denied the growth of pro-Communist feeling or of a Communist take-over,[127] though plainly there was "incontrovertible evidence of a very considerable Communist role among the rank-and-file civilians, who soon outnumbered numbered the original military participants by almost four to one." [128]

Although the Communists may have been too divided among themselves and too much an object of public antipathy to have actually gained control, they still might have been present in sufficient numbers to have promoted and perpetuated a condition of murderous anarchy, which could have cost far more lives than American intervention was to claim. Following this anarchic period, Communists might also have helped to sabotage the newly established Bosch government, in the hope of producing an unstable situation from which they might profit. All of this, of course, is conjecture. But one of President Johnson's main problems was precisely that: he had to act on the basis of rough projections, often grounded on flimsy, incomplete, or erroneous information. In the howling Turner storm of the revolution, perhaps this was inevitable. To this day, descriptions and evaluations of events remain incredibly tangled, sketchy, and contradictory. The analyst, of course, can simply note the informational problems, and possibly suggest that the administration overreacted to a rather minor Communist threat. President Johnson and his advisers, however, could not afford the luxury of such tentative conclusions or benefit from the advantages of hindsight.

To some extent, they seem to have been congnizant of the generally inadequate nature of their information. Yet they felt, nonetheless, that if they were going to act at all, they had to act then. The Bay of Pigs fiasco had demonstrated how difficult and imprudent was the ouster of a Communist government once in power.[129] President Johnson's decision, in short, appears to have been critically determined by the weight he gave to the possibility of an error in judgment. The consequences of unjustifiably depriving an ineffective leader like Bosch of his office obviously seemed less damaging than permitting the Communists to take control. This was the calculation of a cautious man, with little respect for Dominican politics and much respect for Communist organization.

The thinking behind that calculation was rooted in the President's perception of Dominican and American political realities. Yet thinking consists not only of selective perceiving, but in addition of combining parts

---

[127] See, e.g., *ibid.,* chap. 7.

[128] Slater, *op. cit.,* p. 36.

[129] Johnson as Vice-President, however, had been completely left out of Kennedy's Bay of Pigs deliberations. Leonard Baker, *The Johnson Eclipse: A President's Vice Presidency* (New York: Macmillan, 1966), pp. 44–46.

of previous experience into new patterns.[130] Remembrance, in other words, also forms an essential input. Here, too, stress must be placed upon selectivity; [131] for not all events are remembered and not all memories seem relevant to solving the problem at hand. There is always a tendency to apply familiar solutions—the "lessons" of the past—to new problems. The question inherent in this approach, of course, is: was the older problem so different from the newer one that the older solution no longer works? Since each event is unique, the older and newer problems can never be identical, and the President must be forced merely to analogize the present with the past.[132] When, he must ask himself, can different problems be treated as having essentially the same solution? When can the "lessons" of the past be applied?

These questions—as crucial as they are—will not submit to precise, quantifiable replies. Ultimately, it seems, decision makers rely upon the "feel" of the situation, sometimes with disastrous results. For Dulles and Bissell prior to the Bay of Pigs invasion, the problem confronting them "felt" similar to that posed by the Communist-dominated Guatemalan government of Jacob Arbenz Guzmán in the early 1950s.[133] Toward the end of 1953, President Eisenhower decided that Arbenz must be replaced, and instructed the CIA to draw up a plan of action. As implemented the following June, the plan essentially followed this outline: a few planes bombed and strafed the capital, Guatemala City; the frightened Arbenz resigned; and a tiny American-outfitted "army" of 150 Guatemalans moved in from across the border in Honduras, and assumed control of the government. In a matter of days the problem was solved, the "lesson" apparently being that a Communist-oriented Latin American regime, like a splinter in a toe, could be removed quickly, easily, and almost painlessly. As the Bay of Pigs made clear, however, significant differences separated Castro from Arbenz. Arbenz was an ineffective, often publicly ridiculed leader with a narrow popular base,

---

[130] See the two articles by Norman R. F. Maier, "Reasoning in Humans, I: On Direction," *Journal of Comparative Psychology* 10 (April 1930): 115–43; and "Reasoning in Humans, II: The Solution of a Problem and its Appearance in Consciousness," *ibid.,* 12 (August 1931): 181–94. Maier also emphasized the influence of a definite direction in the reasoning as a determinant of the combination.

[131] Frederic C. Bartlett, *Remembering* (Cambridge: Harvard University Press, 1932); Karl Duncker, "On Problem Solving," trans. Lynne S. Lees, *Psychological Monographs* 58 (no. 5, 1945): 84.

[132] This led one journalist to draw his own analogy: "Drawing historical analogies is like eating soup with a fork—messy to begin with and in the end futile." Joseph Kraft, "The American Dienbienphu," *New York Review of Books,* September 16, 1965, p. 5.

[133] On the relation of Arbenz to the Communists, see Ronald Schneider, *Communism in Guatemala: 1944–1954* (New York: Praeger, 1959); on his overthrow, see David Wise and Thomas B. Ross, *The Invisible Government* (New York: Bantam Books, 1965 [c. 1964]), chap. 11.

Castro a charismatic figure with a wide support; Arbenz lacked adequate control over his army, while Castro possessed the loyalty of his army and militia; Arbenz was an obscure figure internationally and not aligned with the Soviet bloc, but Castro was a renowned figure friendly with the Russians. The cumulative effect of these differences was to nullify the "lesson," although neither Dulles nor Bissell noticed this. Thus, when attempts were made to apply it to Cuba, they failed.

During the Dominican revolt, President Johnson's actions similarly seemed to have flowed from his analogizing the Dominican Republic to pre-Castro Cuba. The "lesson" now was: just as American intervention in Cuba would have kept out Castro and saved American political leaders great embarrassment and annoyance, so intervention in the Dominican Republic was warranted in order to prevent another disturbing Communist take-over. The analogy with Cuba, however, is not entirely persuasive, for the Dominican Communists lacked leadership of the stature of the Castro brothers and Guevera, and would have won control not of a relatively prosperous nation but of one with an extremely limited economic future. Even if the Dominican Communists would have been able to settle their internal differences and overcome the tremendous popular antagonism to their cause, there is little reason to suppose that they could have escaped being drowned in the torrent of insoluble problems, despite a presumed influx of Soviet aid.

Were the damaging consequences that President Johnson sought to prevent, then, damaging only to Dominicans? Obviously not; American intervention was not an act of altruism. In the first place, the President wanted to deprive the Communists of another base in the Caribbean from which revolutionary activity could be launched against friendly Latin American nations. And geographically, the Dominican Republic is nearer to Venezuela and Columbia—in addition to Puerto Rico—than is Cuba. In this view, Johnson was "not so much plowing new ground as deepening a furrow dug by his predecessor." [134] After his failure at the Bay of Pigs, Kennedy delivered an address entitled, "The Lesson of Cuba." In it, he declared:

Any unilateral intervention in the absence of an external attack upon ourselves or an ally, would have been contrary to our international treaty obligations. But . . . [s]hould it ever appear that the inter-American doctrine of noninter-

---

[134] Steel, *op. cit.*, pp. 234–35. By this, Steel means that "Kennedy set the stage for the Dominican intervention of his successor by linking American security to the suppression of communist regimes within the hemisphere. He was never able to distinguish clearly between the kind of communism in Latin American that was a threat to American security and the kind that was simply a nuisance. Or if he did make the distinction, it was never translated into policy." *Ibid.*, p. 234.

ference merely conceals or excuses a policy of nonaction—if the nations of this hemisphere should fail to meet their commitments against outside Communist penetration—then I want it clearly understood that this Government will not hesitate in meeting its primary obligations, which are to the security of our Nation.[135]

If Kennedy's interpretation of "outside Communist penetration" had been broad enough to cover Castro's indigenous movement in Cuba, it could certainly have covered the Dominican situation as well.

This unilateral intervention, as Kennedy made clear to his advisers on another occasion, should be carried out only against Communists; totalitarianism of the right was tolerable. Analyzing the situation in the Dominican Republic when Ramfis Trujillo still controlled the military, the President said:

There are three possibilities in descending order of preference: a decent democratic regime, a continuation of the Trujillo regime, or a Castro regime. We ought to aim at the first, but we really can't renounce the second until we are sure that we can avoid the third.[136]

For rightists in the future, the implication of this posture was clear; if you can convince the United States that your opposition is connected with Communists, you can count on American support. And the United States plainly was so worried about Communists that not much convincing was necessary. In the Dominican Republic, in fact, American officials were so worried that *they* helped to convince the "loyalists" to fight.

There was a second and perhaps more important reason for President Johnson's decision to intervene: a Communist take-over would have entailed damaging personal consequences. Solicitous of his own reputation—both in terms of contemporary public opinion and in the broad sweep of history—he recognized the harm that could be done it if a hemispheric Communist outpost were established for which he could be

---

[135] John F. Kennedy, "The Lesson of Cuba: Address by President Kennedy," *Department of State Bulletin* 44 (May 8, 1961): 659. (Address of April 20.) Kennedy reiterated this position in a speech to the Inter-American Press Association less than a week before he was killed. "The Battle for Progress with Freedom in the Western Hemisphere," *Department of State Bulletin* 49 (December 9, 1963): 903. (Remarks of November 18.) Walt W. Rostow, assistant to both Kennedy and Johnson, does not doubt that Kennedy would have applied the "lesson of Cuba" in the form of military intervention in the Dominican Republic. Kennedy, Rostow told *Times* correspondent Henry Raymont, "was very, very tough . . . he was determined that there would not be another Cuba. . . . We had a small task force, of which I was a member, to find what would be the legal basis for using military power. That was Kennedy. So when people say he never would have done it in the Dominican Republic, you're goddamn right he would have!" *New York Times*, April 21, 1969.
[136] Quoted in Schlesinger, *op. cit.*, p. 769.

blamed. With such small incentive to tolerate the possible political embarrassment and annoyance of a rebel victory, he moved to smother the revolution at birth.

All the evidence suggests that these considerations seemed so obvious and overriding to the President that he quite literally felt, as his supporters were later to argue, that "he really had no choice." The question, in other words, seems to have been prejudged to the extent that it is difficult even to speak of his actually deciding among alternatives; his mind had already been made up in favor of suppressing Caribbean revolutions in which Communists might be involved, and the Dominican revolution merely provided the occasion for the implementation of that prior decision. This helps to explain why virtually no attention seems to have been paid either to the disadvantages of intervening in support of the junta or to the advantages of intervening on the side of the rebels. The only disadvantage of the intervention that Johnson appears to have noticed was that it might alienate a number of liberals at home. He tried to counter this, as was said earlier, by relying upon the strategy of presenting the intervention as a purely humanitarian, nonpolitical act, designed solely to save American lives. Reality quickly overran this defense, however, and made the administration look hypocritical and deceitful. It had naively attempted to sell a simplistic appearance to a knowledgeable, attentive public, and had failed. "Somehow," Reedy recalls of his boss, "he had lost his instinctive sense of what people would and would not believe." [137]

Possibly, because Johnson was oriented primarily to the domestic political system where Dominicans were without influence, he seems to have been little concerned with their reactions to the intervention. What had been an extremely pro-American attitude became, as the President's personal emissary, Martin, admitted, violently anti-American. The Dominicans, who had overwhelmingly supported the rebels, saw the United States side with the junta; popular opposition to the junta thus quickly became opposition to America, too. This attitude was expressed by Rafael Molina Morillo in the Santo Domingo weekly, *¡Ahora!* After praising the United States and declaring that Dominicans wanted a similar system for their own country, he wrote, acidly:

We hate the way the men who are now governing the U.S. treat their Latin American neighbors. Unfortunately, we must say that they have a low opinion of us and of our dignity. We are disgusted by the way they use military force just because they think they enjoy special interests in all our Latin American countries.

---

[137] Reedy, *op. cit.*

Even acts of charity often were resented. When the United States distributed food to hungry Dominicans, for example, one woman's reply was, "We are your prisoners, so of course you must feed us." There can be no question that a legacy of bitter anti-Americanism remains in the Dominican Republic, particularly among the large number of persons who supported Juan Bosch. By promoting an international image of the United States as a self-righteous defender of the status quo, the intervention seemed to have validated many Communist interpretations of American behavior, and thus to have been of considerable propaganda value to them.

The President's view in this regard seems to have been that, in the last analysis, considerations of world opinion, image, and propaganda were too ephemeral to take precedence over the tangible threat of a Communist take-over—which would bring in its wake, he would add, damage to the United States in terms of world opinion, image, and propaganda, anyway, by making the nation seem weak and indecisive. The administration's position generally was that the rebel leaders were not themselves Communists, but had taken Communist support under duress and thereby had become dominated by them. If, for the sake of argument, one grants the validity of this position, then one may conclude that American aid for the rebels would have rendered Communist aid superflous and the Communists, therefore, nearly powerless. The administration might then have had the opportunity to support and influence "the decent democratic regime" that both Washington and the rebels professed to desire.[138]

Siding with the rebels may have benefited not only Dominicans, but Americans as well; for it may have made communism less likely to win power in the Dominican Republic by attempting to alleviate some of the social causes of extremist victories.[139] In addition, this alternative may have promoted an international image of the United States as an advocate of reform and democracy in deed as well as in word, and thereby have helped this country to retain and expand its influence within the

---

[138] Slater, in his unusually fair-minded study of the crisis argues that "from the very outset of the intervention the Johnson Administration was not only committed to re-establishment of democratic government through genuinely free elections in the near future, but also intended to use the opportunity to begin gradually to reform and restructure the Dominican military establishment, the main bulwark of the status quo." *Op. cit.,* p. 48. Yet minimizing the risk of a "second Cuba" was unquestionably a more important goal, and clearly took precedence over altruistic considerations regarding internal Dominican Republic politics. This is not to say that the President's concern with Dominican democracy was insincere or shallow, but rather merely secondary.

[139] Yet social reform and economic progress may not placate a people, but instead make them more restless by adding an element of hope, which leaves the poor's sense of relative deprivation, vis-à-vis the nonpoor, sensitized and explosive.

underdeveloped world.[140] A further advantage of this choice lay in the fact that it would have been easier to implement than intervention on behalf of the junta. For one thing, since the rebels were already on the verge of victory, few if any American troops would have been needed. And for another, the United States would not have had to deal with troublesome popular antagonism. Dominicans seem not to have been opposed to intervention per se—the belief that the United States helped to ease Ramfis Trujillo into exile increased Dominican admiration for America—but simply to intervention supporting unpopular forces.

It may be argued that it would have set a dangerous precedent for the United States to have sided with rebels against a duly constituted government. The "loyalists," however, were no such government nor had they even been loyal to Reid. They were simply a faction in a revolution, and the administration showed little reluctance to back factions, as its support of Wessin indicates. Moreover, inasmuch as the rebels installed a Provisional President—the President of the Chamber of Deputies, who was empowered to succeed Bosch under the constitution—as soon as Reid was deposed, they clearly had first call on any support due a legitimate government. Such legalistic arguments, however, ignore the fact that the United States has not always been a respecter of duly constituted governments, as CIA-engineered overthrows of the Arbenz regime in Guatemala and the Mossadegh regime in Iran attest.

It could also be argued that Bosch had proved himself so unsatisfactory that it would have been folly to permit his return. Even granting this, a simple solution was at hand, namely, pressuring the rebels to hold new elections. Many of the rebels, in fact, preferred this alternative to Bosch's resuming control. These elections, as the administration should have known, would have eliminated Bosch just as surely as would have American intervention on behalf of the junta, for a United States Information Agency survey showed him running behind Balaguer by a margin of two to one.[141] The accuracy of this poll was borne out a year later, when in the free election of 1966 Balaguer triumphed easily, much to the

---

[140] Much of the underdeveloped nations' hostility to America, however, may be due less to what it does than to what it has and to what it is.

[141] Balaguer scored fifty-two percent and Bosch twenty-six percent. *New York Times,* November 14, 1965. Balaguer, although a former frontman for Trujillo, became popular when, as chief executive in 1962, he distributed Trujillo properties to peasants and workers. In this regard, the findings of social psychiatrist Bryant Wedge are pertinent. Five months after the violence, he interviewed thirty-three Dominican students individually and 248 in eighteen groups, with a weighting in favor of the politically active reformists. He concluded that Bosch lacked "charismatic influence on the young people . . . it is true that his return was sought as the symbol of legality, but he personally was the object of careful critical judgment by revolutionary youth throughout the Dominican Republic. . . ." Bryant Wedge, "The Case Study of Student Political Violence: Brazil, 1964, and Dominican Republic, 1965," *World Politics* 21 (January 1969): 187.

Johnson administration's delight. By supporting the rebels and insisting upon free elections, therefore, the same end probably could have been achieved, but with much less cost in terms of lives, money, and national prestige. Yet the administration, as Senator Fulbright suggested, was "unduly timid and alarmist in refusing to gamble on the forces of reform and social change." [142] Thus, whatever the pros and cons of intervening on the side of the rebels, there is no evidence to suggest that this alternative was even considered. The feeling probably was that to help the rebels would be to help the Communists—a masochistic goal, which, not surprisingly, no one favored.

V

In sum, President Johnson's actions seem to have been based upon his evaluations, first, of Dominican political reality and the extent of its similarity with Cuba and, second, of American political opinion and the nature of its reaction to another Communist triumph in the Caribbean. Probably, many of the similarities he and his advisers noted between the Dominican Republic and Cuba were less real than apparent, resulting from inadequate information and premature commitment to a policy alternative. This may have led to a tendency to exaggerate the accuracy and significance of facts supporting their policy choices, ignoring or dismissing contrary evidence. As appearance diverged from reality, the range of possible choices was stripped away, leaving the decision as predetermined as the tide.

The decision of how to present the intervention to the people also saw a conflict between appearance and reality. Television, newspapers, and other media were utilized in an effort to create a permissive consensus. And it is no exaggeration to say that the administration at times played the role of deceiver, not deceived. First, the intervention was depicted as a humanitarian act of saving lives, a goal to which it was almost impossible for Americans to be opposed. Later, intervention was sold as necessary to prevent a Communist take-over, again an aim with which few disagreed, although some thought unwarranted by the evidence. Government attempts to suppress unwanted information seem not to have been dictated by tactical exigencies, but instead were part of the effort to justify the intervention to the public and to protect the reputations of the officials and organizations involved from the charge of unpreparedness.

The press seems to have played an ambivalent role in this episode. Part of it reported all the various administration versions of events like a loyal terrier following its fickle master, without doubt or hesitation. Many of these same elements of the press earlier had been wont to com-

---

[142] U.S., *Congressional Record,* 89th Cong., 1st Sess., 1966, 111, pt. 15: 23858.

plain about the administration's lack of forthrightness, and even upon occasion to reveal hostility toward the President. At the very least, they had announced as a matter of fact that the President's press relations "had broadened into an actual feud." [143] Yet whether motivated by patriotism or a new-found belief in official candor, these publications faithfully transmitted official tales of the Dominican revolt to the public, acknowledging no flaws and raising no questions. Undoubtedly, this "administration press" was important in convincing the majority of the population of the rightness of the President's decision.

Another part of the press, however, was unwilling to be merely a passive receptacle for official recitals of events, and, instead, contrasted the administration's interpretations with the facts before them. The "critical press" included some of the nation's most influential publications: "prestige papers" [144] like the *New York Times,* the *New York Herald Tribune,* the *Christian Science Monitor,* and the *Wall Street Journal*; and the popular liberal magazines like the *New Republic, Commentary,* the *New Leader,* and the *Nation.* Thus, much of the liberal and intellectual community came to see the official versions as self-serving appearances, not reality. This marked the first major split between the President and the liberal-intellectual community, which had supported him so vigorously in the election barely five months earlier. It was a split which was to deepen and widen in the days ahead, with momentous consequences for the President and the nation. "The whole episode," writes Reedy with weary irony, "was quite a contribution to White House credibility." [145]

---

[143] "The Widening No Man's Land: President vs. the Press," *Life,* May 7, 1965, p. 34.

[144] Bernard C. Cohen, *The Press and Foreign Policy* (Princeton: Princeton University Press, 1963), pp. 134–40.

[145] Reedy, *op. cit.*

4

Vietnam: The Gulf of Tonkin

It was on the dignity of the Senate that Augustus and his successors founded their new empire. . . . In the administration of their own powers, they frequently consulted the great national council, and seemed to refer to its decision the most important concerns of peace and war. . . . The masters of the Roman world surrounded their throne with darkness, concealed their irresistible strength, and humbly professed themselves the accountable ministers of the Senate, whose supreme decrees they dictated and obeyed . . . Augustus was sensible that mankind is governed by names; nor was he deceived in his expectation that the Senate and the people would submit to slavery, provided they were respectfully assured that they still enjoyed their ancient freedom.

Edward Gibbon,
Decline and Fall of The Roman Empire

The gulf of Tonkin crisis takes its illustrative importance less from what it reveals about appearance and reality in the decision-making process than from what it discloses about the public relations of deception. Thus, this chapter's main concerns will be an investigation of the techniques used to create a permissive consensus and their effectiveness, and the probable motivations of officials who withheld, distorted, or falsified information. Perhaps, the Gulf of Tonkin crisis was only a "pseudocrisis"; but it was certainly viewed by many as a genuine crisis at the time, and its history supports W. I. Thomas's famous apothegm: "What man perceives as real is real in its consequences."

I

The summer of 1964 saw the position of the South Vietnamese government move from bad to worse. Domestic dissent and unrest grew, while the regime of General Nguyen Khanh became steadily less effective.[1] The military pace of the war, too, was stepped up. "The month of July," a well-known military historian observed, "was the bloodiest of the war up to that time, with 900 RVN personnel killed in action, 500 missing, and nearly 1,800 wounded as the number of enemy ambushes, attacks, and acts of terrorism increased sharply."[2]

Khanh, meanwhile, perhaps in order to boost the sagging prestige of his government and the declining morale of his armed forces, retaliated against these developments with increasing belligerence, on July 19 even calling for a march "to the North."[3] This belligerence did not take only a verbal form. The *Saigon Post* reported a marked increase in South Vietnamese commando raids against the North beginning July 10,[4] and on July 25 Radio Hanoi declared that the allies had fired at Northern fishing boats. Six days later, the North complained to the International Control Commission about a similar incident in the Tonkin Gulf and the subsequent bombardment of two Northern coastal islands. An American destroyer, the *Maddox,* was alleged to have provided protection for the South Vietnamese patrol boats.[5] When asked about these charges, Secretary McNamara declined comment, saying simply that his government was not in touch with Saigon on these matters.[6]

None of these developments seems to have had a significant impact on American public opinion, attentive or mass, for the media did not give them concentrated exposure. But in South Vietnam, the atmosphere was one of conflict, tension, and perhaps even desperation—and to a substantially smaller extent, this atmosphere extended to concerned officials in Washington, as well. In this context, the Gulf of Tonkin crisis began to take shape.

II

On August 2, the administration later explained before a congressional hearing, three North Vietnamese torpedo boats attacked the *Mad-*

---

[1] John Mecklin, *Mission in Torment* (Garden City: Doubleday, 1965), p. 290.

[2] Kenneth Sams, "Airpower—The Decisive Element," *Air Force Space Digest* 49 (March 1966).

[3] *New York Times,* July 20, 1964. South Vietnamese Air Force Commander Nguyen Cao Ky followed Khanh's remarks with an announcement that Ky's pilots were undergoing jet bombing training, and were ready and willing to bomb North Vietnam "this afternoon." *New York Times,* July 23, 1964. The next day, United States Ambassador to Saigon, Maxwell Taylor, criticized the imprudence of Ky's announcement. *New York Times,* July 24, 1964.

[4] *Saigon Post,* July 23, 1964, reprinted in *I. F. Stone's Weekly,* September 12, 1966, p. 3. Ky himself confirmed South Vietnamese "air, sea, and land" sabotage forays against North Vietnam at a public news conference, *New York Times,* July 23, 1964.

[5] This kind of protection had been provided for some time, although the South Vietnamese coastal attacks had lately become more effective. *New York Times,* August 10, 1964.

[6] *Le Monde,* August 9 and 10, 1964, cited in Franz Schurmann, Peter Dale Scott, and

dox in the Tonkin Gulf off North Vietnam. "The *Maddox* was operating in international waters," Secretary McNamara told the congressmen, and "was carrying out a routine patrol of the type we carry out all over the world at all times." The destroyer had been engaged in no provocative actions, he said, either alone or in conjunction with "any South Vietnamese actions. . . ." [7] American planes were quickly dispatched from a nearby aircraft carrier, with the result that one enemy boat was sunk and the other two damaged. Hanoi admitted that its boats had attacked, saying that the *Maddox* had violated North Vietnamese coastal waters, and had been involved in the shelling of North Vietnamese islands.

The President reacted swiftly, seeking explanations for Hanoi's action from his top advisers, principally, McNamara, Rusk, and Deputy Secretary of Defense Cyrus Vance. There was, however, no sense of major crisis. One Pentagon spokesman called the situation "unwelcome but not especially serious," [8] and Rusk noted calmly that "the U.S. Seventh Fleet had been patrolling the area for some time, would continue its patrols and had sufficient strength on hand." Underlining his tone of assurance, he said, "The other side got a sting out of this. If they do it again, they'll get another sting." [9] General Khanh, however, did not make light of the incident. "The Americans, he declared, should seize this occasion to dissipate the enemy's belief according to which the United States is only a paper tiger." [10]

President Johnson's public response was a strongly worded protest to Hanoi, warning of "grave consequences" that would follow the attack's repetition. He also stiffened the Navy's orders, telling them "to attack any force which attacks them in international waters, and to attack with the objective not only of driving off the force but of destroying it." [11] A

Reginald Zelnik, *The Politics of Escalation in Vietnam* (Boston: Beacon Press, 1966), pp. 39–40, n. 3.

[7] U.S., Congress, Senate, Committee on Foreign Relations and on Armed Forces, *Hearing on Joint Resolution to Promote Maintenance of International Peace and Security in Southeast Asia*, 88th Cong., 2d Sess., August 6, 1964, p. 23. Copies of the hearing transcript were not released to the public for over two years. By the time they were finally released to the public on November 24, 1966, disputing the Tonkin Gulf Resolution seemed a dead issue. The transcript, moreover, was released Thanksgiving Day, when presumably public and press interest in other matters would be at a maximum. Not surprisingly, then, the transcript attracted little attention, let alone critical scrutiny. In addition, I. F. Stone has pointed out that the transcript was censored on the question of whether "the Tonkin Gulf incidents might have been provoked by commando raids against North Vietnam." I. F. Stone, "Fulbright: From Hawk to Dove (Part 2): Book Review of *Senator Fulbright: Portrait of a Public Philosopher*, by Tristram Coffin," *New York Review of Books*, January 13, 1967, p. 10.

[8] *New York Times*, August 3, 1964.

[9] *Washington Star*, August 3, 1964.

[10] *Le Monde*, August 5, 1964, quoted in Schurmann *et al.*, *op. cit.*, p. 41.

[11] Lyndon B. Johnson, "U.S. Protest to North Vietnam, August 3," *Department of State*

second destroyer, the *C. Turner Joy,* joined the *Maddox,* and, pursuant to presidential order, the two ships resumed an altered patrol the next day. The former route was replaced by a shorter one of forty-five miles in the vicinity of the two North Vietnamese islands which had been attacked a few days earlier.

On August 4, according to the government, North Vietnamese boats attacked the destroyers again, although this time Hanoi denied having done so. The ships, the administration said, had made radar contact with unidentified boats and planes, and had been fired on with torpedoes. The destroyers, however, had successfully evaded the enemy, sinking two of its boats.

The President, upon learning of the second attack, convened the National Security Council for one of its rare meetings, and it recommended retaliation. A later lunch with McNamara, Rusk, and Bundy produced the same conclusion.[12] Johnson then dispatched a retaliatory strike against the North consisting of sixty-four bombing missions. The American response, however, also had a more long-range aspect, as Secretary McNamara disclosed at a news conference held the following morning. Here he stated that the following steps had been taken:

a.   Transfers of an attack carrier group from the Pacific coast to the Western Pacific.

b.   Movement of interceptor and fighter bomber aircraft into Thailand.

c.   Transfer of interceptor and fighter bomber aircraft from the United States to advance bases in the Pacific.

d.   Movement of an antisubmarine force into the South China Sea.

e.   The alerting and readying for movement of selected Army and Marine forces.[13]

The President's decision having been made and the order given, Johnson called in congressional leaders to inform them of his action and to request their support. Senators Mansfield, Dirksen, Fulbright, and Russel, and House Speaker McCormack were involved, and they were faced

---

Bulletin 51 (August 24, 1964): 258; "Statement of President Johnson, August 3," *ibid.,* p. 259.

[12] Johnson and Gwertzman, *op. cit.,* p. 195. Rusk may have been the most "hawkish" of the advisers. One writer has implied that Rusk was so convinced that the South Vietnamese government should not be permitted to collapse that he hid from the President's knowledge a fall, 1964, proposal from Hanoi for secret talks. The assumption was that such talks would destroy the morale of the Saigon government. Norman Cousins, "How the U.S. Spurned Three Chances for Peace in Vietnam," *Look,* July 29, 1969, pp. 45–46. Yet since Johnson did not replace Rusk after learning of the incident, perhaps the President shared Rusk's viewpoint or had even been informed of Hanoi's offer, despite Cousins's story.

[13] "Statements by Secretary Rusk and Secretary McNamara, August 6," *Department of State Bulletin,* 51 (August 24, 1964): 267.

with a high-powered delegation from the administration. In addition to the President, who spoke "gravely" [14] of recent events, they heard from McNamara, Rusk, CIA Director John McCone, and General Earle G. Wheeler of the Joint Chiefs of Staff. The members of Congress were convinced; none objected to the retaliation. The support the President requested was of a tangible kind, consisting of a congressional resolution "making it clear that our Government is united in its determination to take all necessary measures in support of freedom and in defense of peace in Southeast Asia." [15] Fulbright, as chairman of the Senate Foreign Relations Committee, was given the task of shepherding the resolution through the Senate. The President wanted it enacted immediately.

As the President was meeting with congressional leaders, the Defense Department was issuing a statement to the press:

A second deliberate attack was made during darkness by an undetermined number of North Vietnamese PT boats on the *USS Maddox* and *USS C. Turner Joy* while the two destroyers were cruising in company on routine patrol in the Tonkin Gulf in international waters about 65 miles from the nearest land . . . The attackers were driven off with no U.S. casualties, no hits, and no damage to either destroyer. It is believed that at least two of the PT boats were sunk and two others damaged. [16]

Later that night, in a televised address to the nation, Johnson defended the air strikes as "limited and fitting," and said that he had been given "encouraging assurance" that the desired congressional resolution "will be promptly introduced, freely and expeditiously debated, and passed with overwhelming support." [17]

The next day, President Johnson delivered a well-publicized speech at Syracuse University, in which he termed the North Vietnamese attacks "deliberate and unprovoked." Finally, he declared, "Aggression—deliberate, willful, and systematic aggression—has unmasked its face to the entire world." [18]

---

[14] Johnson and Gwertzman, *loc. cit.*

[15] Lyndon B. Johnson, "Statement of President Johnson, August 3," *Department of State Bulletin* 51 (August 24, 1964): 259.

[16] *New York Times,* August 5, 1964.

[17] Lyndon B. Johnson, "Address to the Nation by President Johnson, August 4," *Department of State Bulletin* 51 (August 24, 1964): 259. Although the President spoke of strikes "now in execution," the planes did not actually reach their targets and drop their bombs until an hour and forty minutes later. His announcement, then, may have warned the enemy of the impending attack. The strikes did not commence until 1:15 A.M. Eastern Standard Time, however, and this would have been a very poor time to have made a television address, for most of the Eastern portion of the country would have been asleep, and its television stations off the air. The importance and urgency of the situation, as presented in the President's televised speech, was further underlined by Secretary McNamara's holding a midnight press conference later that same night.

[18] Lyndon B. Johnson, "Address by the President, Syracuse University, August 5," *De-*

Ambassador Stevenson, meanwhile, presented the United States' case at the United Nations Security Council, informing it of the American response. The destroyers had been engaged in "routine operations in international waters," he said, when attacked "about 30 miles at sea from the mainland of North Vietnam." [19] That night, Secretary Rusk appeared on a nationwide television program, and maintained that the destroyers had not been involved in maneuvers in support of South Vietnamese vessels, as Hanoi had claimed. Instead, said Rusk, "Here is a vast expanse of international waters in which we have a perfect right to be." Why, then, did the North Vietnamese attack the destroyers? "I can't come to a rational explanation of it," he admitted, plainly baffled.[20]

Newspaper reaction to the administration's activities was almost unanimously laudatory. The *New York Times* and *Washington Post*—later to be the leading journalistic advocates of the "dovish" position—described the retaliation in terms of "firmness," "balance," and "restraint." "Hawkish" newspapers were plainly enthusiastic, the *New York Daily News* savoring "the unexpected singe dealt by us to [Ho Chi Minh's] wispy whiskers" and the *Charlotte Observer* applauding the response as "a heavy punch on the nose of Asian Communists." [21]

On this day in the midst of this rhetoric, President Johnson formally asked Congress for a joint resolution, assuring him full support "for all necessary action to protect our armed forces and to assist nations covered by the SEATO treaty." [22] Speedy passage was necessary not simply because of the press of events in the Gulf of Tonkin, but also because "we are entering on three months of political campaigning. Hostile nations must understand that in such a period the United States will continue to protect its national interests, and that in these matters there is no division among us."

On August 6, closed-door hearings were held in each house in an atmosphere of intense patriotic urgency. Secretaries Rusk and McNamara

---

partment of State Bulletin 51 (August 24, 1964): 260.

[19] Adlai Stevenson, "Security Council Hears U.S. Charge of North Vietnamese Attacks," *ibid.*, pp. 272–73.

[20] Dean Rusk, "Secretary Rusk Discusses Asian Situation on NBC Program," *ibid.*, p. 269. Similarly, when asked at a press conference, "How do you explain these attacks?" Secretary McNamara replied, blandly, "I can't explain them." *New York Times,* August 6, 1964.

[21] *New York Times,* August 4 and 6, 1964; *Washington Post,* August 4 and 7, 1964; *New York Daily News,* August 6, 1964; *Charlotte* (N.C.) *Observer,* August 6, 1964. Other newspapers registering support for the administration included the *Los Angeles Times,* August 6, 1964; *New York Herald Tribune,* August 7, 1964; *Philadelphia Bulletin,* August 7, 1964; *Miami Herald,* August 6, 1964; *Richmond Times-Dispatch,* August 6, 1964; *New York Journal-American,* August 6, 1964. Later, the appropriateness of the American reponse was echoed in a book by an eminent theorist of international conflict. Thomas C. Schelling, *Arms and Influence* (New Haven: Yale University Press, 1966), pp. 141–45.

[22] Lyndon B. Johnson, "President's Message to Congress, August 5," *Department of State*

again declared the destroyers to have been "in international waters." [23] McNamara, in fact, repeated this contention twice, and termed the North Vietnamese attack "deliberate and unprovoked" three times.[24] The "destroyers relayed messages stating that they had avoided a number of torpedoes," he said, and had been "under repeated attack," with "many torpedoes" having been fired at them. The President's retaliatory strike, McNamara estimated, had destroyed ninety percent of North Vietnam's petroleum storage capacity. Only Oregon's Wayne Morse, Congress's most vocal critic of the war, attempted to subject the witnesses' testimony to serious scrutiny—and he had been secretly informed by a Pentagon official that the *Maddox* was neither in international waters nor on a routine mission.[25] Chairman Fulbright asked no questions at all.

The "perfunctory" [26] nature of the hearings is suggested by the fact that the Senate hearing, which involved two committees and three witnesses, lasted one hour and forty minutes from beginning to end. This even included the time used to poll the members concerning their approval of the resolution. The press of time, in any case, made it impossible to print the hearings and distribute them to other members of Congress before the floor vote.

Floor debate, too, was insubstantial, though both floor leaders were careful to limit the ramifications of the resolution. Representative Thomas E. Morgan, the Pennsylvania Democrat who chaired the House Foreign Affairs Committee, stated that the resolution

is definitely not an advance declaration of war. The Committee has been assured by the Secretary of State that the constitutional prerogative in this respect will continue to be scrupulously observed.[27]

For his part, Fulbright conceded that the resolution would "not prevent" the landing of large American armies in Vietnam, but added, reassuringly:

Bulletin 51 (August 24, 1964): 262.
[23] "Statements by Secretary Rusk and Secretary McNamara, August 6," *ibid.,* pp. 263, 267.
[24] *Ibid.,* pp. 265, 266, 267. This points up the fact that the administration attempted to convince Congress and the public of the accuracy of the official version of events by essentially the same means private individuals might use in ordinary conversations, namely, repetition of unequivocal statements. Apparently, this was an effective communications tactic.
[25] Joseph C. Goulden, *Truth Is the First Casualty: The Gulf of Tonkin Affair—Illusion and Reality* (Chicago: A James B. Adler, Inc., Book, published in association with Rand McNally Co., 1969), p. 48.
[26] The term is Wayne Morse's from a June 17, 1969, speech reprinted in U.S., *Congressional Record,* 91st Cong., 1st Sess., June 26, 1969, p. S7243. (Daily ed.)
[27] U.S., *Congressional Record,* 88th Cong., 2d Sess., 1964, 110, pt. 14: 18539.

Speaking for my own committee, everyone I have heard has said that the last
thing we want to do is to become involved in a land war in Asia.[28]

Not satisfied with the resolution's failure explicitly to disavow a war,
Senator Gaylord Nelson proposed amending the measure:

Our continuing policy is to limit our role to the provision of aid, training assistance, and military advice, and it is the sense of the Congress that, except when
provoked to a greater response, we should continue to attempt to avoid a direct
military involvement in the Southeast Asian conflict.[29]

Fulbright persuaded Nelson to withdraw his amendment, not on the
ground of any substantive objection but simply because it "would delay
matters. . . ." The House was then voting on the original resolution, and
if the Senate were to adopt Nelson's amendment, there would have had
to be a conference with the House and revotes by both chambers.

On August 7, the House by a vote of 416–0 and the Senate by 88–2
adopted a resolution supporting the President's determination "to take
all measures to repel any armed attack against the forces of the United
States and to prevent further aggression." [30] The language was, as Clark
Clifford later termed it, "stern." [31]

And so the matter stood for over three years, during which time the
Tonkin Gulf Resolution came to be treated, in Undersecretary of State
Nicholas Katzenbach's words, as a "functional equivalent" of a declara-
tion of war upon North Vietnam.[32]

III

The use of the resolution should not suggest that everyone was satisfied
with the rectitude of the affair. Doubts had been raised soon after the

---

[28] *Ibid.,* p. 18403.

[29] *Ibid.,* p. 18459.

[30] H. J. Res. 1145; S. J. Res. 189.

[31] Clark M. Clifford, "A Vietnam Reappraisal: The Personal History of One Man's View
and How it Evolved," *Foreign Affairs* 47 (July 1969): 605.

[32] Quoted by Senator Albert Gore, U.S., *Congressional Record,* 91st Cong., 1st Sess., June
24, 1969, p. S7083. (Daily ed.) Katzenbach added that declarations of war have become
"outmoded in the international arena," for they would limit the President's flexibility in
limited wars and would, by their slowness, preclude a response in a nuclear war. U.S., Congress, Senate, Committee on Foreign Relations, *Hearing, United States Commitments to
Foreign Powers,* 90th Cong., 1st Sess., 1967, p. 81. This echoed the judgment of State's legal
adviser to the effect that the President had constitutional authority to commit troops to
Vietnam without a congressional declaration of war. Leonard Meeker, "The Legality of
United States Participation in the Defense of Vietnam," *Department of State Bulletin* 54
(March 28, 1966): 484. The desirability of limiting the President's "flexibility" in limited
wars was not considered.

resolution's passage,[33] and before long disturbing reports and allegations began to appear in the press. Rear Admiral Robert B. Moore, commander of the task force that had supported the *Maddox* during the first attack, for example, was said to have indicated that the ship "might have been two or three miles inside the 12-mile limit set by Hanoi for territorial waters." [34] *Times* columnist James Reston wrote, "It is even possible now to hear officials of this Government talking casually about how easy it would be to 'provoke an incident' in the Gulf of Tonkin that would justify an attack on North Vietnam...." [35] The *Times* Washington bureau chief noted, suspiciously, that Johnson "had been carrying" a draft of the resolution "in his pocket for weeks waiting for the moment." [36] A number of books appeared which also were skeptical of the administration's version of events. [37]

Senator Fulbright, too, had developed qualms about the resolution. Partly, this may have reflected his rapidly growing dissatisfaction with the Johnson foreign policy, generally. Soon after the resolution's passage, Fulbright had enthusiastically seconded Johnson's nomination at the Democratic national convention, and during the presidential campaign had contrasted his sensible foreign policy emphasizing the forces "that unite the human race," with Goldwater's "radical new policy of relentless ideological conflict aimed at the elimination of communism and the imposition of American concepts of freedom on the entire world." [38] Johnson's postelection escalation of the war, however, began to raise some doubts, and the President's handling of the Dominican Republic uprising the following April eventually brought on a blistering speech on the Senate floor.[39] Though Fulbright blamed the President's subordinates for the "overtimidity" and "over-reaction" allegedly characterizing the intervention, Johnson was not so easily mollified. The old friendship, personal and political, had ruptured.[40]

---

[33] E.g., Richard H. Rovere, "Letter from Washington," *New Yorker,* August 22, 1964, pp. 105–6; "Tonkin Gulf: Round II," *Nation,* October 5, 1964, p. 177.

[34] *New York Times,* August 11, 1964. The next day the *Times* printed a Pentagon denial of Moore's remarks; but how a Rear Admiral could have mistaken thirty miles offshore (the *Maddox's* location, according to the Pentagon) for only ten miles remained unexplained.

[35] *New York Times,* October 2, 1964.

[36] Tom Wicker, "Lyndon Johnson vs. the Ghost of Jack Kennedy," *Esquire,* October 1965, p. 152. Assistant Secretary of State William P. Bundy later told the Senate Foreign Relations Committee meeting in executive session in September 1966, that he had drawn up several resolution drafts prior to the actual attacks, explaining his actions as normal contingency planning. *New York Times,* November 25, 1967.

[37] E.g., Schurmann *et al., op. cit.,* chap. 3; George McT. Kahin and John W. Lewis, *The United States in Vietnam* (New York: Dial Press, 1967), pp. 156–59; Theodore Draper, *The Abuse of Power* (New York: Viking Press, 1967), pp. 63–66.

[38] U.S., *Congressional Record,* 88th Cong., 2d Sess., 1964, 110, pt. 16: 21677. See also *ibid.,* pt. 17: 21916-18.

[39] U.S., *Congressional Record,* 89th Cong., 1st Sess., 1965, 111, pt. 15: 23855-61.

[40] Gwertzman and Johnson, *op. cit.,* pp. 219–21.

As American involvement in Vietnam grew, Fulbright became increasingly critical of the war, and dubious of any claims made on its behalf. In January 1966, in fact, his committee held a series of hearings on the war, at which time he noted that he had not believed while working for its passage that the Tonkin resolution would be used to justify action on the scale that the President had taken. The hearings themselves may have been intended to stir widespread public interest in the escalation and legitimate opposition to it, but the publicity they engendered also had at least one unanticipated effect: it transformed Fulbright into a kind of political lightning rod, attracting war policy doubters and cynics from among current and past officialdom. In May, for example, he received an unsolicited letter from a retired World War II destroyer expert, Rear Admiral Arnold E. True, who contended that the *Maddox*'s firing a warning shot across the North Vietnamese boats' bows was a hostile action:

It seems to me that if the [press] accounts I read are correct, the U.S. fired the first shot in the war with N. Vietnam and then bombed the torpedo base because they retaliated, and that the resolution was passed on false premises.[41]

This letter—the first of several Fulbright was to receive from apparently knowledgeable skeptics—heightened his own doubts.

Fulbright also had come to resent the administration's use of the resolution to bypass Congress, and in particular, the Senate Foreign Relations Committee of which he was chairman. His sense of frustration was evident in his 1966 remarks to reporter Eric Sevareid concerning the second Tonkin Gulf attack.

... the Gulf of Tonkin incident, if I may say so, was a very vague one. We were briefed on it, but we have no way of knowing, even to this day what actually happened. I don't know whether we provoked that attack in connection with supervising or helping a raid by South Vietnamese or not. Our evidence was sketchy as to whether those PT boats, or some other kind of boats were coming to investigate or whether they actually attacked. I have been *told* there was no physical damage. They weren't hit by anything. I heard one man say there was one bullet hole in one of these ships. One bullet hole![42]

Shortly thereafter, Fulbright wrote of his own role in the passage of the resolution in confessional tones rare for a politician.

I ... served as floor manager of the Southeast Asia resolution, and did all I could

[41] Goulden, *op. cit.,* p. 176.
[42] Eric Sevareid, "Why Our Foreign Policy Is Failing: an Interview with Senator Fulbright," *Look,* May 3, 1966, pp. 25–26.

to bring about its prompt and overwhelming adoption. I did so because I was confident that President Johnson would use our endorsement with wisdom and restraint. I was also influenced by partisanship: an election campaign was in progress and I had no wish to make any difficulties for the President in his race against a Republican candidate whose election I thought would be a disaster for the country.[43]

A top secret Pentagon briefing in 1966 had left him unconvinced. Meanwhile, disturbing evidence was beginning to accumulate from unlikely sources. One of these was the Little Rock *Arkansas Gazette,* which, unlike the Eastern prestige newspapers, carried an in-depth Associated Press article on the attacks. Crew members were interviewed, and they reported a rumor that the *Maddox* had had equipment designed for "checking on radar and communications on shore," and that the ship's radar and sonar operations might have been unreliable.[44]

As Fulbright's doubts grew, so, too, did the administration's reliance on the resolution. Accompanying both were an increase in American military involvement in Vietnam and an expansion and intensification of "hawkish" sentiments among the mass public at home. In a reaction against these developments, Fulbright introduced a "national commitments resolution" into the Senate, resolving

that it is the sense of the Senate that a national commitment of the United States to a foreign power necessarily and exclusively results from affirmative action taken by the Executive and Legislative branches of the United States government through means of a treaty, convention, or other legislative instrumentality specifically intended to give effect to such a commitment.[45]

For a variety of reasons,[46] the resolution was broadly popular within the Senate, and the Foreign Relations Committee hearings on the measure

---

[43] J. William Fulbright, "The Fatal Arrogance of Power," *New York Times Magazine,* May 15, 1966, p. 104. Fulbright's viewpoint reflected a widespread liberal attitude, in which "partisanship for Johnson as against Goldwater was so intense among precisely those in the United States and elsewhere who would have been most likely to criticize, that most of them hesitated to express their dissent." Maurice J. Goldbloom, "Johnson So Far: III; Foreign Policy," *Commentary,* June 1965, p. 49. Later, in a newspaper interview on the occasion of his eleventh anniversary as committee chairman, Fulbright unhesitatingly chose his support of the resolution as the action he would most like to do differently, if he had the years to live over again. But though castigating the President for his "misrepresentation," Fulbright failed to mention that only his own and his colleagues' suspension of their critical faculties permitted such misrepresentation to succeed. *Washington Star,* April 19, 1970.

[44] Little Rock, *Arkansas Gazette,* July 16, 1967. Racial violence in Newark had squeezed the article out of the prestige newspapers. The incident is recounted in Goulden, *op. cit.,* p. 201.

[45] S. Res. 151, U.S., *Congressional Record,* 90th Cong., 1st Sess., 1967, 112, pt. 15: 20702.

[46] E.g., the resolution defended the integrity of the Senate, the President had been treating the Senate with ill-concealed contempt, and the resolution did not affect substantive policy directly, minimizing the occasions for concrete disagreements to shatter the abstract consensus.

broadened this sentiment, for the administration treated them with open disdain. Secretary McNamara refused even to testify, Undersecretary Katzenbach aggressively defended the position that the Tonkin Gulf Resolution constituted a "functional equivalent" of a declaration of war, making further congressional action in this regard superfluous and needlessly divisive, and the President arrogantly said in effect that if Congress no longer approved of the way the resolution was being used, the legislature should repeal it.

Like his hearings the year before, Fulbright's "national commitments resolution" meetings attracted an unexpected bit of correspondence, an unsigned letter—apparently, from a knowledgeable person with access to hitherto unreleased information concerning the incidents. The informant alleged, according to one source, "that there was mass confusion at the Pentagon on the day of the second incident, with receipt and transmission of cables delayed for hours." Furthermore, he continued, "it was 'obvious' the decision to attack was made in the face of contradictory reports from the field." [47]

Fulbright and his staff agreed that the letter's implications were worth pursuing, and asked the Navy for the destroyer's official logbooks. The Navy's delay in making the logs available further aroused Fulbright's suspicions, and when he requested communications mentioned in the logs, "The Defense Department became tighter, and made a policy decision to supply only the cables that were specifically requested, and to volunteer no information, written or otherwise." [48] These communications contained a number of mentions of "34–A Operation," which seemed to refer to South Vietnamese patrol boat raids against certain North Vietnamese islands. In other contacts with the committee, the informant passed on additional information. [49]

In December, Fulbright's staff concluded that, far from being certain of a second attack, the Joint Chiefs were still seeking confirmation from the *Maddox's* commander even after the retaliation sorties had started. About that time, too, the committee received a letter from a former Navy junior officer. The officer, Lieutenant (j.g.) John W. White, had served on a seaplane tender which had come to the *Maddox's* aid after the second incident. He charged that Johnson, McNamara, and the Joint Chiefs had provided "false information" to Congress regarding that incident. "I recall clearly the confusing radio messages sent at that time by the destroyers," he later wrote the *New Haven Register,* "confusing because the de-

---

[47] Goulden, *op. cit.,* p. 203.

[48] *Ibid.*

[49] The Navy later discovered the identity of the informant, and had him declared psychiatrically unfit for duty. *Ibid.,* p. 205.

stroyers themselves were not certain they were being attacked." [50] White conceded that North Vietnamese boats might have harassed the ships, but maintained that the enemy had fired no torpedoes or shells. The *Maddox*'s chief sonarman, wrote White, had informed him that the sonarscopes had picked up no torpedoes during the August 4 encounter. White admitted, however, that he had spoken with the sonarman six full months after the incident during a "casual encounter" in a shipyard, and could not even remember the sonarman's name. The charges, then, were intriguing, but hardly conclusive. [51]

Thus, as useful as all of these unconventional sources of information were, Fulbright recognized that an exposé would be vastly more convincing if it were based on official documents and statements. Although he knew that the Defense Department would hardly be an enthusiastic accomplice in this enterprise, he felt that it could not prevent enough information from being disclosed to assure its failure. Thus, an attempt by Undersecretary of Defense Paul Nitze to dissuade Fulbright from pursuing the matter further was foredoomed to defeat.

A few days later, on December 26, another anonymous informant contacted Fulbright, telling him of a top secret study, "Command and Control of the Tonkin Gulf Incident, 4–5 August 1964," carried out by members of the Office of the Secretary of Defense. The study, the informant said, concluded that "The first attack . . . was very probably made because the NVN [North Vietnamese] confused the *Maddox* . . . with operations which were covering SVN [South Vietnamese] hit-and-run attacks against NVN coastal areas." As for the second attack, it was "probably imaginary." [52]

Fulbright planned to present his findings to his committee on January 24, 1968, in the hope that it might be convinced of the advisability of beginning a formal investigation. But he was troubled by the recognition that he could not "advocate this step too forcefully" to the other members, "without being accused of wanting to undertake a personal vendetta against the Administration on its Vietnam policy." [53]

On January 23, North Korea seized an American intelligence ship, the *Pueblo*, which had been engaged in activity near the North Korean coast. The parallel with the *Maddox* and *Turner Joy* was obvious, and many reservations individual members had had about the Tonkin affair surfaced. "Just as the Tonkin incidents led to war," argued Fulbright, "so possibly could the *Pueblo* incident." Even Karl Mundt of North Dakota,

[50] *New Haven Register,* December 6, 1967.
[51] *New York Times,* December 21, 1967.
[52] Goulden, *op. cit.,* p. 208.
[53] *New York Times,* January 21, 1968.

a strong supporter of the war, admitted, "Bill, you have a point." [54] The *Pueblo* capture, in other words, permitted the committee to reopen the Tonkin affair, not ostensibly to criticize past behavior, but rather to learn from it—a much more publicly acceptable motive.

On February 20, this second hearing was held. And if the first hearing had been dominated by the administration's implicit appeal to patriotism, the second was characterized by a critical impatience with emotionalism, and a desire for facts. It was soon obvious that the administration had been less than candid.

Instead of being in "international waters," McNamara admitted that the *Maddox* had been within the twelve-mile limit claimed by North Vietnam.[55] McNamara explained this discrepancy by saying that it had been assumed that North Vietnam had claimed only a three-mile limit, as the French colonialists before them had done. In support of this, McNamara pointed out that North Vietnam itself did not announce the twelve-mile limit until nearly a month after the attacks.[56]

It is difficult to take such facile disclaimers seriously. More than fifteen months prior to the incidents, the Director of Naval Intelligence had informed the American naval attaché in Saigon that there was "a good possibility" Hanoi would claim a twelve-mile limit "if issue were raised." [57] Several weeks before the encounter, the CIA had gathered evidence that North Vietnam asserted a twelve-mile limit,[58] and five days preceding the first attack Radio Hanoi had protested allied activity nine miles off North Vietnam's coast.[59] In fact, on August 8, the day after the passage of the resolution, Vance said on a Voice of America broadcast interview, "I think that they [North Vietnam and China] do claim a twelve-mile limit . . ." [60]—and Vance had been present at and taken part in the retaliation decisions made barely four days earlier. Even if one were to believe the McNamara version, there would remain the question of why the three-mile limit were merely assumed, and not properly checked out. If this type of mission required approval at the highest levels of the Defense Department, State Department, and CIA, as McNamara claimed, this "assumption" plainly did not speak well of the adequacy of their review.

McNamara also maintained that this country "recognizes no claim of a territorial sea in excess of three miles." Yet as Senator Morse has

[54] *New York Times*, February 4, 1968.
[55] *Hearing*, p. 69.
[56] *Ibid.*, p. 13.
[57] *New York Times*, December 20, 1968.
[58] Goulden, *op. cit.*, p. 225.
[59] *Ibid.*, p. 227.
[60] *Ibid.*, p. 230.

shown, the *Maddox* was ordered to stay at least fifteen miles from China's shore, indicating that the administration had acceded to Peking's claim of a twelve-mile limit.[61]

Nor could the patrols accurately be termed "routine." The word denotes customary activity, a phrase hardly in accord with the fact that there had been only two similar patrols in the preceding thirty-two months.[62] Routine, further, connotes a commonplace lack of danger, a view at odds with that of the *Maddox*'s commander, who had complained to superiors even before the first attack that "continuance of patrol presents an unacceptable risk." [63] The second patrol, in which two destroyers passed near recently shelled North Vietnamese islands, plainly was even less "routine" than the first.

More importantly, the hearing uncovered considerable evidence suggesting that the destroyers' actions may, indeed, have been "provocative." The *Maddox*, it developed, had initially been involved in a "DeSoto" operation for American intelligence agencies. That is, the *Maddox*, like a number of other vessels, was equipped with sophisticated electronic intelligence apparatus, and engaged in a single ship patrol off a hostile coast. The *Maddox*, in particular, had been directed to "stimulate Chicom-North Vietnamese electronic reaction" by heading toward shore with its gun control radar equipment in operation. These feints, as McNamara conceded, led "the Chicoms or the North Vietnamese to turn on the radars so that we can measure the radar frequencies. . . ." [64] If these mimicked attacks were not enough to cast doubt on the "unprovoked" nature of the first incident, it might be remembered that it was the *Maddox* which entered Hanoi's territorial waters and fired the first shot in the encounter. After the first attack, in any event, the ship's commander had cabled the commander of the Seventh Fleet, telling him that North Vietnam considered the *Maddox* to be part of "34–A Operations," raids by American-supplied South Vietnamese patrol boats involving bombardment of two North Vietnamese coastal islands. The *Maddox*'s commander concluded from this that Hanoi classed his ship as an "enemy." [65] The Navy, thus, was not unaware that the *Maddox* might have appeared "provocative" to North Vietnam.

Yet the second patrol was more "provocative" still, for by this time the DeSoto operation had been replaced by an order to the destroyers to

---

[61] U.S., *Congressional Record,* 90th Cong., 2d Sess. (February 29, 1968), p. S1948. (Daily ed.)

[62] Remarks of Senator Morse, U.S., *Congressional Record,* 90th Cong., 2d Sess. (February 29, 1968), p. S1948. (Daily ed.)

[63] Goulden, *op. cit.,* p. 130.

[64] *Ibid.,* p. 124.

[65] *Hearing,* p. 33.

"possibly draw NVN [North Vietnamese] PGM [patrol boats] to north-ward away from area of 34–A Ops. . . ." This brought the *Maddox* and *Turner Joy* "close to the shore within four miles of the [North Vietnamese] islands under orders in the daytime, retreating at night. . . ." In other words, the ships violated North Vietnam's twelve-mile limit, and became, as Morse put it with characteristic bluntness, "decoys." [66]

It also developed at the hearing that some question existed as to whether the second attack had even taken place. According to a communiqué from the Naval Communications Center sent about four hours after the second attack had allegedly occurred:

Review of action makes many recorded contacts and torpedoes fired appear doubtful. Freak weather effects and overeager sonarman may have accounted for many reports. No actual visual sightings by *Maddox*. Suggest complete evaluation before any further action.[67]

The Navy later admitted in its report that "extensive interrogation of all potential knowledgeable sources reveals they have no info concerning NVN attack on U.S. ships on 4 August 1964." Nor was any debris found in the area.[68] Nor were any radio communications or radar emanating from the enemy picked up by the destroyers. Tennessee's Senator Albert Gore concluded that McNamara had been unable to establish the second attack, adding, "I think there is more question now than when you

---

[66] *Ibid.*, pp. 31, 102, 50, 83.

[67] *Ibid.*, p. 57. In this regard, a message from the *Turner Joy* read in part, "No sonar indications of torpedo noises. . . . Self noise was very high." *Ibid.*, p. 70. The ship was traveling at a speed in excess of thirty knots, at which self noise may interfere with the operation of sonar equipment. The ship's evasive maneuvers further hampered sonar operations. Nor was the *Maddox* aided by the facts that its sonar had been "totally on the blink" earlier in the day, and its operator was notably lacking in experience. Goulden, *op. cit.*, pp. 142, 144. The efficiency of the radar operations on this tense, dark, and stormy night is suggested by this reminiscence of seaman Patrick N. Park, main gun director of the *Maddox*. As Goulden relates it:

Around midnight Park . . . was given a range on a target spotted by the main radar room, "the firmest target we've had all night." He directed his own radar toward the target. "It was a damned big one right on us, no doubt about this one. About 1,500 yards off to the side, a nice fat blip." Park asked for . . . control of the triggering device on the five-inch gun mounts and for permission to open fire. . . . "Just before I pushed the trigger, I suddenly realized—that's the *Turner Joy*. This came right with the order to open fire. I shouted back, 'Where's the *Turner Joy*?' There was a lot of yelling of 'Goddamn' back and forth, with the bridge telling me to 'fire before we lose the contact,' and me yelling right back at them . . . I finally told them, 'I'm not opening fire until I know where the *Turner Joy* is.' The bridge got on the phone and said, 'Turn on your lights, *Turner Joy*.' Sure enough, there she was, right on the crosshairs. I had six five-inch guns right at the *Turner Joy*, 1,500 yards away. If I had fired, it would have blown it clear out of the water. All I had to do was squeeze the trigger. In fact, I could have been shot for *not* squeezing the trigger!" (Goulden, *op. cit.*, pp. 146–47)

[68] *Hearing*, pp. 75, 58.

came." [69] Most of the other committee members conceded that an attack had occurred, perhaps so as not overly to embarrass the administration and the Secretary of Defense, who was to resign in nine days.

In any case, McNamara conceded that the administration had not always been certain. On August 4, the Secretary had met with Assistant Secretary of Defense Vance and the Joint Chiefs of Staff for two and a half hours "to determine whether, in fact, an attack on the destroyers had occurred." For about four and a half hours, said McNamara, "we were reviewing the information that bore on whether an attack had taken place." He informed the committee that Vice Admiral Roy L. Johnson, then Commander of the Seventh Fleet, had reported that he was "convinced beyond any doubt that *Maddox* and *Turner Joy* were subject to an unprovoked torpedo attack on the night of 4 August 1964." [70] But McNamara neglected to mention that this statement had been made on August 14, and, therefore, could hardly have been used to support the bombing decision taken nine days earlier.[71]

Any battle whose very existence is subject to debate is unlikely to have been of much importance. And, in fact, the United States suffered "no damage" to men or property. Why, then, asked Senators Gore and Pell, did this country retaliate with such force? [72]

Why, for example, was the matter not taken to the UN? Secretary McNamara's answer was that "we had no reason to believe the United Nations could have acted in any effective manner." [73] This response itself raises several problems. In the first place, while the UN may have only limited relevance in a situation in which a major power feels its vital interests are at stake, it may be quite useful in preventing a minor incident from ballooning into a major one. In this case, the delay afforded by UN discussion might have permitted tempers to cool and doubts concerning the attack to be settled.

Secondly, in the UN the administration's evidence might have been forced to submit to greater scrutiny. The other member nations would

---

[69] *Ibid.,* p. 102. In later televised remarks Fulbright was less equivocal. "I am personally convinced in my own mind," he said, "that no attack took place on the fourth [of August]." "Sixty Minutes," CBS telecast, March 16, 1971.

[70] *Ibid.,* pp. 58, 59, 93.

[71] David Halberstam has recounted an incident which suggests the value the administration laid on precise information. After the second attack, McGeorge Bundy, the President's assistant for national security affairs, brought together his staff, and told them that Johnson intended to seek passage of a congressional resolution. Douglass Cater, a White House adviser with long experience as a Washington reporter, asked Bundy, "Isn't it a little precipitous? Do we have all the information?" Bundy answered, "The President has decided and that's what we're doing." When Cater persisted, Bundy cut him off curtly. David Halberstam, "The Very Expensive Education of McGeorge Bundy," *Harper's,* July 1969, p. 34.

[72] *Hearing,* pp. 93, 105.

[73] *Ibid.,* p. 70.

not be moved by patriotic demands, as congressmen were, and there would have been an opportunity for Hanoi to present its side of the story. Perhaps the administration's unwillingness to go to the UN, then, betrays a fear that the flimsy nature of its evidence might have been exposed.[74]

Thirdly, what is meant by "effective manner"? If the United States could present its case adequately, presumably Hanoi would suffer a setback before "world opinion." Admittedly, this would not be a grave punishment; yet the offense—if we can properly term it that—was not grave, either. Certainly the UN would not have approved military sanctions against North Vietnam; but was this the only "effective manner" of handling the situation? For the UN's strongest verbal and financial supporter to admit this is to call into question the sincerity or relevance of America's entire commitment to the UN as a peace-keeping organization. If policy makers believe that the UN cannot deal with a minor event like this, what can it deal with?

IV

Why, given the incomplete and ambiguous character of much of the evidence, did the administration choose to impose a most explosive and dubious interpretation upon events? According to Secretary Rusk's statement at the 1964 hearing, "These attacks were not an isolated event but are related directly to the aggressive posture of North Vietnam and to the policy that the United States has been pursuing" in Vietnam and Southeast Asia.[75] Did the evidence support such a view? In a brief paroxysm of candor on a television program the night before, Rusk implied that it did not; for he confessed that he was unable to offer a "rational explanation" for North Vietnam's actions, when that was precisely the function his "aggressive posture" statement was supposed to serve when he delivered it the following morning.

In any event, one is entitled to ask how this "aggressive posture" was manifested. It is certainly true that the Vietcong had repeatedly made it clear that they were unawed by the United States and would not easily be frightened off. In one ten-day period in May, for instance, terrorists had sunk an American aircraft transport in Saigon harbor, tossed a bomb into a crowd of Americans viewing the wrecked ship, and planted explosives under a bridge on which the visiting Secretary McNamara

---

[74] Related to this, had the incident been brought to the UN, several member nations probably would have tried to pressure the United States into agreeing to the convening of a fourteen-nation conference on Southeast Asia, a plan much discussed at the time. The Johnson administration had been on record as opposing the conference as futile.

[75] Dean Rusk, in U.S., Congress, House, *Promoting the Maintenance of International Peace and Security in Southeast Asia*, 88th Cong., 2d Sess., 1964, H. Rept. 1708, p. 5.

was expected to travel. Probably, it was this kind of determination not to be cowed by the United States that impelled North Vietnamese boats to attack the *Maddox* in the first place.

Yet do these terrorist attacks amount to an "aggressive posture" on the part of Hanoi? A positive answer would have to assume a very substantial degree of control to have been exercised by North Vietnam over the Vietcong during this period. Is this assumption warranted? It seems clear that, as Bernard Fall concluded in 1965, the Vietcong were not puppets of Hanoi.[76] But if the relationship were not one of master to puppet, what was it? A year later, Douglas Pike, a supporter of the war and the author of the most detailed analysis of the Vietcong, provided a different metaphor. The National Liberation Front (the Vietcong's political structure) and North Vietnam, he said, "were separate entities with separate lives. The NLF was not an independent, indigenous organization as it asserted. But neither was it simply a hammer in the long arm of the DRV [i.e., North Vietnam]." [77] Thus, while the evidence is not overwhelming, it is probably fallacious to identify Vietcong actions with North Vietnamese intentions, and thereby declare Hanoi to have assumed an "aggressive posture" by proxy.

It is certainly difficult to argue that *by its own actions,* North Vietnam had assumed an "aggressive posture" toward the United States. Nor is this surprising, for why should Hanoi deliberately set out to provoke a wider war with the United States? For a nation with resources as meager as North Vietnam's, such a strategy would have been "quixotic," [78] if not actually masochistic. It also would have been needless: the Vietcong already were making impressive gains in the South at very little cost in men and supplies to the North.[79] Did Hanoi, then, seek only to cause America to lose face in Southeast Asia? That, too, is difficult to defend, for had that been North Vietnam's aim, it scarcely would have denied its involvement in the second attack.

Two possible explanations may be suggested for the administration's interpreting events as it did. Both explanations assume that decision makers welcomed the incident, a proposition to be examined shortly.

---

[76] Bernard B. Fall, *Viet-Nam Witness 1953-66* (New York: Praeger, 1966), chap. 18.

[77] Douglas Pike, *Viet Cong: The Organization and Techniques of the National Liberation Front of South Vietnam* (Cambridge: M.I.T. Press, 1966), p. 236. This judgment is echoed in Donald Zagoria, *Vietnam Triangle: Moscow, Peking, Hanoi* (New York: Pegasus, 1967), pp. 112–22.

[78] This is, in fact, what Geyelin termed the attack. *Op. cit.,* p. 79.

[79] "Most of the supplies for the Vietcong, like the recruits, came from the villages of the *South*—the Vietcong required only five or six tons of supplies a day from the outside world." Hilsman, *op. cit.,* p. 533. Similarly, Pike concludes that "material aid by the DRV in the period before mid-1964 probably was minimal . . . because it did not consider such aid necessary." Pike, *op. cit.,* p. 325. Indeed, "aid was largely confined to two areas—doctrinal know-how and leadership personnel. . . ." *Ibid.,* p. 321.

First, consciously or unconsciously, policy makers felt that the incident's usefulness would increase with its seriousness. This guided their judgment and perceptual selectivity as they examined the evidence. Other explanations may perhaps have been more plausible to policy makers of more open minds; but the conclusion of North Vietnamese aggression permitted these policy makers to find what they had been looking for.

Second, the administration had no illusions about the "aggressive" nature of Hanoi's attacks, but deliberately exaggerated them in order to provide an excuse to bomb the North and to obtain a broad supporting resolution from Congress. This is a very serious charge, and if true, the Tonkin incident could hardly be treated as a true crisis: it would stand as readymade and artificial as a public relations gimmick. The very seriousness of this charge precludes direct supporting evidence. For public officials to suggest such behavior on the part of the administration, as McNamara said, would be "monstrous." Nor would the press have great incentive to risk the enormous outpouring of official invective in order to make such a point.

Consequently, the supporting evidence necessarily is highly circumstantial and inferential. But the relevant question may not be whether this contention is adequately demonstrated, but rather whether it is more persuasive than the alternatives, particularly that offered by the administration itself.

It may be noted that if either of the attacks was to be interpreted as serious, it should have been the first, since it was clearly more substantial than the second. And yet the essence of the unguarded remarks of officials after the initial attack was that it had been of no major military or political significance. If this were true of the first, it should have been truer still of the second. But instead of the second attack being pictured as a relatively minor incident, it was depicted as being of such importance that immediate military and congressional retaliation was necessary. Unless one believes that Johnson felt that a repetition of a minor incident transformed it into a major one, his interpreting the second attack as important becomes inexplicable.

Alternatively, one might suggest not that Johnson actually interpreted the second attack as important, but merely that he saw that it would serve his purposes if he were perceived to so interpret it.

What, then, were these purposes? In the first place, the incident and the administration's response gave the President a virtual blank check from Congress regarding future actions in Vietnam. Through his public statements and the sixty-four bombing missions, he made it almost impossible for Congress to reject his resolution. Top officials, both on national television and before the congressional committee, appeared absolutely convinced of the "deliberate, uprovoked" nature of the attacks, and the air strikes underlined this certitude with the *fait accompli* of commitment. In this atmosphere of patriotic urgency with elections barely three months away, politicians had little inducement to raise doubts. Instead, the necessity of national unity in support of the commander-in-chief seemed all important. A demand for the critical examination of the evidence would have been seen as obstructionist, divisive, and blatantly "political." As Fulbright was to put it, "It just seemed sort of really treasonable to question that damn Tonkin Gulf resolution at the time." [80]

Secretary McNamara, of course, explicitly denied that the Tonkin "incident was provoked in order to have a reason to come to the Congress," and the very suggestion of such a motive was evidently considered too indelicate to explore. But it may be significant that, although famed for his memory, the Secretary claimed that he was unable to recall such important facts as whether the administration had already planned an "intensification of U.S. involvement" in the war or the "bombing of North Vietnam" [81]

If the administration did not exaggerate the incident to obtain a congressional resolution, a number of questions remain:

First, why was the nature of the incidents significantly misrepresented to Congress and to the public?

Second, why did the destroyers violate North Vietnam's twelve-mile limit a second time?

Third, why was the President's retaliation so rapid, so irrevocable, and so grossly out of proportion?

Fourth, why were American aircraft dispatched to Thailand, if not to bomb the North in the future?

Why should the President want such a blank check? The answer is obvious. It was plain that a significant American military escalation was required to ward off disaster. A June CIA study informed Washington that there was "serious doubt that a victory can be won." [82] And the situation continued to deteriorate, so that when American ambassador to South Vietnam Maxwell Taylor reported to Washington three months later his message was very gloomy. "The Administration was left with the fundamental question," the *Times* commented: "Would there be, and how much longer, a South Vietnamese structure for the United States to support." [83] For as one scholar of Asian affairs has written:

---

[80] Quoted in Johnson and Gwertzman, *op. cit.,* p. 198.
[81] *Hearing,* pp. 89, 24. .
[82] *New York Times,* August 23, 1964.
[83] *New York Times,* September 13, 1964.

By the fall of 1964, South Vietnam was on the verge of collapse. The Vietcong were threatening to cut the country in half, and the South Vietnamese army and civil administration were shattered.[84]

The administration was well aware of these developments, and wanted to reverse them.

In any case, what happened, of course, was that three months after the 1964 presidential election bombing of the North began in earnest, and the Tonkin Gulf Resolution was used to legitimate this escalation.[85] It proved an effective instrument with which congressional critics of the war could be flailed; for nearly all, as the President never ceased pointing out, had voted for the resolution.[86] If the crisis were not deliberately exaggerated for the administration's benefit, then certainly it stumbled upon a series of fortunate coincidences.

There is a second—and somewhat less persuasive—reason to believe that the administration may have welcomed the incident. The sixty-four retaliatory bombing missions dulled much of the point of the charges of Senator Barry Goldwater and other conservatives that the President had been pursuing a "no win" policy in Vietnam. The American response demonstrated with blistering clarity that Johnson was neither reluctant nor squeamish about the use of force. At the same time, however, because there was only one series of air strikes and no immediate massive escalation, the response did not significantly damage the President's claims to restraint. The Johnson image of controlled strength was thus fortified by his reaction, and with a presidential election in November there was ample incentive to improve the image.

In this regard, it is pertinent to recall the nature of public opinion on the war. It was, in the first place, perceived as an important issue. In fact, as measured by the number of comments it elicited from the University of Michigan's Survey Research Center's national sample, Vietnam was the most salient of electoral issues.[87] More than that, popular sentiment was decidedly "hawkish." For example, among SRC's respondents choosing one of the offered alternatives, forty-eight percent selected taking "a stronger stand even if it means invading North Vietnam," thirty-eight percent favored keeping "our soldiers in Viet Nam but try[ing] to end the fighting," and only thirteen percent chose pulling "out of Viet Nam en-

---

[84] Zagoria, *op. cit.,* p. 44.

[85] By this time, not only Khanh but also his successor had been replaced as rulers of South Vietnam.

[86] The lone exceptions were Senators Morse of Oregon and Gruening of Alaska. Representative Powell of New York had neither supported nor opposed the resolution, but had merely voted "present."

[87] John H. Kessel, *The Goldwater Coalition: Republican Strategies in 1964* (Indianapolis: Bobbs-Merrill, 1968), p. 277.

tirely." [88] This hawkishness, moreover, was considerably more wide-spread among political activists—the most influential portion of the population—than among nonactivists.[89] And yet the general hawkishness was not such as to demand an enormous immediate increase in American military presence in Vietnam. Quite the opposite, in fact, was the case. Thus, the same survey found that eighty-nine percent of those choosing among designated alternatives were "not at all worried" or only "somewhat worried" concerning "the chances of our country getting into war"; a mere ten percent were "pretty worried." Moreover, eighty-two percent said that "during the last few years . . . our chances of staying out of war" were "getting better" or had "stayed the same"; eighteen percent believed that they were "getting worse." [90] Popular hawkishness, coexisting so comfortably with a widespread desire for continued peace, was largely without bite, and thus could easily be appeased. It is not surprising, then, that a Louis Harris poll taken a "few days" after the retaliatory air strike "revealed a striking growth of public confidence" in the President's handling of Southeast Asia. This contrasted with an "earlier poll," which had seemed to show that Goldwater and other critics had been "quite successful in undermining confidence." [91]

Of course, it may be replied, Johnson was certain of victory in November, anyway. Why, then, should the election be on his mind when contemplating a suitable reaction to the attacks? There are two possible answers. First, the President, a crafty politician, was taking no chances. If he could with relative ease deflate one of his opponents' chief issues, why not? That Johnson was in fact not taking any chances in 1964 is illustrated by his extremely orthodox campaign, and his selection of Hubert Humphrey as his running-mate in order to placate the party's liberals.[92]

---

[88] Inter-University Consortium for Political Research, "1964 Election Study," SRC Study 473 (University of Michigan Survey Research Center, Post-Election Study, September–November, 1964), Deck 12, p. 6. (Mimeographed.)

[89] Kessel, *op. cit.,* p. 333.

[90] Inter-University Consortium for Political Research, "1964 Election Study," SRC Study 473 (University of Michigan Survey Research Center, Pre-Election Study, September–November 1964), Deck 5, p. 33. The irony, of course, was that the United States *was* then at war. Public ignorance of this fact was a tribute to the success of the administration's policies of deception (e.g., repeatedly speaking of "peace" in the present tense, utilizing professional army men rather than draftees in Vietnam).

[91] Richard H. Rovere, "Letter from Washington," *New Yorker,* August 22, 1964, p. 104.

[92] Nelson W. Polsby and Aaron B. Wildavsky, *Presidential Elections: Strategies of American Electoral Politics,* 2d ed. (New York: Scribners, 1968), pp. 200–1. Polsby and Wildavsky suggest that Johnson chose Humphrey in order to increase his support from party liberals, a segment who had opposed Johnson's own selection as vice presidential candidate in 1960. And yet, the passage of the Civil Rights Act of 1964 meant that liberals had already, by and large, been converted to Johnson supporters. Moreover, if they still disliked him, to whom else could they turn? Certainly, Goldwater horrified them, and there was no talk of establishing a liberal-oriented third party or of denying Johnson his renomination.

Second, the President did not merely want to win—he wanted to win by landslide proportions. By so doing, he could gain the opportunity to compile a remarkable record in office, bringing him contemporary adulation and a place of honor in American history.[93] A great victory would provide him with a popular mandate to initiate and have passed his major programs; and the larger his margin, the better his chance of facing a Congress willing to follow his lead.

Yet why did the President choose a congressional resolution for these ends? Why this device? Why not another? A glance at the alternatives reveals the answer. On the one hand, had Johnson refrained from obtaining some act of congressional acquiescence before escalating the war, he would certainly have left himself open for charges of having usurped Congress's authority to declare war.[94] If Congress had not thus disarmed itself by enacting the resolution, congressional and partisan criticism would have been far more intense and early in coming. This was a lesson from recent history of which he could hardly, as a senator and vice-president during the previous sixteen years, have been unaware. President Truman had intervened in the Korean conflict without bothering to obtain formal congressional approval, and later had found himself under heated domestic attack for his action. Johnson did not wish to repeat the blunder.

On the other hand, had Johnson attempted to have truly strong conlems would have arisen: it would have been very difficult to argue that the Tonkin "incidents" warranted such a measure; it might have aroused searching public and congressional debate and criticism, which might have threatened to expose the Tonkin incidents' reality or discredit the administration's war policies; it would have jarred with the Johnsonian electoral emphasis on *controlled* strength.

What was needed, then, was an approach like Goldilocks's porridge: not too cold, not too hot, but just right. Such an alternative, fortunately for the administration, was readily available, complete with recent historical precedents, in the form of the congressional resolution. Presidents Eisenhower and Kennedy had had Tonkin-type resolutions passed concerning Formosa and Cuba, respectively, without difficulty. Thus, by 1964 the congressional resolution was an accepted and obvious tool with which Presidents compelled Congress to legitimize their freedom in deal-

---

If Johnson were playing the campaign this close to the vest, in short, the possibility of using the Tonkin incident for electoral advantage cannot be altogether ignored.

[93] Another factor here might have been the desire to out-distance Kennedy's narrow margin of victory in 1960. Certainly, there was no love lost between the two men, and envy and resentment may not have been entirely alien to the relationship.

[94] To some extent, of course, Johnson did face these precise charges from the war's opponents, but surely they would have been more frequent and effective had he not been able to utilize the resolution as a "functional equivalent."

ing with international emergencies. In short, the resolution far out-distanced the alternative approaches.

V

In retrospect, it is difficult to believe that the Tonkin Gulf crisis presented significant difficulties to decision makers regarding the distinguishing of appearances from reality. If the precise nature of the incidents were unclear, if the existence of the second attack were open to question, these were problems only of detail. That the incidents were militarily and politically trivial there could be no doubt.

From the vantage of the public, mass and attentive, the crisis raised perceptual problems of a more serious nature. Using the media effectively, the President and top officials helped to create an atmosphere of urgency and impatience. In this concentrated public relations attack, television seems to have been especially useful. Righteous indignation was perhaps the main theme of the oratory, but a humanitarian concern for South Vietnam and a stress on the importance of the American image of strength were also present.

It is fair to say that a good deal of the administration's public relations efforts were directed toward suppressing or distorting unwanted information—facts that would have cast doubt upon the official version's emphasis on the "unprovocative" activities of the destroyers in "international" waters. An exposé would have undermined the basic response attitude of indignation, thus eliminating the rationale for military and congressional retaliation. Information was suppressed, in other words, mainly out of decision makers' policy convictions: a congressional resolution would smooth the way for a military escalation, which was felt to be necessary to prevent defeat in South Vietnam. More personal motivations may also have been present, specifically, the President's desire to reinforce his image of cautious strength in order to better his performance in the coming election.

And yet most of the public—and congressional—relations efforts seem to have been directed less at falsifying facts than at falsifying an atmosphere. For the administration succeeded in creating an atmosphere of urgency and crisis even though its own version of events hardly justified such a view. Even had the destroyers been wantonly and arbitrarily attacked in international waters, a crisis calling for the administration's response could not be said to have existed.

To speak of "atmosphere" is to suggest something ephemeral, easily dissipated or penetrated. And yet the atmosphere protecting the official version of events was remarkably durable, at first consisting of patriotic urgency and later of patriotic support for the war effort. Much of the atmosphere had to be dispelled before the official version could effectively be questioned.

Ultimately, of course, it was questioned and shattered. The facts—or many of them, anyway—have emerged from the Tonkin crisis. Does it, then, support the belief that the public's information about crises is not only voluminous, but also largely accurate? If yes be the answer, it must be so trussed with qualifications as to be of very limited importance. For if the truth did finally out, it was very late in coming. Both major effects of the event—aiding Johnson's election effort and providing him with a congressional blank check on Vietnam—were history. For Johnson carried forty-four states in November, and many Democratic members of Congress recognized that they owed their seats to his great victory and the "coat tails" effect. From this sense of obligation came a great deal of support for presidential programs in this Congress. Johnson's support from freshman congressmen, in particular, was so powerful that they have been "credited with the successful record of the 89th Congress." [95] And following soon after the electoral triumph and accompanying the impressive outpouring of legislation was the military escalation in Vietnam. Bombing of the North began in earnest less than three weeks after the President's inaugural address, and by the end of 1965 troop strength was up from 23,000 to 181,000; Americans killed in Vietnam from 195 to 1,728; and Americans wounded from 1,039 to 6,114. [96] And these increases were just the beginning.

It may be, of course, that the usefulness of the Tonkin crisis with respect to the President's election and his subsequent decision to escalate the war each represented a happy accident. Lyndon Johnson, however, was not renowned for leaving such important matters to chance.

If it is true that the Fulbright Committee's ultimate disclosures damaged the administration's prestige, widened the "credibility gap," and made it unlikely that the resolution would in the future be referred to as a "functional equivalent" of a declaration of war, it is also true that these disclosures would never have been made except for the happenstance of the *Pueblo* seizure. Misleading appearances were corrected too late to change events significantly, and their correction itself was in the last analysis dependent upon an act of fate.

By the end of 1968, the resolution, reeking with notoriety, had been banished from official rhetoric like a kitchen odor following an assault by an air freshener.

Critics of the war, however, refused to let it be forgotten, and numer-

[95] Thomas P. Murphy, "The Extraordinary Power of Freshmen in Congress," *Trans-action*, March 1968, p. 35.

[96] U.S., *Congressional Record*, 91st Cong., 1st Sess., October 8, 1969, p. S12160. (Daily ed.)

ous resolutions were introduced in Congress calling for its repeal.[97] With the rhetoric of deescalation becoming politically *de rigeur,* the new Nixon administration moved from a position of hostility toward the Tonkin Gulf Resolution's repeal to one of neutrality. And when it became apparent that a repeal move by Senate "doves" was assured of success, the administration acted quickly in order to forestall a fresh outburst of congressional antiwar criticism, and to gain credit for an antiwar (and not coincidentally, a retrospective anti-Democratic administration) measure of its own. The resolution, which earlier hardly anyone could oppose, now could hardly be supported.

Robert Dole of Kansas, a freshman senator but already one of the administration's chief spokesmen, on June 22, 1970, abruptly proposed a repeal motion in the form of an amendment to the fairly minor Foreign Military Sales Act. Cosponsors included such leading senatorial "hawks" as Arizona's Barry Goldwater and California's George Murphy. The administration had prepared the way for this maneuver by announcing that the President's authority to act in Vietnam was based not on the Tonkin Gulf Resolution, but on his constitutional role as commander-in-chief, which permitted him to take action to safeguard American troops as they were being withdrawn. Thus, soon after the Senate overwhelmingly approved another amendment acknowledging the President's authority "to protect the lives of United States Armed Forces wherever deployed," Dole introduced his repeal measure, denouncing the "superfluous nature and irrelevancy of the so-called Tonkin Gulf Resolution." [98] A handful of Southern "hawks" disagreed, and argued that the resolution was "the only authority given by Congress to the President under the Constitution," [99] and that its repeal "would jerk the rug out from under the authority that has been exercised for all these years. . . ." [100] Fulbright, ironically, joined these "hawks" in opposing the Dole amendment, ostensibly because it had not been offered "in the regular fashion," complete with committee hearings and reports, as had a repeal resolution which his Foreign Relations Committee had already approved for floor action. "I think this procedure, without notice, with-

---

[97] See, e.g., S. Con. Res. 32, S.J. Res. 166 (1969).

[98] U.S., *Congressional Record,* 91st Cong., 2d Sess., June 22, 1970. p. S9444. (Daily ed.) When pressed by Missouri's Democratic Senator Thomas Eagleton as to the legal basis for the American military presence in Vietnam, however, Dole resorted to a series of highly elaborate evasive maneuvers. *Ibid.,* June 23, 1970, pp. S9591-603.

[99] Senator Sam Ervin, *ibid.,* June 26, 1970, p. S10005.

[100] Senator John Stennis, *ibid.,* June 22, 1970, p. S9449. Ervin, known for his legalistic approach to lawmaking, also contended that the Dole amendment was inappropriate, since the Tonkin Gulf Resolution could be repealed only by another concurrent resolution, and not "by an amendment to an act of Congress having no connection with the subject." *Ibid.,* p. S9490.

out discussion, at least as so far as are available in connection with this bill," he said, "is a bad procedure." [101] Plainly, though, it was less the procedural shortcut than the smothering of repeal as a political issue that rankled. The Dole amendment, in any event, passed easily, with only Fulbright and nine "super-hawks" [102] out of the ninety-one senators voting dissenting. The Senate's action of repeal, like that of passage, took only two days. On New Year's Eve, House members of a Senate-House conference committee agreed to include the amendment as part of the bill, and it was enacted and signed by President Nixon on January 13 at his Western White House in San Clemente, California. The *New York Times* noted the event with a brief article on page fourteen.

As an embarrassing anachronism, the Gulf of Tonkin Resolution was dispatched to a status of well-earned oblivion with all the cynicism and haste attending its birth. Its repeal was very nearly as popular as had been its adoption, and with mostly the same people. The Dole amendment, then, leaves the observer with a sense of returning to the beginning, but the visual metaphor is not a newly cleaned blackboard but rather a snake which has swallowed its tail and is gagging on the back of its own neck. The Gulf of Tonkin episode, at any rate, is over. Yet the feeling of *déjà vu* surrounding its demise was so pronounced that it seems reckless to predict that it could not recur.

---

[101] *Ibid.,* June 23, 1970, p. S9590; June 22, 1970, p. S9491. For an acrimonious Fulbright-Dole confrontation, see *ibid.,* p. S9495.

[102] Senators Allen, Eastland, Ellender, Hollings, Long, McClellan, McGee, Bellman, and Stennis.

5

Vietnam: The Tet Offensive

All life and brightness seem an ancient dream.

Feodor Tyutchev, "The Abyss"

Perhaps the most important crisis posed by the Tet offensive was a crisis in confidence. Unexpectedly, the veracity and competence of the Johnson administration were subjected to one of their most serious challenges. This chapter will be concerned, first, with the problem of appearance and reality as it plagued decision makers trying to determine the nature and extent of the enemy's threat. Particular emphasis will be placed upon preexisting organizations, which had been designed to keep the President and his advisers adequately informed of events but had, in fact, an uneven record of performance. Second, the administration's attempt to purvey to the public pleasing appearances as reality will be treated. Included will be discussions of appeals made, apparent motivations for the public relations effort, and an evaluation of its success.

I

As 1967 drew to a close, President Johnson and his advisers expressed growing confidence in the progress of the war in Vietnam. In October, Secretary Rusk declared that "military success in the South . . . is now beyond [the enemy's] reach." [1] Addressing American servicemen at the mbssive military installations at Cam Ranh Bay two months later, President Johnson called attention to "just how far we had come from the valleys and the depths of despondency to the heights and the cliffs, where we know now that the enemy can never win." The enemy "is holding on

---

[1] Dean Rusk, "Firmness and Restraint in Viet-Nam," *Department of State Bulletin* 57 (November 27, 1967): 705.

desperately," Johnson added, and "even as the enemy is being met, a nation is also being built." [2]

Meanwhile, in the United States Vice-President Humphrey was declaring that "the situation in Vietnam is better militarily and politically, and in terms of developing rural areas in the country." [3] The Defense Department let it be known that its experts had devised an "index of victory," [4] and later General William C. Westmoreland, commander of American forces in Vietnam, in a post-Christmas radio interview, described 1967 as "a year of great progress in the Vietnam war." [5] Robert W. Komer, chief American adviser of the pacification program, interpreted "the increase in Vietcong terrorism during the year" as suggesting "increasing enemy desperation." [6] And in the President's State of the Union address to Congress, he declared:

The enemy has been defeated in battle after battle. The number of South Vietnamese living in areas under government protection tonight has grown by more than a million since January of last year. These are all marks of progress.[7]

These announcements were reinforced by generally supportive news media. Editorially, they were optimistic regarding war developments, and increasingly critical of domestic opponents of the conflict. More importantly, the media's emphasis upon objectivity and topicality practically disarmed the press as a critical force. "Objectivity" was taken to preclude meaningful evaluation of official claims; and topicality cut

---

[2] Lyndon B. Johnson, "Remarks to U.S. Service Personnel, Cam Ranh Bay, December 23," *ibid.*, 58 (January 15, 1968): 76. This speech was perhaps the high point of the President's globe-trotting trip on behalf of his war policy, ostensibly occasioned by his desire to attend the funeral of Australian prime minister Harold Holt. In addition to appearing in South Vietnam and Australia, Johnson addressed American fliers in Thailand and had an audience with the Pope in the Vatican. The President's trip had followed by a few days the airlifting of 10,000 additional Army troops from Fort Campbell to Vietnam, an escalation which raised the number of American troops in Vietnam past that which had been dispatched to Korea. Johnson had flown to Fort Campbell to see the latest contingent off personally.

[3] *New York Times*, December 24, 1967.

[4] The index was constructed from the numbers of enemy killed, hamlets pacified, enemy infiltrated and recruited, and miles of roads safely cleared in South Vietnam. *Wall Street Journal*, October 27, 1967.

[5] *New York Times*, December 27, 1967. Six weeks earlier, Westmoreland had led a contingent of top Saigon-based policy makers who had journeyed to Washington to deliver well-publicized optimistic appraisals of the war. Joining the general had been the more subdued Ambassador to South Vietnam, Ellsworth Bunker, and the chief adviser of the pacification program, Robert W. Komer.

[6] *New York Times*, January 6, 1968.

[7] Lyndon B. Johnson, "The State of the Union," *Department of State Bulletin* 58 (February 5, 1968): 161. (Address delivered January 17.) Many observers felt that the President's "language was firmer and sterner" with respect to possible negotiation terms. His aides, of course, denied any change. *New York Times*, January 21, 1968.

reality into individual events and incidents and deemphasize[d] the long-term processes of which these events are only a part.[8]

Thus, the war was "covered in terms of daily battles and body counts," with little independent effort exerted in examining the nature and progress of the war from a larger perspective. The major mass news media, in short, were of invaluable assistance to the administration in its propagandizing operations on the home front.

The official and press optimism was reflected in three interrelated trends with respect to American public opinion.[9] First, the mass public shifted toward a "harder" line on the war. The nationwide Harris poll, for example, found that the percentage of Americans agreeing that the best way to negotiate peace is "to convince the Communists they will lose the war if they continue fighting" rose from forty-five percent in July to fifty-eight percent in December. More significantly, perhaps, the percentage disagreeing dropped sharply from forty-two percent to twenty-four percent. Similarly, the suggestion that the United States halt its bombings of North Vietnam to see if Hanoi would negotiate was overwhelmingly rejected by a margin of sixty-three percent to twenty-four percent. In October the halt had been rejected fifty-three percent to twenty-nine percent; and in September the figures stood at forty-eight percent opposed and thirty-seven percent in favor.[10] A *New York Times* survey of eight western states disclosed a "hearty optimism" concerning the war.[11]

Second, the public increasingly came to identify the President with this "harder" line. In the public's view, no major candidate for the presidential nomination rivaled him as a "hawk," not even the militant former governor of Alabama, George C. Wallace. A Gallup poll revealed how

[8] Herbert J. Gans, "How Well *Doest* TV Present the News?" *New York Times Magazine,* January 11, 1970, p. 40.
[9] It would be misleading, however, to suggest that mass public opinion was characterized by great clarity. Barely half the population said that it had a clear idea of what the United States was fighting for in Vietnam, for example, compared with eighty-three percent during World War II. *Gallup Opinion Index* (Report 25, July 1967). In fact, confusion, ignorance, and emotionalism so dominated public opinion regarding the war that most people seemed more impressed by presidential leadership than by the direction that leadership took. Thus, another poll concluded, "The President's support increases no matter what he does—increase the war or talk of negotiations—as long as he does something." Sidney Verba *et al.,* "Public Opinion and the War in Vietnam," *American Political Science Review* 61 (June 1967): 333. It is safe to say, however, that official and media treatments of the war during the last part of 1967 significantly reinforced President Johnson's stature as a leader, thereby helping to satisfy the widespread popular desire to be led. His success in developing a leadership image, though, was still quite shaky and uneven. Events were to make its vulnerability painfully apparent.
[10] *New York Times,* December 24, 1967.
[11] *New York Times,* January 21, 1968.

Americans classified the four most "hawkish" possible nominees (Table 2).[12]

TABLE 2

COMPARISON OF THE PUBLIC'S PERCEPTIONS
OF LEADING PRESIDENTIAL CANDIDATES'
ATTITUDES TOWARD THE WAR IN VIETNAM,
JANUARY, 1968

	Hawk	Dove	No opinion	Hawk Index*
Johnson	66%	18%	16%	48
Nixon	46	26	28	20
Reagan	39	27	34	12
Wallace	37	20	43	17

* The "Hawk Index" is the percentage of respondents classifying a nominee as a hawk, less the percentage classifying him as a dove.

Third, as a consequence of its increasing approval of the "hard" line and its classification of the President as a "hawk," the public came to adopt a more favorable view of Johnson. Only thirty-eight percent of Americans approved of his performance in October, according to the Gallup poll, but this rose to forty-one percent in November and to forty-six percent in December.[13] The President's popularity showed steady and impressive improvement.

In late January, dispatches from South Vietnam indicated that American troops were pulling out of Saigon,[14] and that a major attack was expected at a Marine base in the north near Khesanh. On January 24, the base was hit by heavy artillery fire for the first time, and many American military officials concluded that General Vo Nguyen Giap, the North Vietnamese Defense Minister, was trying to repeat his 1954 triumph over the French at Dienbienphu. General Westmoreland publicly predicted a "sizable invasion" by the North Vietnamese,[15] and privately told a visiting senator "that without a doubt the Vietcong would try to overrun Khesanh during the Tet lunar holiday" at the end of January, and "that 40,000 fighting men had been withdrawn from the interior and central highlands and that the Vietcong were being encircled and would be annihilated when they attacked. . . ." [16] The *Times* agreed that a "large

[12] *New York Times,* January 14, 1968. The "Hawk Index" is mine.
[13] *New York Times,* January 3, 1968.
[14] By January 21, the shifting of American troops from Saigon was about eighty-five percent complete. The movement, begun in July, was known as Operation Moose (i.e., "Move Out of Saigon Expeditiously"). *New York Times,* January 22, 1968.
[15] *New York Times,* January 28, 1968.
[16] Remarks of Senator Stephen Young of Ohio, who talked with Westmoreland

battle may be about to begin" at Khesanh. "The whole center of balance of power in Vietnam is being moved steadily north to meet the threat." [17]

This was in line with General Westmoreland's dual aims of maximizing the area under allied control, and inflicting casualties sufficiently "unacceptable" in number to cause the enemy to withdraw. More precisely, this shift was in accord with Westmoreland's "forward strategy" of positioning American troops "in a much wider radius to maintain contact with enemy forces," leaving the "South Vietnamese Army to undertake most of the security duty in the five provinces surrounding Saigon." [18] The heart of this strategy was the belief that the enemy consisted primarily of main force battalions of Vietcong and North Vietnamese troops in these forward areas. If these battalions could be defeated, presumably, in Henry Kissinger's words, "the guerrillas [would] wither on the vine." [19]

Three days after the first heavy shellings of Khesanh, the enemy proclaimed a ceasefire in honor of the traditional Buddhist lunar holiday, Tet, the greatest celebration of the year in Vietnam. About half of the effective personnel in South Vietnamese units were on official leave, probably another twenty to thirty percent were actually absent, and many of those remaining were celebrating in the barracks. A number of American units, too, had twenty to thirty percent of their effective personnel on official leave, and perhaps forty to sixty percent more absent or celebrating.[20] Despite the holiday spirit, however, there seemed to be little prospect for the halting of hostilities.

II

On January 29, Vietnamese bargirls in Saigon complained about the absence of the usual American customers, who had been forbidden by military order from going downtown during Tet. Earlier in the day elsewhere in Vietnam, "Vietcong raiders drove into the center of seven major . . . cities . . . burning Government buildings, freeing prisoners from provincial jails and blasting military installations and airfields with rockets and mortars." [21]

This was merely a prelude. The following day, a tiny band of Vietcong seized parts of the supposedly invulnerable American Embassy in Sai-

within four days of Tet. U.S., *Congressional Record*, 91st Cong., 2d Sess., February 10, 1970, p. S1515. (Daily ed.)

[17] *New York Times,* January 28, 1968.

[18] *Ibid.*

[19] Henry A. Kissinger, *American Foreign Policy: Three Essays* (New York: Norton, 1969), p. 102. Kissinger here is voicing the army's viewpoint, and not his own.

[20] Herman Kahn, "A Special Prefatory Note," *Can We Win in Vietnam?* ed. Frank E. Armbruster *et al.* (New York: Praeger, 1968), pp. vii–viii.

[21] *New York Times,* January 30, 1968.

gon, and held them for over six hours; another Vietcong squad nearly took the heavily fortified Tansonnhut airport and the new multi-million dollar American military command building there; the three-month old Presidential Palace was almost captured; Saigon radio was knocked off the air; raiders struck in the central market and the Chinese quarter; a police station and bridges to the city were also hit.

A *New York Times* reporter on the scene concluded that, "despite public warnings by the Saigon police that a terroristic assault could be expected . . . the raiders seem to have caught both the Americans and the South Vietnamese by surprise." [22] In words of an anti-Communist Catholic, "At first everyone in Saigon thought it was another coup d'état, with Ky trying to overthrow Thieu. Then they realized it was the Communists." [23]

Nor were Saigon's suburbs spared. One weeping suburban housewife described her fear upon seeing guerrillas on the street:

But the Viet Cong reassured me they wouldn't come into my house. They went into my front yard—and then an American helicopter started firing into my house and killed three of my children. [24]

Enemy assaults were not limited to the Saigon area. Also attacked in the south were Cantho, Vinhlong, Mytho, the Bienhoa airbase, and the American headquarters at Longbinh; in central Vietnam, Vietcong struck at Nhatrang, Banmethruont, Truyhoa, Quinhon, Pleiku, Kontum, and the resort city of Dalat, where over half the police and government troops were home for the holidays; in the north, the enemy hit at Hainan, Danang, and Hue, in addition to continuing their firing at the Marine outpost at Khesanh. The Vietcong also seized or purchased huge quantities of precious rice. By February 2, the "guerrillas, with apparently only minor assistance from North Vietnamese units, had made major assaults on twenty-six provincial captials and uncounted numbers of district towns and American and Vietnamese airfields and bases." [25]

---

[22] Tom Buckley, *ibid.*, January 31, 1968.
[23] Unnamed Vietnamese, quoted by Beverly Deepe, *Christian Science Monitor*, February 4, 1968.
[24] Unnamed suburban housewife, quoted by Deepe, *ibid.* Presumably, it was this kind of complaint which led Secretary Rusk to admit that:

there are some people in South Vietnam who are grumpy, as there are some people here who are grumpy, because it was not possible to give them complete protection against what happened in the last few days.

"Secretary Rusk and Secretary of Defense McNamara Discuss Vietnam and Korea on 'Meet the Press,' " *Department of State Bulletin* 58 (February 26, 1968): 264. (Telecast of February 4.)
[25] *New York Times*, February 4, 1969. Eventually, according to Senator Young, thirty-eight of the forty-four provincial capitals were attacked. U.S., *Congressional Record*, 90th

III

On February 2, President Johnson held a press conference at which the enemy's Tet offensive was discussed. The President made two basic points during his opening formal statement, and repeated each of them several times in his extemporaneous replies to reporters' questions. First, the allied forces were not unprepared. "We have known for several months now that the Communists planned a massive winter-spring offensive," he said, later adding that the allies' "information has been very clear" [26] about the offensive, which "has been anticipated, prepared for, and met." Finally, he said simply, "we have been expecting it."

Second, Johnson announced that the enemy's military and psychological goals "have failed" because they found little or no popular support in the cities. As if to emphasize this point, he referred twice again to the attacks as "failures." Of course, the President conceded, "there have been civilian casualties and disruption of public services," but what he said he found truly impressive was "the vigor with which the Vietnam Government and our own people are working together to deal with the problems. . . ." In answering a reporter's question, Johnson continued this general line of argument:

It's just like when we have a riot in town or when we have a very serious strike or bridges go out or lights—power failures and things. They [the Vietcong] have disrupted services. A few bandits can do that in any city in the land.

Later, the President drew an implicit comparison between the Tet offensive and a peace march on the Pentagon and the 1967 summer riots in Detroit. Throughout the press conference, the President expressed his desire "to keep the American people informed as these matters develop."

That sanguine assessment of events was echoed by the President's principal advisers. His chief foreign affairs consultant, Walt W. Rostow, judged the performance of the South Vietnamese Government as "very good," and that of its army as "magnificent." In fact, Rostow implied that the offensive might have been a blessing in disguise. "In these weeks . . . in the cities of South Vietnam," he said, "you come closer to a sense of nationhood than you ever have before." [27] Secretary of Defense

---

Cong., 2d sess., February 15, 1968, p. S1284. (Daily ed.) A year later David Hoffman of the *Washington Post* reported that "some 120 South Vietnamese population centers and military installations" had been attacked during the week ending February 10, 1968. Four hundred Americans had been killed and another 934 seriously wounded; South Vietnamese losses were put at 1,032 killed; and enemy deaths were estimated at 13,118. *Des Moines Register*, March 7, 1969.

[26] Lyndon B. Johnson, "President Johnson's News Conference of February 2," *Department of State Bulletin* 58 (February 19, 1968): 221, 224.

[27] U.S., *Congressional Record*, 90th Cong., 2d Sess., February 21, 1968, p. H1263. (Daily

McNamara was somewhat more restrained. Still, he was careful to note that "We did have advance intelligence of the winter-spring campaign offensive," and that "the South Vietnamese had sufficient intelligence to maintain their forces in a state of alert such that they were able to inflict these very heavy penalties on the Vietcong and the North Vietnamese. . . ." [28]

Senate hawks agreed. John Tower of Texas interpreted the raids as the "death rattle" [29] of the Vietcong; Birch Bayh of Indiana called the offensive "a desperate, inconclusive Communist lunge at the cities"; [30] Thomas McIntyre of New Hampshire was certain that "history . . . will show that the Communists committed a decisive error—that they failed to make a dramatic impact on the people of South Vietnam and the American public; [31] and Daniel Brewster of Maryland argued that not only had the enemy "failed in its basic objectives," but in addition had destroyed the myth that the South Vietnamese army cannot and does not fight." [32] General Westmoreland declared flatly that "the enemy's well-laid plans ran afoul." [33]

Joining this encouraging chorus were the war's supporters among the press. Columnist William S. White likened the offensive to the "last Nazi

---

ed.) Similarly, when interviewed on television two years later, Johnson declared that Tet "for the first time brought about a unity that never existed before in South Vietnam and brought about a degree of determination that never existed before." *New York Times,* February 7, 1970.

[28] "Secretary Rusk and Secretary of Defense McNamara Discuss Vietnam and Korea on 'Meet the Press,' " *Department of State Bulletin* 58 (February 26, 1968): 267, 268. (Telecast of February 4.)

[29] Quoted by Ward Just, *Washington Post,* February 4, 1968.

[30] U.S., *Congressional Record,* 90th Cong., 2d Sess., February 14, 1968, p. S1227. (Daily ed.) A week before the offensive, the *Times* reported, a cynical young officer in Saigon satirized the prevailing military attitude that the enemy planned to attack in a last gasp effort. "In desperation," he wrote in an official report, "the Vietcong today overran Saigon and won the war." His superior, the *Times* noted, "was not amused." *New York Times,* January 21, 1968.

[31] U.S., *Congressional Record,* 90th Cong., 2d Sess., February 8, 1968, p. S1155. (Daily ed.)

[32] *Ibid.,* p. S1148.

[33] *Los Angeles Times,* February 1, 1969. He has continued to maintain this position. See William C. Westmoreland and Admiral Ulysses S. Grant Sharp, *Report on the War in Vietnam* (Washington: Government Printing Office, 1969). Westmoreland here treats the Tet offensive solely in military terms, admitting that its extent had been unanticipated, but concluding nonetheless that it had constituted a military failure for the enemy. More recently, speaking at a Senate news conference, he assessed the psychological impact of the offensive on the South Vietnamese: "The Tet offensive unified the people as never before. It was their Pearl Harbor." *Des Moines Register,* June 11, 1969. It is interesting that, though maintaining that Tet was an allied victory, he analogized its effects to those following the most stunning of military setbacks. Westmoreland's tenacious optimism is not, however, unique. Army Major General R. G. Ciccolella, for example, in a speech a year after Tet characterized it as "a great Communist disaster," which "Communist propaganda with its obvious influence in the non-Communist press, succeeded in" depicting "as a great Communist vic-

spasms at the Bulge";[34] William Randolph Hearst, Jr., termed the attacks "Communist hell raising," and asserted that "anybody who says we have been caught with our pants down is simply in error"; Crosby S. Noyes felt that Hanoi had "miscalculated on the outcome of the showdown"; [35] and Earl W. Foell suggested that the offensive "may have freed rather than frozen President Johnson's hand in the long run . . . because Washington now is bound less by the threat of back talk from the Thieu government in Saigon." [36]

Not all observers found the administration's arguments this convincing. The President's first contention—that the allies knew of the attack beforehand—was doubted by Senator John Sherman Cooper of Kentucky [37] and ridiculed by Senator Stephen Young of Ohio.[38] Hanson Baldwin, chief military analyst for the *New York Times* and an administration supporter, conceded parenthetically that the South Vietnamese had "had their guard down," and the *Times* editorialized that "American preparedness for the unexpected" must be considered a "critical failure." [39] In any case, as Everett G. Martin of *Newsweek* pointed out, "Statements that U.S. military men knew in advance that the enemy would attack, while intended to be reassuring, have in reality exactly the opposite effect." For they raise the obvious and unanswerable question: "If you knew, why couldn't you do something about it?" [40]

The President's contention that Vietcong efforts had been a military and psychological failure also buckled beneath the evidence. Weeks be-

---

tory. . . ." R. G. Ciccolella, "The United States Role in Vietnam and Prospects for Peace," address of February 27, 1969, reprinted in U.S., *Congressional Record*, 91st Cong., 1st Sess., December 5, 1969, p. S15841. (Daily ed.) Another rhetorical tactic is that utilized by American officials in Vietnam, who, according to a *New York Times* reporter, describe "The enemy offensives in 1968 . . . as a 'great victory' or a 'salutary shock,' depending on the point they are trying to make. . . ." Tom Buckley, "The ARVN is Bigger and Better, But——" *New York Times Magazine,* October 12, 1969, p. 130. The reaction of General Creighton W. Abrams, Westmoreland's successor as U.S. Commander in Vietnam, to an upbeat analysis of the Tet attacks was more candid. "Gentlemen," he said, "we got our asses handed to us." Abrams quoted in Kevin P. Buckley, "General Abrams Deserves a Better War," *New York Times Magazine,* October 5, 1969, p. 35.

[34] *Washington Star,* February 12, 1968.

[35] *Washington Star,* February 6, 1968.

[36] *Christian Science Monitor,* February 6, 1968. To the extent that these private and public statements accurately reflect the speakers' feelings, they illustrate that the strength of a belief can be maintained or even increased, despite the emergence of evidence to the contrary. For more extreme examples of this well-known psychological phenomenon, see the classic work by Leon Festinger, Henry W. Reicken, and Stanley Schachter, *When Prophecy Fails* (Minneapolis: University of Minnesota Press, 1956).

[37] U.S., *Congressional Record,* 90th Cong., 2d Sess., February 5, 1968, p. S890. (Daily ed.)

[38] U.S., *Congressional Record,* 90th Cong., 2d Sess., February 15, 1968, p. S1283. (Daily ed.)

[39] *New York Times,* February 1, 4, 1968.

[40] Everett G. Martin, "The Devastating Effects on the People," *Newsweek,* February 12, 1968, p. 32.

fore the offensive, Hanoi had made it clear that its military operations were primarily means to the psychological end of proving to the allies and to the civilians of Vietnam that the Vietcong and the North Vietnamese were still strong and could strike at will. At least, this was the understanding of American officials.[41] There can be no question that this psychological objective was achieved. The offensive, in the words of a reporter on the scene, constituted "a political-psychological setback of unprecedented magnitude. . . ." [42] As Max Frankel of the *New York Times* put it:

> . . . the real name of the game out there is "Who can provide safety for whom?" And haven't they in a very serious way humiliated our ability in major cities all up and down this country to provide the South Vietnamese population that is listed as clearly in our control with a degree of assurance and safety that South Vietnamese forces and American forces together could give them?[43]

The offensive, said Senator Young, "demonstrated once again the hollowness of the Saigon regime's pretensions of sovereignty over South Vietnam, and the fraudulence of claims of imminent victory" by American generals and civilians.[44]

The skepticism with which administration claims of triumph were greeted was perhaps best summarized in the column by the political humorist Art Buchwald, entitled, " 'We Have Enemy on the Run,' says General Custer at Big Horn." [45] When Undersecretary of State Nicholas Katzenbach declared on television, "I don't believe that in any sense at

---

[41] *New York Times,* December 26, 1967.

[42] Beverly Deepe, *Christian Science Monitor,* February 4, 1968. *The New York Times* also agreed that "the psychological implications of the attacks are incalculable." *New York Times,* February 4, 1968. Hawkish Australian columnist Denis Warner, writing a year later, admitted that Tet "was the most daring, audacious and well-coordinated political and psychological action of the war." It brought the enemy, he said, "almost to the point of psychological victory." *Des Moines Register,* January 26, 1969.

[43] "Secretary Rusk and Secretary of Defense McNamara Discuss Vietnam and Korea on 'Meet the Press,' " *Department of State Bulletin* 58 (February 26, 1968): 266. (Telecast of February 4.) See also Kissinger, *op. cit.,* pp. 106–7.

[44] U.S., *Congressional Record,* 90th Cong., 2d Sess., February 15, 1968, p. S1283. (Daily ed.)

[45] *Washington Post,* February 6, 1968. The Battle of the Bulge provoked a similar attempt by the Allies to minimize its impact. This attempt was satirized contemporaneously by the London *Daily Express:* "While it cannot be said that Runstedt's offensive achieved its object of changing the Allied timetable, it has undoubtedly made some alteration necessary in the timetable. It has rather postponed than delayed the offensive, and in that sense alone, may be said to have lengthened, but not prolonged, the war. The Allies were not surprised, because they knew the possibility of a surprise attack. What surprised them was that the Germans thought it worthwhile to make a surprise attack in spite of the fact that such an attack, though deemed possible, was not deemed probable, in view of the fact that we knew they would try to surprise us." Quoted in Washington Platt, *Strategic Intelligence Prediction: Basic Principles* (New York: Praeger, 1957), pp. 69–70.

all the administration has misled the American people," [46] he did not end the doubting. The swamp of misstatements and halftruths could not be filled in with rhetorical refuse.

A demand then arose for greater presidential candor. "The American people must be told the truth about Vietnam," said Senator James Pearson of Kansas,[47] and much of the press agreed. The *Washington Daily News* spoke of a "Whitewash Test," and termed the administration's story "unconvincing." John Hughes in the *Christian Science Monitor* saw a parallel between the Tet offensive and the British escape from Dunkirk, and suggested that it was "time for Churchillian candor." The *Denver Rocky Mountain News* used punctuation to make its point: "The President 'explains.' " [48]

In succeeding days, the administration retreated gradually but significantly from its earlier position, conceding that events had not gone well for the allies. It was, after all, difficult to continue to call the offensive "a complete failure" in the face of the Vietcong's holding parts of Hue for twenty-four days,[49] and forcing the South Vietnamese government's pacification teams to abandon the countryside for a month.[50] Usu-

---

[46] "Under Secretary Katzenbach Interviewed on 'Face the Nation,' " *Department of State Bulletin* 58 (February 26, 1968): 273. (Telecast of February 4.)

[47] U.S., *Congressional Record*, 90th Cong., 2d Sess., February 19, 1968, p. S1448. (Daily ed.)

[48] *Washington Daily News*, February 5, 6, 1968; *Christian Science Monitor*, February 7, 1968; *Denver Rocky Mountain News*, February 5, 1968.

[49] *Times* correspondent Charles Mohr recalled that after Tet, "Hue appeared to be a dead city. Approximately 100,000 of its 160,000 people were homeless. At least 14,300 of its 24,000 residences had been more than 50 percent destroyed and 8,000 others had been damaged. Perhaps 5,000 civilians had been killed," many by the Vietcong. *New York Times*, February 4, 1969.

[50] The offensive's effects on pacification were neither minor nor temporary. It was soon evident that rural insecurity would lead to a sharp decline in the Agency for International Development's rice plan in South Vietnam. *New York Times*, April 10, 1968. Shortly thereafter, the whole emphasis of pacification shifted from the development of schools, dispensaries, roads, and agriculture to the providing of basic physical security for the hamlets. *New York Times*, June 2, 1968. Perhaps even more significant, "not only did the Tet offensive give impetus to the Alliance [of National Democratic and Peace Forces, a middle-class front group established in the South by Hanoi after Tet] and numerous other local and regional 'revolutionary' bodies but it also created a new and serious vacuum in the rural areas, where the Communists were able to form new 'autonomous' and 'people's' committees in scores of villages. The new committees . . . are likely to be the real instruments of the Communist political power thrust in the future, with the [National Liberation] Front and Alliance serving as broad national spearheads." Robert Shaplen, "A Reporter at Large: Seats at the Table," *New Yorker*, November 16, 1968, p. 197. Sir Robert Thompson, a British counterinsurgency expert held in high esteem by President Nixon, concluded after Tet that pacification would have to start from the beginning again "in a time frame of at least twenty years." Quoted in Townsend Hoopes, *The Limits of Intervention* (New York: David McKay, 1969), p. 149. Pacification had, Thompson felt, been "brought to a grinding halt" by the offensive. Sir Robert Thompson, *No Exit from Vietnam*, updated ed. (New York: David McKay, 1970), p. 74.

ally, the bad news was made public through anonymous official American sources: a high-ranking official with the pacification mission admits that there had been "a significant psychological setback";[51] a senior military officer tells a *Times* reporter at the end of February that Saigon remained vulnerable to renewed attacks;[52] an embassy official observes that "Tet proved just how hollow so many of our past achievements really were";[53] and one pacification adviser calls his area "a Vietcong picnic ground," while another says simply, "I don't think we're getting anywhere." [54] Past praise for South Vietnamese troops was damaged by stories of widespread looting and terrorism; in one instance, government troops sold water supplied by Americans to parched and homeless refugees.[55]

All this took its toll on President Johnson's growing popularity; for as his close adviser and later Secretary of Defense, Clark Clifford, was to note, "The confidence of the American people had been badly shaken." [56] The Gallup poll reported that Johnson's January twelve percentage point lead over Richard Nixon was completely wiped out by February,[57] and his ten percentage point lead over Robert Kennedy was entirely eliminated by early March.[58] On March 12 in the New Hampshire presidential primary, the President barely escaped defeat at the hands of Senator Eugene McCarthy in a stunning reversal of form. By the end of the month, the Gallup poll showed that approval of Johnson's general performance in office and of his handling of the war had fallen to new lows.[59]

To return to one of our original questions: is the information available to the public on crisis events not only voluminous, but also largely accurate? Judging from the Tet offensive, the answer might be a qualified "yes." While the administration failed to provide an adequate picture, the press and Congress emerged as fairly effective correctives. That these critical views touched the public consciousness is reflected in the polls showing renewed skepticism concerning the war effort, and waning support for the President's performance in office.

---

[51] *New York Times,* February 25, 1968.

[52] *Ibid.*

[53] Unnamed embassy official, quoted by Robert Keatley and Peter R. Kann, *Wall Street Journal,* March 5, 1968.

[54] *Wall Street Journal,* March 8, 1968.

[55] *Wall Street Journal,* March 5, 1968. South Vietnamese troops were also responsible for most of the looting at Hue. *New York Times,* February 4, 1969.

[56] Clark M. Clifford, "A Vietnam Reappraisal: The Personal History of One Man's View and How It Evolved," *Foreign Affairs* 47 (July 1969): 609.

[57] *New York Times,* February 25, 1968.

[58] *New Orleans Times-Picayune,* March 17, 1968.

[59] *New Orleans Times-Picayune,* March 21, 1968. Only thirty-six percent of the sample

But if the general thrust of the administration's propaganda effort had the effect of reducing public confidence in the government and support for the war, why was the information it gave to the public not more accurate? Clearly, its inadequacies served only to exacerbate a difficult situation. One answer may be that the President and his advisers themselves had defective perceptions of reality. Partly, this may have been due to organizational difficulties relating to the quality and quantity of their data. In the first place, much of the information transmitted to them simply turned out to be erroneous. Certainly the entire Tet offensive bespeaks a woefully incompetent American intelligence operation in Vietnam. For when the allies shifted their emphasis to "forward positions" and the reinforcement of Khesanh, the Vietcong responded by unleashing a "blitz war" against key cities, towns, and military installations. Obviously, as Senator Young charged, "The VC outwitted and outgeneraled our generals," [60] and some of the blame for this must rest with the allied information-gathering apparatus.

The allies were not unaware of their problem in this regard, and it is worth investigating in some detail one of their attempted solutions. Prior to Tet, Komer had recognized informational difficulties relating to the pacification program, and had taken steps he had hoped would correct them. In particular, a computerized Hamlet Evaluation System (HES) was set up. Questionnaires were constructed purporting to measure development and physical security in the pacification hamlets, and American advisers were required to fill out and return the forms each month. The data were then analyzed, and the results released to the press and used by government officials.

Whatever the theoretical merits of the questionnaire, [61] the manner of its administration assured the inadequacies of its results. Representative

---

approved of the way Johnson was handling his job as President, and a mere twenty-six percent approved of his handling of the war.

[60] U.S., *Congressional Record*, 90th Cong., 2d Sess., February 15, 1968, p. S1284. (Daily ed.) Young called for General Westmoreland's replacement. Thompson agrees that "the Americans were strategically outmaneuvered and the doors were left wide open for the Tet offensive." Thompson, *op. cit.,* p. 142.

[61] Its merits are open to dispute. Gerald Hickey, a RAND Corporation social anthropologist and Vietnam expert, was moved to attack the whole idea of a standardized questionnaire. "You can't just set up a set of indicators that are applicable to the whole of Vietnam society," he declared, arguing that such an approach ignored crucial variations within the society itself. Zalin Grant, "Counting on Strength That Isn't There," *New Republic,* June 1968, p. 13. More recently, Dr. James R. Schlesinger, Acting Deputy Director of the Budget Bureau, defense management and strategy analyst and former Director of Strategic Studies at the RAND Corporation, attacked procedures for measuring hamlet security. They produce "a misleading number . . . that you are likely to take seriously," he said, offering this illustration: "One of the criteria used in measuring security is whether the village chief sleeps in the village at night. To the extent that the village chief does sleep in the village, this has been taken as an indication of pacification. There is no reason to believe that that is

John V. Tunney, a California Democrat who undertook an HES study mission in Vietnam four months after the offensive, has outlined its faults in a short but devastating report to the Foreign Affairs Committee.[62] The American advisers responsible for hamlet evaluation, Tunney points out, were in Vietnam too briefly to develop real familiarity with their hamlets, and were given preparatory training in data-gathering techniques and Vietnamese culture that was far too skimpy to overcome this handicap. Many advisers lacked even a working knowledge of the language. Moreover, there were so many demands on their time that monthly visits to each hamlet they were to evaluate became impossible. Previous—and thus perhaps outdated and erroneous—evaluations were in these instances merely resubmitted, possibly modified by more recent hearsay.

The visits themselves often were very short—sometimes less than an hour—and featured heavy reliance upon local chiefs (who knew that a "secure" rating was a precondition for American development aid) and local inhabitants (whose fear of the Vietcong and distrust of uniformed Americans did not conduce to frankness). Nor were the advisers themselves provided with incentives to overcome the unreliability of their information sources; for HES really was a kind of self-evaluation, and it would be unrealistic to expect advisers to sacrifice their professional reputations in the interest of accuracy. Furthermore, new advisers whose evaluations reflected a significant security decline from those of their predecessors may have found themselves deluged with demands from superiors for explanations of the changes. These demands constituted an added burden for the new advisers, who were probably overworked and desirous mainly of accommodating themselves to their new environment with a minimum of intraorganizational friction. The pressure to conform, then, operated early in the advisers' stay as a deterrent, preventing their submitting pessimistic evaluations in the future.

---

the appropriate inference. It may well be, and frequently is the case, that the fact that the village chief sleeps in the village is simply due to his working out an accommodation with the VC. In many cases sleeping in the village at night simply reflects the fact that the VC is in control of the area. In that event it is the opposite of pacification." U.S., Congress, Senate, Committee on Government Operations, Subcommittee on National Security and International Operations, *Hearings, Planning-Programming-Budgeting,* 91st Cong., 1st Sess., December 10, 1969, pt. 5: 321–22. Hereinafter cited as *Schlesinger Hearing.* On the other hand, the Simulmatics Corporation, an organization of "hawkish" experts on computer operations and systems analysis, studied HES just before Tet, and "concluded the system is good," blaming the trouble on faulty "input and judgment on the American side. . . ." Grant, *loc. cit.* The then Undersecretary of the Air Force also has chosen to criticize not the questions themselves, but instead certain methodological flaws that rendered the peasants' answers misleading. Hoopes, *op. cit.,* p. 71.

[62] U.S., Congress, House, Committee on Foreign Affairs, *Report of a Special Mission by Honorable John V. Tunney, Measuring Hamlet Security in Vietnam,* Report No. 91–25, 91st Cong., 1st Sess., 1969. Hereinafter cited as *Tunney Report.*

If the administration of HES questionnaires was flawed, so, too, was the presentation of HES findings. Several practices contributed to the obfuscation. Hamlets characterized by "effective" tax-levying Vietcong and "nonexistent" or "just beginning" South Vietnamese government programs, for example, were euphemistically listed as "contested." And though advisers were required to distinguish between five grades of hamlets, the top three categories were then combined under the rubric "relatively secure," even though one grade was subject to Vietcong harassment and another to Vietcong threat. Finally, HES data from all the advisers emerged as a single percentage figure of national hamlet security worked out to a decimal point, suggesting a precision which parodied the actual information-gathering procedures.[63]

Partly, it would appear, HES was a tool in the administration's constant battle to create a permissive public opinion on the American homefront. Optimistic reports, dressed up in numbers from computers, might have seemed an effective way of reinforcing public faith in official policy and personnel. In this light, it is difficult to quarrel seriously with the judgment of a Marine pacification officer, who termed HES a "fraud," which "overlooked or papered over the basic structural errors in the program." [64] And yet HES was not merely an elaborate public relations device directed at the attentive public back home. Additionally, conclude Tunney[65] and Corson,[66] it operated as a means of self-deception, buoying officials with flatulent optimism.

The HES experience suggests that one factor contributing to the American information problem may have been a tendency, consciously or unconsciously, for line and staff officers to fit their data to the desires and expectations of their superiors.[67] Information, as a leading analyst of intraorganizational communications has noted:

---

[63] Recent figures further reinforce the allies' reputation for straight-faced humor. Thus, on January 15, 1970, President Thieu reported that 92.7 percent of South Vietnam's population was under the Saigon government's control, 4.5 percent was living in contested areas, and only 2.8 percent was under Vietcong control. Though American officials defensively said that the "figures are intended merely to indicate trends," Saigon officials took them more seriously. The Associated Press noted, however, that the "ratings frequently bear no resemblance to the government's territorial control or to the military situation." citing two supposedly pacified provinces then the scenes of very fierce fighting. A week before Thieu announced that his government controlled 92.7 percent of the Vietnamese population, he had claimed control over 97 percent. No explanation was offered for the discrepancy in the percentages or the apparent loss of 760,000 South Vietnamese. *Des Moines Register,* January 16, 1970.

[64] William R. Corson, *The Betrayal* (New York: Norton, 1968), pp. 232, 239. More recently, several American generals discounted the validity of HES statistics as "just a numbers game we're playing for Paris." David Hoffman, *Washington Post,* January 28, 1969.

[65] *Tunney Report,* p. 9.

[66] Corson, *op. cit.,* p. 242.

[67] Thus, Hoopes speaks of Komer as the "the victim of relentless White House pressure

is a resource that symbolizes status, enhances authority, and shapes careers. In reporting at every level, hierarchy is conducive to concealment and misrepresentation. Subordinates are asked to transmit information that can be used to evaluate their performance. Their motive for "making it look good," for "playing it safe" is . . . the desire not only to please but also to preserve comfortable routines of work. . . .[68]

This problem of distortion in the upward flow of information is a common one in large-scale organizations,[69] but is likely to be especially prevalent in more rigid hierarchies, such as those of the military. Though a leading sociological analyst of the military has concluded that its authority and communication systems are less rigid today than in the past,[70] his peacetime judgment is due for reassessment; for war produces its own special pressures and tensions.[71] General Westmoreland's reaction to the situation—and one which "set the tone for the whole chain of command"—was to characterize critics as " 'nigglers,' who would be proven wrong when 'victory was achieved,' which was just around the corner." [72] Such a posture was hardly likely to encourage the upward communication of unpleasant information.

Moreover, sometimes the military's desire for more complete and precise information may itself have aggravated the distortion problem. Thus, the emphasis upon body counts and kill ratios promoted not accuracy but the misleading illusion of accuracy.[73] This was true partly be-

---

to show dramatic progress in the war," adding, however, that "to some extent, he was the victim of his own compulsive optimism." Hoopes, *op. cit.,* p. 72.

[68] Wilensky, *op. cit.,* p. 43. Cohen found that the subordinate's desire for advancement in the organization was the key motivating factor behind his suppression of critical information. A. R. Cohen, "Upward Communications in Experimentally Created Hierarchies," *Human Relations* 11 (No. 1, 1958): 41. This was supported by Reed, who, after investigating three industrial organizations, concluded that "mobility aspiration is negatively related [-.41] to accuracy of upward communications." This information distortion was said to be due to the subordinate's wanting "to withhold or refrain from communicating information that is potentially threatening to the status of the communicator." W. H. Reed, "Upward Communication in Industrial Hierarchies," *Human Relations* 15 (No. 1, 1962): 13.

[69] See, e.g., Burleigh B. Gardner, *Human Relations in Industry* (Homewood, Ill.: Richard C. Irwin, 1944).

[70] Morris Janowitz, "Changing Patterns of Organizational Authority," *Administrative Science Quarterly* 3 (March 1959): 473-93.

[71] Thus, the Army's report on the alleged My Lai massacre "concluded that each successive level of command received a more watered down account," in which "the reported number of Vietnamese killed became smaller," comprising only twenty-eight by the time it reached division headquarters. The actual figure is said to have been between 175 and 200. *New York Times,* March 27, 1970.

[72] Kevin P. Buckley, "General Abrams Deserves a Better War." *New York Times Magazine,* October 5, 1969, p. 35.

[73] The stress on body counts may also have led American soldiers to kill larger numbers of enemy soldiers and Vietnamese civilians than would otherwise have been the case. This, at least, was the main defense offered for a soldier court martialed for the alleged pre-

cause in the hurly-burly of combat, statistics are difficult to gather, and partly because promotions were tied to such statistics, creating an incentive for inflation by the officers on the scene. Lieutenant William Calley, Jr., for example, testified at his My Lai court martial, "You just make an estimate off the top of your head. There is no way to make a body count. You just take VC, water buffalo, pigs, cows, anything. If something is dead, you put it in the body count." He characterized his superior officers' attitude in these terms: "Everybody else is getting a high body count. Why aren't you? Why aren't you shooting anything?" [74] The army's stress on numbers, in addition, had the dysfunctional effect of deflecting official attention away from larger matters of policy analysis.[75]

All of this may help to explain why the American command had been convinced prior to Tet that "the Vietcong are on their last legs." [76] It may also help to explain why the hearty optimism of Westmoreland was replaced by the wary skepticism of his successor, General Creighton Abrams. "Whenever we get a report of some good news," he said, "we wait twenty-four hours and then if we're really lucky, it turns out to be twenty-five percent correct." [77]

Aggravating the distortion problem still further may have been the unpopular nature of the war and Johnson's growing annoyance at the opposition it had engendered. These factors may have made high level optimism almost obligatory by stigmatizing criticism as a sign of hostility and allegiance with domestic dissidents.[78] Moreover, the nature of the war—coupled with the President's bullying ways as a boss—contributed to an exodus of moderates and doves, or at least a severe diminution in their influence.[79] Goodwin, Moyers, Goldberg, even McNamara lost out.

---

meditated murder of an unarmed Vietnamese civilian. The Pentagon naturally denied that its body count emphasis had such effects. *New York Times,* March 28, 1970.

[74] *Des Moines Register,* March 7, 1971.

[75] *Schlesinger Hearing,* p. 321.

[76] *New York Times,* January 21, 1968.

[77] Abrams, quoted in Kevin Buckley, *op. cit.,* p. 130.

[78] According to columnist Joseph Kraft, "For years, high advisers galore have harbored the sharpest doubts and gravest misgivings about Vietnam policy, but in deference to the President, as a mark of loyalty, they have adjusted, or swallowed, or buried, these views." *Des Moines Register,* October 15, 1969. Thus preferring "loyalty to the President over loyalty to the truth," these advisers—and especially, Secretary Rusk—"have shown their mettle in backing to the hilt positions they doubted rather than in raising doubts about the President they served. The upshot has been deception on a grand scale—an assertion of constant progress in Vietnam." *Des Moines Register,* October 10, 1969. Hoopes, on the other hand, contends, "Control of the war effort remained tightly held by the inner group, and they were, with the exception of McNamara, united . . . in their conviction about the *rightness* of present policy. . . ." Hoopes, *op. cit.,* p. 150. (Emphasis added.)

[79] One writer has contended that, since the introduction of the modern White House staff under President Franklin Roosevelt, "probably . . . Johnson had the highest turnover rate. . . . [O]f President Johnson's own eleven early appointees in 1963 and 1964, only three

Remaining were those who believed in the goals and conduct of the war, perhaps to the extent of staking their public careers on it. With such a deep personal investment in good news from the war, they could hardly be expected to welcome pessimism from below.

Thus, informational distortions could not be effectively weeded out as they passed upwards in the bureaucracy; for not only did higher officials lack adequate weeding criteria, but in addition were themselves subject to the same natural proclivity to see primarily what one wants or expects to see.[80]

A key figure at the top level of the organization seems to have been Rostow, who "had become the channel through which President Johnson received almost all written communications on foreign affairs," and had assumed "a large hand in determining who, outside the closed circle of advisers, the President would see or not see."[81] Such a crucial communications role suggests a remarkable capacity for detachment and impartiality. Yet by all accounts Rostow was a man of "boundless optimism,"[82] a "dedicated partisan whose mind automatically filtered out evidence that did not support his own established beliefs."[83] More "easily impressed than anyone else in the Administration by the questionable statistics sent from U.S. officials in Vietnam on the 'kill-ratio,' enemy weapons captured, enemy deserters, hamlets pacified, and so on,"[84] Rostow constituted an important incentive for lower officials to accentuate the positive. Thus, one columnist has reported that George Carver, head of the CIA unit in charge of briefing Rostow, "largely served up to Rostow what he wanted to hear."[85] And a former *Times* correspondent, who

---

remained to the end. Those who left included key men like Bill Moyers, Walter Jenkins, Jake Jacobson, Jack Valenti, and Horace Busby." Alex B. Lacy, Jr., "The White House Staff Bureaucracy," *Trans-action*, January 1969, p. 52.

[80] Nor was this tendency a recent development. Prior to the Tet offensive, former Kennedy aide Arthur Schlesinger, Jr., had complained that "the Administration in Washington was systematically misinformed by senior American officials in Saigon in 1962–63 regarding the progress of the war, the popularity of Diem, the effectiveness of the 'strategic hamlet' program and other vital matters. It was not that these officials were deliberately deceiving their President; it was that they deceived themselves first. Ordinary citizens restricted to reading the American press were better informed in 1963 than officials who took top-secret cables seriously." Arthur Schlesinger, Jr., "The U.S. Ignorance About Vietnam," *San Francisco Chronicle*, September 28, 1966.

[81] Hoopes, *op. cit.*, p. 59. "Shielded by Rostow," Hoopes adds, Johnson "'was probably unaware that his subcabinet group and an influential segment of the foreign-military bureaucracy were increasingly disenchanted with his leadership, frustrated by their own impotence, and incipiently rebellious." *Ibid.*, p. 116.

[82] Anderson, *op. cit.*, p. 273.

[83] Hoopes, *op. cit.*, pp. 60, 21.

[84] Anderson, *op. cit.*, p. 384.

[85] Joseph Kraft, *Des Moines Register*, February 3, 1969. This may help to explain why National Intelligence Estimates of Vietcong political cadre in the South had been only 75–85,000 prior to Tet; soon thereafter, the estimate was revised upwards to 110–120,000. *New York Times*, March 19, 1968.

received a Pulitzer Prize for his articles from Vietnam, has written, "If a field officer wants to report to Rostow, he must get the positive news in first because Rostow will turn off once the darker side comes on." [86] Exhibiting "a natural deference to authority," [87] and having constructed his career as top adviser from favorable assurances on the war, Rostow probably could not avoid the tendency to brighten the Tet news still further as he passed it on to the President.[88] Certainly, it is difficult to dispute the judgment of a former Pentagon official, who found Rostow "exactly the wrong man for the job of helping a President to delineate the profound issues of the war and to identify with precision the hard core of U.S. national interest in Asia." [89]

Not only was the quality of information such as to insure distortion. In addition, the quantity of information being passed upwards through the various military, civilian, and CIA hierarchies appears to have been so vast that it caused an overload within the organization's communications system. As one government analyst bluntly put it:

One of the most significant problems is the pressure for numbers. What happened in Vietnam is that we were simply drowned in statistics; we were drowned in information. A very small proportion of this information was properly analyzed. We would have been much better off to have a much smaller take of information and to have done a better job of interpreting what that information meant. But the system that was developed in Vietnam was geared to the massive outpouring of data, data that drowned all of us, I think.[90]

The Tet experience, then, illustrates the system's failure to solve what Guetzkow has termed "a central problem in communications systems: How may fullness of meaning be carried without overload?" [91] In this case, of course, the system failed both to provide fullness of meaning and to avoid overload. Miller has identified several possible consequences of

[86] David Halberstam, quoted in Anderson, *op. cit.*, p. 385.
[87] Hoopes, *op. cit.*, p. 20.
[88] Stuart H. Loory, *Los Angeles Times*, May 31, 1968. Hoopes reports that Rostow, along with Rusk and Wheeler, made the President "the victim" of " 'selective briefings'—the time-honored technique of underlining within a mass of material, those particular elements that one wishes to draw to the special attention of a busy chief...." Hoopes, *op. cit.*, p. 218. Yet given the nature of briefings, a good deal of "selectivity" is, of course, unavoidable and desirable.
[89] *Ibid.*, p. 61.
[90] *Schlesinger Hearing*, p. 322. The Vietnam experience supports Richard Neustadt's view. "Choking people to death with information," he said, "is one of the oldest bureaucratic techniques known to man. Never have there been such opportunities as now." U.S., Congress, Senate, Committee on Government Operations, *Hearings, Administration of National Security*, 88th Cong., 2d Sess., 1964, p. 99. A war situation would serve only to underscore the accuracy of these statements.
[91] Harold Guetzkow, "Communications in Organizations," *Handbook of Organizations*, ed. James G. March (Chicago: Rand McNally, 1965), p. 553.

such information overload,[92] and, as two theorists of organizations have argued, most of the system's responses tend to be maladaptive defensive mechanisms, such as arbitrarily failing to process some of the information or processing it incorrectly.[93]

It is hardly surprising, then, to find that for weeks preceding Tet, President Johnson and his staff had pictured the enemy as desperate. Carver's reports to Rostow, for example, "justified the continuing military effort on the ground that success was not too far away." [94] There may, therefore, have been a tendency to view the offensive as a last gasp, in order to harmonize it with preconceptions. And from this, it is but a small step to dismissing the attacks as "a complete failure," [95] for, after all, they *were* beaten back.[96] In line with this, the *Times'* Washington columnist, James Reston, certainly no supporter of the war, indicated that the "most popular" interpretation in the capital was that "the enemy is desperate." [97] He noted that for the first few days the President refrained from bombing Hanoi or Haiphong as an overture to peace talks. Reston concluded, therefore, that Johnson was "operating for the time being on the assumption that this really is a desperate last effort on the part of the enemy, and if it can be contained, Hanoi will finally withdraw and negotiate." [98] Because the President had been predisposed toward this view of desperation, then, he may have made it the touchstone of his perceptions, although it was plainly not the most plausible of the possible alternative explanations.

Another factor helping to distort the President's evaluation of the situation in Vietnam may have been his belief in the prevailing American military doctrine. This doctrine emphasized the goals of gaining territory and killing the enemy, and *on these terms,* certainly the enemy had failed; for it had not seized the cities or escaped heavy losses. The problem was, of course, that the doctrine did not fit the war. In a guerrilla action with a major civil war component, pursuit of these goals may be ir-

---

[92] James G. Miller, "Information, Input Overload, and Psychopathology," *American Journal of Psychiatry* 116 (1960): 695–704.

[93] Daniel Katz and Robert L. Kahn, *The Social Psychology of Organizations* (New York: Wiley, 1966), pp. 231–34.

[94] Kraft, *loc. cit.*

[95] Lyndon B. Johnson, "President Johnson's News Conference of February 2," *Department of State Bulletin* 58 (February 19, 1968): 222.

[96] The attacks, however, were not all beaten back at the time of the President's statement. In fact, the Vietcong held parts of Hue until February 4, over three weeks after the press conference.

[97] *New York Times,* February 4, 1969.

[98] In this regard, another journalist described the crisis week as one "in which the Johnson Administration more than ever resembled a Chinese Court, with the mandarins assembled to tell the leadership what it wanted to hear." Ward Just, *Washington Post,* February 4, 1968.

relevant, if not actually counterproductive. For guerrillas may be less interested in holding territory than in promoting a feeling of psychological insecurity among the population, thereby undermining the legitimacy of the regime;[99] and a counterinsurgency emphasis on killing the enemy may antagonize many of the natives, for as this aim is sought, numbers of innocent civilians inevitably become casualties, too.

But if, as Kissinger has observed, "the Tet offensive overthrew the assumptions of American strategy,"[100] it did not do so all at once. The President, in other words, probably evaluated ongoing events in terms of this strategy, and this helped to mislead him as to the nature of Vietnamese reality during Tet.

V

Plainly, the Tet offensive posed stiff problems for decision makers, rendering an accurate perception of events difficult and a successful public relations campaign impossible.

The decision makers' own perceptual problems seem to have stemmed from two major factors: the nature of the information given them before and during the offensive, and their capacity for evaluating it. These factors interacted, reinforcing each other and making the ultimate problem insoluble. The apparatus responsible for keeping the decision makers informed had for some time been transmitting an unrealistically optimistic image of developments in Vietnam. The apparent "scientific" character of some of the devices used—like HES—served to add to the credibility of the information, though the surface precision was actually misleading; for assertions only *seem* truer if dressed in numbers and decimal points. Decision makers, thus, were quite unprepared for the nature of the offensive. The surprise, anger, and frustration it engendered were all distorting factors of no small importance. Preexisting beliefs about the progress of the war effort and the value of the prevailing military doctrine compounded the difficulty, and the great quantity of information brought on by the offensive was simply indigestible.

Yet the decision makers were not simply victims of a faulty information gathering and analyzing apparatus, for its defects could be attri-

---

[99] That Westmoreland never fully appreciated this is suggested by his adherence to conventional warfare tactics as well as by a story told by a *Newsweek* reporter in Vietnam: "On Westmoreland's last day in Vietnam, several Soviet-manufactured 122-mm. rockets, with 41-pound warheads, crashed into Tu Do Street. Others landed near the Presidential Palace and in working-class neighborhoods. Westmoreland was consistent to the last. He brushed them aside, saying the attacks were 'of no military significance.' They were not—to the extent that they did not hit military installations, just civilian homes." Abrams, by contrast, saw the rockets' harmful effects on public confidence in the Saigon government, and successfully sought to stop the attacks. Kevin Buckley, *op. cit.,* p. 126.

[100] Kissinger, *op. cit.,* p. 101; Thompson, *op. cit.,* p. 144.

buted partly to their actions. If the organizations had been excessively
optimistic, this probably had been due mainly to the decision makers'
demand for good news. And they desired positive reports not only because they could be publicized, and thereby used to help create a permissive consensus supporting the administration's behavior regarding
the war. In addition, decision makers themselves seem to have wanted
and expected to be told of progress. Many of these individuals had committed their careers and public reputations to their belief in eventual
Vietnamese success, and would clearly become displeased by pessimism
or skepticism from any source—especially from within their own organizations. Given such a situation, it is no more to be wondered that the decision makers got the kind of information they wanted than that the information itself was inadequate. The decision makers' attitude, which
had discouraged doubt at lower levels, also drove critics from the highest
levels. Thus, no one with ready access to the President remained to question the veracity of the preoffensive reports. All of this meant that any attempt to penetrate appearances during the actual crisis would, at least in
the short run, be doomed to failure.

The President's main nonmilitary reaction to Tet, of course, was his attempt to convince the non-antiwar mass and attentive publics that the
enemy's offensive had failed. The motivation for this public relations effort seems to have been both personally and policy oriented. Presumably, that is, the President desired to ward off the great personal political
defeat that would inevitably accompany widespread knowledge of the
Tet setback; and he felt that such a setback would seriously reduce public confidence in his war policy, perhaps even leading to a polarization in
which ever larger numbers favored rapid withdrawal or an all-out military response, leaving his middle-ground approach abandoned like a di-
vining rod discarded because it found no water.

Partly, for these calculating personal and policy purposes, but partly,
too, because they reflected the administration's own point of view, the
Vietcong's objectives were defined in a strictly military sense. And in this
sense—with the help of some inflated rhetoric—it could be shown that the
enemy had not in fact succeeded. Not stopping at this, the administration refused even to grant the Vietcong the achievement of tactical
surprise.

The public, however, could not so easily be convinced, and perhaps
was actually less vulnerable to the seductions of optimistic appearances
than were the decision makers. The mass public, holding its views on the
nature and progress of the war with an unimpressive intensity, could
more easily change its mind. It had not made a sizable personal investment in a particular interpretation of events, and thus was more
open to the obvious conclusion that the offensive had been a stunning

setback. The attentive antiwar public perceived events as reinforcing its earlier convictions regarding the impracticality of the war and the stupidity of its conduct on the American side. Critical reports from the prestige press—particularly those from reporters on the scene—were doubtless important in this regard. The attentive prowar public probably tended to adhere to the administration's interpretation, although the defection of the future Secretary of Defense Clark Clifford from the "hawks" camp suggests that the offensive may have had some effect in this quarter as well.

For those not already strongly committed to the administration, the spectacular, unexpected offensive, following a months-long crescendo of good news, resurrected older not yet moribund doubts about the credibility and competence of Johnson and his advisers. Possibly recognizing this activation of latent uneasiness, the administration gradually retreated from its highly positive assessment, hinting that the offensive had been larger and more costly than officials had earlier admitted. Whether this modified approach was ignored by the public or simply had the effect of confirming its rising suspicions, it was clearly ineffective. Polls soon showed sharp drops in Johnson's popularity, and in public confidence in his handling of the war. Still larger opinion reverses were on the horizon. Misperceptions as to events and the public's gullibility were to be costly indeed.

Thus far we have concentrated on the substance of crises: what was the nature of the Tet offensive and the allied response? What really happened in the Gulf of Tonkin in the beginning of August in 1964? What was the character of the chaotic revolutionary situation in the Dominican Republic? Why was the Bay of Pigs invasion force organized as it was? Public information on all these matters is substantial, and if one is sometimes willing to wait a few years, reasonably accurate.

But what of the decision-making process itself—the procedures and deliberations from which policy emerges? About this behind-the-scenes activity the public knows little of value. Partly, this may be because the decision-making process can never be carried out effectively in public. The pressures of democratic posturing would be too great, and any element of surprise would have to be eliminated from the strategy.

It is hardly surprising, then, to find that the secrecy of crisis decision making is often exploited to the advantage of the participants, as writers grasp for facts like goldfish wriggling for breadcrumbs. With elbows braced on window ledges, we observe far away the melodrama of a political showdown, larger than life because in some sense the spectacle is not true to life. Perhaps the romanticization of the protagonists is necessary in order to convince the public of the wisdom of its omission from crisis decision making. Perhaps it is simply a means *ad majoram gloriam* the President. But, in any case, crisis decision making is too important to be left to mythologists, however lofty their motives. So we turn now to decision making in the greatest of all Cold Wars crises, that surrounding the emplacement of Soviet nuclear missiles in Cuba in 1962.

6

Cuba: The Missile Crisis

*No war is begun, or at least no war should
be begun if people acted wisely, without
first finding an answer to the question:
what is to be attained by and in war?*

Clausewitz, *On War*

This case study focuses primarily on decision makers' efforts to distinguish appearance from reality.[1] Special emphasis is placed upon the importance of presidential advisers, and their interaction as a group. The nature of presidential leadership in the evaluative process is also stressed. To a lesser extent, the decision makers' relations with the public are treated; specifically, the use of secrecy during the early crisis phase and of open diplomacy during the acute phase. The effectiveness of these techniques is assessed, and speculation as to presidential motivation is offered.

THE PRE-CRISIS PHASE: THROUGH OCTOBER 13

Ye shall hear of wars and rumors of wars.

Matthew 24:6

For at least two years prior to the crisis, and especially during the months following the abortive invasion attempt at the Bay of Pigs, Cuba

---

[1] The chronological periodization of the crisis follows the schema of Ole R. Holsti, Richard A. Brody, and Robert C. North, "Measuring Affect and Action in International Reaction Models: Empirical Materials from the 1962 Cuban Crisis," paper read before the International Peace Research Society Conference, Ghent, Belgium, July 18 and 19, 1964. (Mimeographed.)

was perhaps "the rawest nerve in our body politic. . . ." [2] Calls for a United States invasion or blockade became so numerous as to be almost commonplace. In the last week of July, 1962, a Soviet military buildup in Cuba evidently began,[3] and on September 2, Moscow acknowledged this development, although attributing its initiative to the Cubans.

But even before this announcement, suspicions heightened by the imperatives of an American election year had added to the tension of the domestic political scene. On August 27, for example, Republican Senator Homer E. Capehart of Indiana had declared, "It is high time that the American people demand that President Kennedy quit 'examining the situation' and start protecting the interests of the United States." [4] Four days later Senator Kenneth Keating, a Republican from New York, had told the Senate "that the Soviet buildup is 'deliberately designed' to enable Russia to build missile sites and to interfere with U.S. troops at Cape Canaveral." [5] Former Vice-President Nixon, campaigning for the governorship of California, called for an American "quarantine" of the island.[6] The Republican senatorial and congressional campaign committee announced that Cuba would be "the dominant issue of the 1962 campaign," [7] and popular news magazines agreed.[8] Representative William Miller, chairman of the Republican National Committee, speaking of the coming elections, emphasized the role of Cuba: "If we were asked to state the issue in one word, that word would be Cuba—symbol of the tragic irresolution of the Administration." [9]

Meanwhile, several public opinion polls revealed an increasing frustration concerning American policy with respect to Communist influence

---

[2] Karl E. Meyer, "The Cuban Torment," *New Leader,* October 1, 1962, p. 3.

[3] Theodore Draper, "Castro and Communism," *Reporter,* January 17, 1963, p. 38.

[4] Homer E. Capehart, "Capehart: U.S. Should Act, Stop 'Examining' Cuba," *U.S. News and World Report,* September 10, 1962, p. 45. Later, after the government's discovery of the missiles, the President quipped, "This will make Capehart look like the Churchill of the 'sixties." John F. Kennedy, quoted in Joseph Kraft, *Profiles in Power: A Washington Insight* (New York: New American Library, 1966), p. 3. Capehart, however, was defeated in his reelection battle.

[5] Kenneth B. Keating, quoted in "Is Castro's Cuba a Soviet Base?" *U.S. News and World Report,* September 10, 1962, p. 43. One conservative analyst has contended that Senator Keating's repeated warnings mark him—and not the President—as the true hero of the missile affair. Thomas A. Lane, *The Leadership of President Kennedy* (Caldwell, Idaho: Caxton Press, 1964), p. 97.

[6] Richard M. Nixon, quoted in *New York Times,* September 19, 1962; also quoted in John N. Plank, "Monroe's Doctrine—and Castro's," *New York Times Magazine,* October 7, 1962, p. 30.

[7] Data Digest, *Cuban Crisis* (New York: Keynote Publications, 1963), p. 35.

[8] See, e.g., "The Campaign," *Time,* October 26, 1962, p. 23; "How U.S. Voters Feel About Cuba," *Newsweek,* October 22, 1962, p. 21.

[9] William E. Miller, quoted in "Notes of the Month: Cuba: A U.S. Election Issue," *World Today* 18 (November 1962): 453.

in the Caribbean.[10] Yet this should not be overstated. *Newsweek*, for example, after interviewing two thousand persons on a nationwide basis, concluded:

That nearly all Americans are deeply concerned—but not panicked—by the presence of Russian arms and "technicians" 90 miles from the Florida Keys.

That about 90 per cent don't want to invade Cuba now.

That there is widespread confusion about which actions "short of war" would work against Fidel Castro or would be acceptable under international law.[11]

Similarly, both the Gallup nationwide poll of October 14 and the *San Francisco Chronicle* October 12 poll of northern California showed that only a minority favored aggressive action against Cuba.

Foreign observers, who had heretofore belittled the importance of Cuba to the United States, now overcompensated, drenching their assessments in alarm. The Soviet buildup, one of them declared, had "set off an emotional reaction among Americans." Others commented on "the popular frustration" and the mood of "furious impatience," which they interpreted as a "widespread demand for President Kennedy to 'do something' and damn the consequences. . . ." One left-wing Washington correspondent remarked, "The truth is that everybody seems to be afraid of everything but war." [12] The end of September saw a near-unanimous Congress pass a joint resolution declaring the United States' determination

(a) to prevent by whatever means may be necessary, including the use of arms, the Marxist-Leninist regime in Cuba from extending, by force or the threat of force, its aggressive or subversive activities to any part of this hemisphere;

(b) to prevent in Cuba the creation or use of an externally supported military capability endangering the security of the United States. . . .[13]

When the President arrived in Chicago on a campaign tour in mid-October, one "welcoming" sign read: "Less Profile—More Courage." [14]

---

[10] Quincy Wright, "The Cuban Quarantine of 1962," *Power and Order*, ed. John G. Stoessinger and Alan F. Westin (New York: Harcourt, Brace and World, 1964), p. 184.

[11] "How U.S. Voters Feel About Cuba," *Newsweek*, October 22, 1962, p. 21.

[12] "Cold War on the Doorstep," *Economist* 205 (October 13, 1962): 138; Karl E. Meyer, "Time Marches on Cuba," *New Statesman* 64 (September 21, 1962): 349; "Obsessed by Cuba," *Economist* 205 (October 6, 1962): 15; "Afraid of Everything But War," *I. F. Stone's Weekly*, September 17, 1962, p. 1.

[13] S. J. Res. 230; passed by the Senate on September 20 by a vote of 86 to 1, and by the House of Representatives on September 26 by a vote of 384 to 7.

[14] Wright, *op. cit.*, p. 186.

The American press, by and large, supported the administration's policy. Of those magazines that dissented and assumed a "harder line," the most influential were unquestionably the Luce publications. In a special cover article on the Monroe Doctrine, *Time* advocated "a direct U.S. invasion of Cuba, carried out with sufficient force to get the job done with surgical speed and efficiency"; inter-American pacts against intervention were dismissed as "multilateral flypaper." In that same week, *Life* editorialized in favor of a blockade; two weeks later, Mrs. Luce accused the administration of queasiness in the face of danger.[15] Most of the press, however, refrained from expressing alarm, usually viewing the new developments in limited terms. One magazine, for example, felt that the Soviet arms were "brought in to crush the growing rebellion, in all social classes, of a people that less than four years ago was cheering Fidel Castro as its liberator";[16] a second contended that the purpose was to "discourage Cuban rebels from making plans for another invasion of Cuba."[17] The possibility that the Soviets had shipped offensive weapons to Cuba was widely discounted. The pressure for American intervention, while significant and vocal, was, in short, not as great as a first glance might indicate.

Generally, the administration was able to resist the agitation for action, part of its firmness no doubt deriving from the assurances of American intelligence officials. These analysts, as a Senate subcommittee subsequently put it, "were strongly influenced by their philosophical judgment that it would be contrary to Soviet policy to introduce strategic missiles into Cuba."[18] Only CIA Director John McCone had considered the possibility of the installation of offensive missiles, but even he "did not take this thought seriously enough to prevent his going off for a three weeks' honeymoon in Europe."[19] The President, then, acting on faulty

---

[15] "The Presidency: The Double Doctrine," *Time,* September 21, 1962, p. 21. Cf., Basil Dontryskyn and Jesse L. Gilmore, "The Monroe Doctrine: A Soviet View," *Institute for the Study of the USSR* 11 (May 1964): 3. "Editorial: What Should Monroe Doctrine Mean? Blockade," *Life,* September 21, 1962, p. 4. Clare Boothe Luce, "Cuba and the Unfaced Truth: Our Global Double Bind," *Life,* October 5, 1962, pp. 53–56.

[16] Leo Sauvage, "Castro's Foreign Legion," *Reporter,* September 10, 1962, p. 45.

[17] "Is Castro's Cuba a Soviet Base?" *U.S. News and World Report,* September 10, 1962, p. 45.

[18] U.S., Congress, Senate, Committee on Armed Services, Subcommittee on Preparedness, *Interim Report on the Cuban Military Buildup and Investigation of the Preparedness Program,* 88th Cong., 1st Sess., 1963, p. 11. This conclusion is disputed by Klaus Knorr, "Failure in National Intelligence Estimates: The Case of the Cuban Missiles," *World Politics* 16 (April 1964): 455–67.

[19] Arthur M. Schlesinger, Jr., *A Thousand Days: John F. Kennedy in the White House* (Boston: Houghton Mifflin, 1965), p. 799; Abel, *op. cit.,* pp. 17–18; Edward Weintal and Charles Bartlett, *Facing the Brink: An Intimate Study of Crisis Diplomacy* (New York: Scribner's, 1967), p. 60. McCone's suggestion, in any event, was based on wholly deductive, nonempirical grounds. Roger Hilsman, *To Move a Nation: The Politics of Foreign Policy in*

information, pointedly rejected proposals for "unilateral military intervention," noting that "rash talk is cheap, particularly on the part of those who did not have the responsibility" for action.[20] He did, however, reiterate the United States' resolve to "do whatever must be done to protect its own security and that of its allies." And when, on September 23, Castro announced that the Soviet Union had agreed to help Cuba build a new fishing port, the administration, in the face of "revived attacks," virtually accepted some of the policies pressed upon it by its critics, in particular by "attempting to enlist support from the Latin American and European allies of the U.S. for certain forms of concerted action against Cuba." [21] These attempts met only limited success.

Yet persistent rumors circulated regarding the emplacement of offensive Soviet missiles and troops in Cuba. In this atmosphere, Robert Kennedy met with Soviet Ambassador Anatoly Dobrynin, and expressed the administration's concern. Dobrynin attempted to allay American anxieties by brushing aside the rumors, and assuring the Attorney General that Khrushchev "liked President Kennedy and did not wish to embarrass him" before elections.[22] Shortly thereafter, a Soviet-Cuban military agreement was announced, and two days later the President denied the missile rumors again, adding a more pointed warning to the Russians. "There is no evidence," he said, "of the presence of offensive ground-to-ground missiles or of other significant offensive capability either in Cuban hands or under Soviet direction and guidance." But, he continued, "were it to be otherwise the gravest issues would arise." [23] In this, Kennedy "was drawing a line, and he was making it extremely unlikely that we would back down if that line were crossed." [24]

the Administration of John F. Kennedy (Garden City: Doubleday, 1967), pp. 172–73. Actually, Schlesinger's remark understates McCone's concern, for even while on the Riviera, he sent a number of cables on the matter to his deputy, General Marshall Carter. They were never shown to the President, however, for Carter did not want to antagonize Kennedy by repeatedly raising an interpretation of events that had already been rejected. Abel, *op. cit.,* p. 23. By the end of September—roughly a month after McCone had spoken with the President—officers within the Defense Intelligence Agency came to a similar conclusion. U.S., Congress, House of Representatives, Committee on Appropriations, Subcommittee on Department of Defense Appropriations, *Hearings,* 88th Congress, 1st Sess., 1963, p. 71.

[20] John F. Kennedy, "President States U.S. Policy Toward Cuba," *Department of State Bulletin* 47 (October 1, 1962): 481, 482. (Statement of September 13.)

[21] "Notes of the Month: Cuba: A U.S. Election Issue," *World Today* 18 (November 1962): 454.

[22] Robert F. Kennedy, "Thirteen Days: The Story about How the World Almost Ended," *McCall's,* November 1968, p. 7. Hereinafter cited as "Thirteen Days," In retrospect, the Attorney General probably attributes a more skeptical administration reaction to Dobrynin's statements than may actually have occurred.

[23] John F. Kennedy, "U.S. Reaffirms Policy on Prevention of Aggressive Actions by Cuba," *Department of State Bulletin* 48 (September 24, 1962): 450. (Statement of September 4.)

[24] Roberta Wohlstetter, *Cuba and Pearl Harbor: Hindsight and Foresight* (RAND Corpo-

The President's position of caution was reinforced a few days later, when a Soviet official relayed Khrushchev's personal assurance that ground-to-ground missiles would never be shipped to Cuba. To this private message, the Soviets added a long public communiqué on September 11. While repeating that it was sending a "certain amount of armaments to Cuba," the Soviet government took unusual care to reassure the President that these armaments were "designed exclusively for defensive purposes." This was underlined by the Soviets' boast that it was not necessary for them to transport offensive weapons to Cuba because Soviet nuclear rockets were so powerful that "there is no need to search for sites for them beyond the boundaries of the Soviet Union." [25]

In response, President Kennedy reiterated his policy of watchful waiting, repeating that "these new shipments do not constitute a serious threat to any other part of this hemisphere." [26] The Intelligence Community, in its report of September 19, supported this position by unequivocally predicting that "the Soviet Union would not make Cuba a strategic base" because it "had not taken this kind of step with any of its satellites in the past and would feel the risk of retaliation from the United States to be too great to take the risk in this case." [27] Other officials echoed this conclusion. General Lucius Clay, for instance, appearing on a September 23 telecast, stated, "I'm not too concerned about the Cuban situation as an offensive threat against the United States." [28] Secretary Rusk restated this view a week later on a nationwide television program.[29] Meanwhile, however, governmental concern had been expressed by a high State Department news official in Washington,[30] and by Ambassador Stevenson at the United Nations.[31] By October 9, even Secretary Rusk acknowledged that he was concerned.[32]

---

ration, RM-4328-1SA, April 1965), p. 23. Yet since it was not made clear what actions the United States would be willing to take if the "line were crossed," the significance of its having been drawn in the first place was necessarily mitigated.

[25] *New York Times,* September 12, 1962.

[26] John F. Kennedy, "President States U.S. Policy Toward Cuba," *Department of State Bulletin* 47 (October 1, 1962): 481. (Statement of September 13.)

[27] Paraphrased by Robert F. Kennedy, "Thirteen Days," p. 8.

[28] Lucius Clay, quoted in "How *Do* You Crush an Inspiration?" *I. F. Stone's Weekly,* October 1, 1962, p. 1.

[29] Dean Rusk, "Secretary Discusses Cuban Situation on 'News and Comment' Program," *Department of State Bulletin* 47 (October 22, 1962): 595.

[30] "Concern Expressed by United States in Matter of Cuban Fishing Port," *Department of State Bulletin* 47 (October 15, 1962): 560–61. (Statement of September 26 of Lincoln White, Director of the Office of News.)

[31] Adlai Stevenson, "U.S. Replies to Charges on Cuba in U.N. General Assembly," *Department of State Bulletin* 47 (October 15, 1962): 583. (Statement of September 21 made in plenary session.)

[32] Dean Rusk, "United States Presents Facilities at Fort McNair to Inter-American Defense College," *Department of State Bulletin* 47 (October 29, 1962): 643. (Address delivered October 9.)

On the eve of the crisis, several points may be noted. First, while suspicious of the new developments regarding Cuba, American decision makers essentially believed Soviet assurances about the "defensive" character of the weapons. Second, as Kennedy realized, the popular demand for invasion or blockade was more mirage than reality. In sum, the President's actions—except if they resulted in national humiliation—would obtain widespread support, whatever they were.

THE EARLY CRISIS PHASE: OCTOBER 14–21

> *He measures necessity*
> *With a pikestaff's haft, from his wish's circumference*
> *To the center of violence.*

> Ben Belitt, "Encounter"

On October 13, President Kennedy spoke scornfully of the "self-appointed generals and admirals who want to send someone else's sons to war...." [33] The following afternoon, McGeorge Bundy gave similar assurances in a television interview. Later that day—at least a month after their importation in Cuba—offensive Soviet missiles were indentified by an Air Force U-2 reconnaissance plane.[34] Despite prior expressions of

---

[33] John F. Kennedy, quoted in Draper, *op. cit.,* p. 40.

[34] The precise reasons for this delay have never been adequately explained. Hilsman writes, for example, that no U-2 flights were ordered from September 5 through September 16 because of bad weather, and the fear that surface-to-air missiles in Cuba would shoot the U-2s down, killing the pilot and creating a "political storm." Hilsman, *op. cit.,* pp. 173–74, 190. Yet the weather was not foul the whole time, and stories of suspicious activities in Cuba were so persistent that U-2 flights took place on September 17 and 25, but, oddly, did not cover the entire island.

Graham T. Allison, an academic analyst, offers two possible explanations. First, he suggests that "the discovery took place on October 14 . . . as a consequence of the established routines and procedures of the organizations which constitute the U.S. intelligence community." That is, time was necessarily consumed checking out suspicions, transmitting observations, coordinating apparently disparate facts into a coherent whole, and, finally, determining whether the CIA or the Air Force would make the required reconnaissance flight. Graham T. Allison, "Conceptual Models and the Cuban Missile Crisis," *American Political Science Review* 63 (September 1969): 704-5. Second, Allison points out that on "September 9 a U-2 'on loan' to the Chinese Nationalists was shot down over mainland China. The Committee on Overhead Reconnaissance convened on September 10 with a sense of urgency. Loss of another U-2 might incite world opinion to demand cancellation of U-2 flights. The President's campaign against those who asserted that the Soviets were acting provocatively in Cuba had begun. To risk downing a U-2 over Cuba was to risk chopping off the limb on which the President was sitting. That meeting decided to shy away from the western end of Cuba (where surface-to-air missiles were becoming operational) and modify the flight pattern of the U-2s in order to reduce the probability that a U-2 would be lost." *Ibid.,* p. 713. This almost amounts to saying that the President was publicly committed to the view that there were no missiles on Cuba, intelligence felt constrained to support him, and, consequently, searched for missiles only where they would *least* likely be

concern, the discovery left policy makers with a sense of "stunned surprise" and "shocked incredulity."[35] "The rapidity of the Russians' installation," wrote Roberta Wohlstetter, the perceptive analyst of the Pearl Harbor attack, "was in effect a logistical surprise comparable to the technological surprise at the time of Pearl Harbor."[36] The American "assessment of the warning signs," as one veteran journalist remarked, "was just about one hundred per cent wrong."[37] On October 15, the intelligence photographs were processed and analyzed. The President was informed of the discovery the following morning.[38]

Before considering the United States' reactions to the Soviet challenge, it is necessary to ask how American decision makers viewed the nature of the threat; for they were motivated not by "objective" facts but rather by

found. Allison does not state why, given COMOR's desire to find no missiles, it chose to send any flights at all; presumably, this was due to pressure from McCone and Carter or from a conviction that Kennedy deserved strong but *not unlimited* backing.

In an even more ingenious explanation, Leslie Dewart argues that the United States knew of the emplacement of intermediate range missiles in September because the Soviets had not tried to hide this move. By permitting the United States to learn of the development, he contends, the Soviets sought to observe American reactions and increase the buildup accordingly or terminate the process with small loss if Kennedy appeared intransigent. Since the United States knew of the maneuvers, it was much less likely to retaliate out of surprise, anger, and desperation, and thereby set off a war. The United States, Dewart believes, however, misled the Russians into thinking that "it would accept the deployment of the missiles," while actually, "the U.S. plan was to feign surprise at the later 'discovery' of the missiles and, then, with the backing of an aroused, 'managed' public opinion, to demand the unconditional withdrawal of the missiles." For this plan to work, it was necessary for the early American knowledge of the missiles to be kept secret from the general public. This, Dewart suggests, was easily accomplished by limiting those who knew to a mere handful of trusted men (e.g., Robert Kennedy, CIA Chief McCone, a CIA photographic intelligence officer needed to analyze the U-2 photographs, Robert McNamara and his intelligence assistant John Hughes, and possibly McGeorge Bundy). Leslie Dewart, "The Cuban Crisis Revisited," *Studies on the Left* 5 (Spring 1965): 15–40. Since none of the persons whom Dewart suggests might have been privy to the information has made it public, the deception remains viable today. Needless to say, Dewart's evidence is wholly circumstantial and inferential.

[35] Robert F. Kennedy, "Thirteen Days," pp. 7, 8.

[36] Roberta Wohlstetter, quoted in Schlesinger, *op. cit.,* p. 800. See, in general, Wohlstetter, *op. cit.*

[37] Hanson W. Baldwin, "The Growing Risks of Bureaucratic Intelligence," *Reporter,* August 15, 1963, p. 50. It had been assumed "that with all the means at its disposal and with events taking place so close to home, the intelligence service must be able to supply Washington with more or less accurate information about Cuba." Sauvage, *op. cit.,* p. 21. In 1960 Benno Wasserman had suggested that intelligence failures result from "an uncritical conceptual framework, so that—despite the intelligence service's voluminous detailed information—its estimates of the intentions of other countries are based on inapplicable assumptions." Benno Wasserman, "The Failure of Intelligence Prediction," *Political Studies* 8 (June 1960): 157.

[38] Theodore C. Sorensen, *Decision-Making in the White House: The Olive Branch or the Arrows* (New York: Columbia University Press, 1963), pp. 30–31. Hereinafter cited as *Decison-Making.* Sorensen defends the delay, as does Schlesinger, *op. cit.,* p. 801. For the explanation of Bundy, who had authorized the delay, see Theodore C. Sorensen, *Kennedy* (New York: Harper and Row, 1965), p. 673.

their personal vision of them. As an authority on communication has emphasized:

We do not perceive and know *"things as they are";* we perceive signs, and from these signs make inferences and build up our mental models of the world; we say we see and hear it; we talk about "real" things.[39]

The response to "signs," in turn, "depends upon the past experience from which an individual acquires his particular habits" and "upon the immediate past experience of the perceiver and upon the environment at that time."

Out of his past experience, the President had developed a strikingly pragmatic cast of mind. "A practical liberal," he called himself, "a pragmatic liberal." [40] And when he was criticized for this, his answer was, "At least we do things that work." [41] Restless with formalities and clichés, having "little interest in abstract theories," [42] "impatient with organizational tidiness," [43] the President sought to get at the nub of things. In order to harness this drive, he became "sincerely committed to the more flexible techniques." [44] Kennedy's conviction—it was more than a mental "habit"—was the foundation upon which his crisis strategy was built.

The particulars were filled in by recent events. The President's first reaction upon learning of the offensive missiles "was one of genuine outrage, for one of [his] basic tenets had been that a state of mutual trust between the great powers is an important step toward the problem of relaxing international tension." [45] The Soviets had violated that trust, and in an especially blatant and provocative manner. The anger, in addition, was of a personal kind. As Allison put it:

Kennedy had staked his full Presidential authority on the assertion that the Soviets would not place offensive weapons in Cuba. Moreover, Khrushchev had assured the President through the most direct and personal channels that he was

[39] Colin Cherry, *On Human Communication,* Science Editions (New York: Wiley, 1961 [c. 1957]), p. 260.
[40] John F. Kennedy, quoted in Sorensen, *Kennedy,* p. 22.
[41] John F. Kennedy, quoted in Sorensen, in Steven V. Roberts, "The Two Presidents: Word Pictures by Ten of the Kennedy Advisers Who Left," *Esquire,* November 1965, p. 165.
[42] Sorensen, *Kennedy,* p. 14.
[43] Douglass Cater, *Power in Washington* (New York: Vintage Books, 1965 [c. 1964]), p. 100.
[44] *Ibid.,* p. 102.
[45] Wohlstetter, *op. cit.,* p. 32; Raymond Aron, *The Great Debate: Theories of Nuclear Strategy,* trans. Ernest Powel, Anchor Books (Garden City: Doubleday, 1965), pp. 250–51. This "tenet," of course, had not deterred Kennedy from approving his own Cuban action at the Bay of Pigs a year earlier.

aware of the President's domestic political problem [i.e., attacks from the right on his handling of Cuba] and that nothing would be done to exacerbate the problem. The Chairman *lied* to the President.[46]

"Basically," as Sorensen said later of the President, "he was a man who personally didn't like to come in second." [47]

Despite this, the President's response was not that of a moralist. His first concern was the menace posed to the United States by the missiles, a menace conceived less in military than in political terms. The Soviet missiles, he recalled later, "would have *politically* changed the balance of power...." [48] In the words of one who participated in the crisis decisions, "the military equation was not altered" by the importation of missiles into Cuba because the Soviets already had other missiles, both at home and on submarines, that could perform the same functions. "It was simply an element of flexibility introduced into the power equation that the Soviets had not heretofore possessed." [49]

Other officials, however, were later to emphasize the military implications of the Russian move. Assistant Secretary of Defense Paul Nitze, for example, was to argue that Cuban-based missiles would reduce the period of warning before an attack on Strategic Air Command bombers from fifteen minutes if launched from the Soviet Union to only two or three minutes.[50] And while intelligence experts were to concede that the United States would maintain its nuclear superiority, they contended that emplacing missiles in Cuba would increase "the destructive power the Soviets could deliver on target in the United States by over fifty per

---

[46] Allison, *op. cit.*, p. 713.

[47] Theodore C. Sorensen, quoted in Roberts, *op. cit.*, p. 92.

[48] "A Conversation with President Kennedy," CBS telecast, December 17, 1962, p. 22. (Mimeographed.) Hereinafter cited as "Conversation." (Emphasis added.) This view has also been expressed by Schlesinger, *op. cit.*, p. 796; Sorensen, *Kennedy*, p. 678; Philip Van Slyck, *Peace: The Control of Nuclear Power* (Boston: Beacon Press, 1963), p. 3; Roger Hagen and Burt Bernstein, "Military Value of Missiles in Cuba," *Bulletin of the Atomic Scientists*, February 1963, pp. 8-13; Brian Beedham, "Cuba and the Balance of Power," *World Today* 19 (January 1963): 41; Henry A. Kissinger, "Reflections on Cuba," *Reporter*, November 22, 1962, pp. 21-22; Charles Burton Marshall, "Cuba—Why the Russians Are There," *New Republic*, October 1, 1962, pp. 9-10; David R. Inglis, "Disarmament After Cuba," *Bulletin of the Atomic Scientists*, January 1963, p. 18; Richard Lowenthal, "After Cuba, Berlin," *Encounter*, December 1962, p. 48.

[49] Deputy Secretary of Defense Roswell L. Gilpatric, speaking on a November 11 television program, quoted in Hagen and Bernstein, *op. cit.*, p. 10.

[50] Hilsman, *op. cit.*, p. 195. In this regard, a French observer has commented that the Soviets ought to have known that Americans "are haunted by the idea of a surprise attack and have spent astronomical sums to surround the United States with a warning system which enables them to react to thermonuclear aggression before their retaliatory installations have been hit." Andre Fontaine, "History of a Crisis," *Le Monde*, November 3, 4, 5, 1962, trans. E. W. Schnitzer, *Translations of Political Interest, 1962-1963*, ed. Horst Menderhausen (RAND Corporation, RM-3078-PR, January 1964), p. 61.

cent." [51] Moreover, even if the missiles did not constitute a potent military threat at the time, the President was not unaware that in the future they might raise grave problems, especially if the missiles were augmented by additional weapons.

In either case, the President understood that a great power is one that is treated like a great power; the United States, in his view, therefore, could not accept the emplacement of missiles in Cuba as a *fait accompli*, as it had a year before accepted the erection of the Berlin Wall.

The President was a meticulous student of public opinion, with "an acute awareness of the importance of the 'public image' in a public man." [52] And it was no coincidence that this politician of consummate style was so deeply concerned with his nation's international appearance. "But why?" one political scientist has asked. "Who was in a position to put this country on trial, who doubted its resolve, who was ignorant of its strength (the Soviet Union and China included)? . . . [W]as America's reputation so fragile?" [53]

There are two answers to these questions. First, if America's reputation were secure, the same could not be said of its President or of his party. A defeat in Cuba might have cracked the brittle surface of Kennedy's public image and self-esteem, no small matter for a man as concerned with public opinion as he was. In his 1960 campaign for nomination and election, for example, he had made unparalleled use of polls. This practice continued after he assumed office, to the extent that even a number of sympathetic writers thought that his sensitivity to the public and the press was such that his leadership function had been compromised by a drive for popularity.[54]

A defeat in Cuba would also have damaged the Democrats two weeks before congressional elections. Domestic politics tend to be looked upon as faintly disreputable and out of place in the consideration of issues of major international importance. It is no surprise, therefore, that analysts have denied that President Kennedy paid any attention to the domestic political implications of his crisis decision. Edward Weintal and Charles

[51] Hilsman, *op. cit.*, p. 201. The military implications of the missiles were also stressed by Herbert R. Dinerstein, *The United States and the Soviet Union: Standoff or Confrontation?* (RAND Corporation, P-3046, January 1965), p. 6; Dinerstein, *The Transformation of the Alliance Systems* (RAND Corporation, P-2993, February 1965), p. 21; Albert and Roberta Wohlstetter, *Controlling the Risks in Cuba* (Adelphi Papers No. 17, April 1965), pp. 12–14, where the importance of overseas bases is brought out; and in such journalistic treatments as William Henry Chamberlin's "The Great Confrontation," *The New Leader*, November 12, 1962, p. 21.
[52] Stuart Gerry Brown, *The American Presidency: Leadership, Partisanship, and Popularity* (New York: Macmillan, 1966), p. 52.
[53] George Kateb, "Kennedy As Statesman," *Commentary*, June 1966, pp. 57, 59.
[54] E.g., James M. Burns, "The Four Kennedys of the First Year," *New York Times Magazine*, January 14, 1962, p. 9.

Bartlett, for instance, state that in all the high-level crisis meetings, the subject was raised only once—and then not by Kennedy but by Vice-President Johnson. The President's reaction, they report reassuringly, was "mildly derisive." [55] Roger Hilsman, a participant in the meetings, says simply that domestic political pressures were "not discussed at all." [56] Yet while domestic politics may have seemed too mundane to discuss, they were also plainly too important to ignore. The political implications of the crisis, in fact, were so obvious that there may have appeared to be no need to discuss them at all: everyone felt that a triumph would pay dividends in popular support and at the polls.

Second, decisive action seemed necessary to *maintain* the United States' mighty position; for its might was conceived partly—perhaps primarily—as a function of its national image. The preoccupation with a nation's appearance probably was almost instinctual at the highest levels. For appearances have long pervaded strategic theory, as analysts focus on how other countries view us and what we ought to say and do to make them view us differently. Deterrence is thought to be effective, for instance, not if a nation is ready, willing, and able to use nuclear weapons under certain conditions against other nations, but instead if that nation is widely *perceived* as being ready, willing, and able to use them.[57]

Appearances also pervade practical politics—particularly democratic politics—for voters and politicians react to a leader less in terms of what he has done than in terms of what it *seems* he has done, what it can be *expected* he will do, or what qualities he *appears* to embody. Concern with appearances, above all, is a characteristic of interpersonal and not abstract international relationships. Probably, personal and national considerations were entangled to such a degree during the missile crisis that the President himself was unable always to draw distinctions.

But in any event, it seemed plain to him that the United States had to seize the offensive. "They thought they had us either way," said Kennedy later. "If we did nothing, we would be dead. If we reacted, they hoped to put us in an exposed position, whether with regard to Berlin or Turkey or the U.N." [58] The apparent dilemma, then, involved not only Cuba but the entire international scene as well. Here, notably in Berlin, related issues threatened to distort the perception of Soviet intentions, with a possible result of violence in several theaters, or what Herman

---

[55] Weintal and Bartlett, *op. cit.*, p. 58.

[56] Hilsman, *op. cit.*, p. 196.

[57] Nuclear weaponry, of course, has made appearances seem more important than ever before by raising the stakes of testing intentions and capabilities to the level of unparalleled potential catastrophe.

[58] John F. Kennedy, quoted in Schlesinger, *op. cit.*, p. 811.

Kahn has termed "large compound escalation." [59] A broad view had to
be taken, yet not too broad. But in the first analysis of what Premier
Khrushchev was up to, for example, "Berlin bulked very large," [60] though
as events progressed the Soviets pursued a very cautious course in that
city.[61] One official, in fact, interpreted Khrushchev's emplacement of missiles as "a left hook designed to make him tougher when he comes at us
in November, presumably on Berlin." [62] Nor was this official alone in his
judgment.[63] "Many regarded the Cuba missile deployment as designed
chiefly to improve the Soviet bargaining position in the renewed crisis
that was expected to be raised by the Russians after the 1962 U.S. elections." [64] The existence of these various viewpoints is perhaps more significant than questions relating to their validity, for this diversity indicates that from the beginning Cuba had been seen not in isolation but
in its global context. "The encounter over this small island," Albert and
Roberta Wohlstetter have written, "on the American view, had to do
with the future of the world." [65]

A decision maker's "major area of freedom is in the hypothesis he
chooses to adopt, not in the manner in which he can choose to test." [66] In
this sense, the President's freedom was severely limited from the outset,
for that the United States must maintain its world position was a proposition he accepted without question or chance of reversal. The primary
means to this end, as it turned out, was convincing Khrushchev of America's firmness on this point.[67] With a sizable number of possible alterna-

[59] Kahn, *op. cit.,* pp. 86–87.

[60] Sorensen, *Decision-Making,* pp. 34–35; Abel, *op. cit.,* p. 47; Richard H. Rovere, "Letter from Washington," *New Yorker,* November 3, 1962, p. 118.

[61] Arnold L. Horelick, *The Cuban Missile Crisis: An Analysis of Soviet Calculations and Behavior* (RAND Corporation, RM-3779-PR, September 1963), pp. 57–60; Kenneth Ames, "Prospects for Berlin," *New Leader,* November 12, 1962, pp. 8–9. I. F. Stone reported that "during the crisis these fears [in the United States that the Soviets might retaliate by taking action in Berlin] were diminished by the mutual surveillance of each other's troop movements in the Berlin area by the U.S. and Soviet military commands in Germany. Each side had a military mission on the other's territory, and in the Berlin area was even able to use helicopters with the other's consent to make sure that no threatening buildup was occurring." "A Hopeful Crisis Story the Government Withholds," *I. F. Stone's Weekly,* December 10, 1962, p. 1. These missions dated from an American-Soviet-British agreement of October 1944, formalized by a U.S.-Soviet military agreement signed April 5, 1947 (*ibid.,* p. 4).

[62] Unnamed official, quoted in *New York Times,* November 3, 1962.

[63] See, e.g., W. W. Rostow, *View from the Seventh Floor* (New York: Harper and Row, 1964), p. 9.

[64] Horelick, *op. cit.,* p. 58. Secretary McNamara reiterated this view in testimony before the House Armed Services Committee several months after the crisis. U.S., Congress, House Committee on Armed Services, *Hearings on Military Posture,* 88th Cong., 1st Sess., 1963, p. 300.

[65] Albert and Roberta Wohlstetter, *op. cit.,* p. 14.

[66] Bruner, Goodman, and Austin, *op. cit.,* p. 126.

[67] Thus Secretary McNamara, in reflecting upon the crisis, has spoken of the quarantine

tive instruments, these larger notions of means and ends formed a
" 'quick elimination' strategy," [68] which greatly expedited the President's
decision making by permitting him to discard certain courses almost at
once. It need hardly be added that the overriding, almost mystical re-
striction to which the President was subject was the threat of a thermonuclear holocaust.

> . . . the abyss? the abyss?
> "The abyss you can't miss:
> It's right where you are—
> A step down the stair." [69]

Within ten minutes of his notification by Bundy, the President had
made his first important crisis decision: he had appointed his advisers.
Later, recalling the first active phase of the crisis—from October 14 to
21—President Kennedy acknowledged that "fifteen people, more or less,
who were directly consulted," developed "a general concensus" regarding the major decision to invoke a limited blockade.[70] Among those consulted, the most influential appear to have been:

George W. Ball, Undersecretary of State;
McGeorge Bundy, Special Adviser to the President on National Security Affairs;
C. Douglas Dillon, Secretary of the Treasury;
Roswell L. Gilpatric, Deputy Secretary of Defense;
U. Alexis Johnson, Deputy Undersecretary of Defense for Political Affairs;
Robert F. Kennedy, Attorney General;
Edward M. Martin, Assistant Secretary of State for Inter-American Affairs;
John H. McCone, Director of the CIA;
Robert S. McNamara, Secretary of Defense;
Paul Nitze, Assistant Secretary of Defense for National Security Affairs;
Dean Rusk, Secretary of State;

---

as "not just a blockade," but "a line of communication from President Kennedy to Premier
Khrushchev." Quoted in Brock Bower, "McNamara Seen Now, Full Length," *Life,* May
10, 1968, p. 78. In this vein, General Thomas D. White, former Air Force Chief of Staff,
has cited the missile crisis as an instance in which the will to fight constituted a crucial international "communication." U.S., Congress, Senate, Committee on Government Operations, Subcommittee on National Security and International Operations, *Hearings on the
Conduct of National Security Policy,* Part 2, 89th Cong., 1st Sess., June 16, 1965, p. 88. One
adviser of both Presidents Kennedy and Johnson, in fact, has characterized "the whole enterprise" of American military and foreign policy in the Cold War as "an act of persuasion." W. W. Rostow, *The United States in the World Arena: An Essay in Recent History*
(New York: Harper and Bros., 1960), p. 440.
   [68] Bruner, Goodman, and Austin, *op. cit.,* p. 61.
   [69] Theodore Roethke, "The Abyss," *The Collected Poems of Theodore Roethke* (Garden
City: Doubleday, 1963), p. 49.
   [70] "Conversation," p. 2.

Theodore C. Sorensen, Special Counsel to the President;
General Maxwell D. Taylor, Chairman of the Joint Chiefs of Staff.

Others involved in decision making were:

Admiral George W. Anderson, Chief of Naval Operations;
Lieutenant General Joseph F. Carroll, Director of the Defense Intelligence
   Agency;
Lyndon B. Johnson, Vice-President;
Kenneth O'Donnell, Special Assistant to the President;
Adlai E. Stevenson, Ambassador to the UN;
Llewellyn E. Thompson, Ambassador-at-Large and former Ambassador to the
   Soviet Union;
Donald Wilson, Deputy Director of the United States Information Agency.

That informal considerations—that is, considerations of personal confidence rather than of rank or party position—dominated the President's
choice of advisers there can be no doubt. Both in composition and in operation, his staff reflected his own pragmatic concern and aversion to rigidity.
   Among Kennedy's prime organizational objectives, one of his early
advisers has written, was "To keep the White House Staff flexible, gener-
alist, and tied to the President's personal business," [71] and to this aim the
crisis added a special and compelling urgency. Informality revealed itself
in a number of ways in the President's choice of advisers. While including four department heads among his staff, for example, Kennedy
declined to treat the Cabinet as his advisory body. Not all its members
were qualified to give crisis advice, and his faith in the abilities of several
of them was rather limited. In any case, the Cabinet, as its most careful
analyst has shown, "as a collectivity has only symbolic value, a value
which readily disappears when the need for action supersedes the need
for show." [72]
   If the Cabinet were unsuited to advise, what of the Joint Chiefs of
Staff, one of whose functions was to formulate a unified military
strategy? The President, though he selected Taylor and Anderson as advisers, did not choose to utilize the JCS as an organic body. Partially, this
may be traced to the long-standing lack of awe with which he viewed
generals and admirals. [73] This attitude predated his ascendency to the
presidency, and undoubtedly was reinforced by his experience at the Bay

---

[71] Richard Neustadt, quoted in Cater, *op. cit.*, p. 100; Kurt London, *The Making of Foreign Policy East and West* (Philadelphia: J. B. Lippincott Co., 1965), p. 158.
   [72] Richard F. Fenno, Jr., *The President's Cabinet* (Cambridge: Harvard University Press,
1959), p. 247.
   [73] Sorensen, *Kennedy*, p. 18.

of Pigs. Speaking of Kennedy, Schlesinger suggests that among his advisers at this earlier Cuban crisis, "the Joint Chiefs had disappointed him most for their cursory review of the military plans." [74] Later the President spoke of the JCS in more pungent terms. "They advise you the way a man advises another one about whether he should marry a girl. He doesn't have to live with her." [75]

Having eliminated the Cabinet and the Joint Chiefs, there still remained the "most important single agency in the present organization for coordinating the elements of national [security] policy": [76] this was the National Security Council, which had been created "to assess and appraise the objectives, commitments and risks of the United States in relation to our actual and potential military power. . . ." [77] The Council, said a former Executive Secretary, "gives the President a permanent staff agency in his Executive Office which can, as quickly or as deliberately as the occasion warrants, bring to bear on each grave issue of national security all the talents, resources, and considerations which may help him find the best possible solution." [78] Once again, while the President picked several of his advisers from the Council—including its director, Mr. Bundy—he refused to place his reliance in formal institutions. How is this to be explained? First of all, as Bundy himself has emphasized, "The National Security Council is one instrument among many . . . available to the President in dealing with the problems of our national security." Continuing, he pointed out that "many of the great episodes of the Tru-

---

[74] Schlesinger, *op. cit.*, p. 295. Yet plainly the JCS had hardly been as blameworthy as the CIA. This illustrates Kennedy's peculiar bias against the regular military, which, as his support of the Bay of Pigs operation and counterinsurgency in general indicates, did not extend to the use of force as an instrument of foreign policy. The basis for this stance is not clear, but, judging from his concerns in other political areas, it might have partly been stylistic. For the stodgy regular military lacked the coolness, verve, and *au courant* quality of the CIA, civilian defense strategists, or special forces. It is hardly coincidental, in this light, that one of the few regular military leaders the President respected, Maxwell Taylor, had long been anathema to most other senior officers, and had championed the newer emphasis on counterinsurgency techniques. Taylor, in fact, had gone so far as to resign as Eisenhower's Army Chief of Staff as a protest against the administration's preference for strategic air power.

[75] John F. Kennedy, quoted by Cater, *loc. cit.* Robert Kennedy apparently shared his brother's views regarding the military. "[M]any times," the Attorney General recalled acidly, "I had heard the military take positions which, if wrong, had the advantage that no one would be around at the end to know." Robert F. Kennedy, "Thirteen Days," p. 149.

[76] Timothy W. Stanley with Harry Howe Ransom, "The National Security Council: The Interpretation of Political, Military and Economic Factors in National Policy-making," *Organizing for National Security: Selected Materials Prepared for the Committee on Government Operations, United States Senate, and Its Subcommittee on National Policy Machinery* (Washington: Government Printing Office, 1960), p. 73.

[77] The National Security Act of 1947 101 (b) (1), 61 *Stat.* 495, 497 (1947). This was not the only statutory purpose of the NSC.

[78] James S. Lay, Jr., "National Security Council's Role in the U.S. Security and Peace Program," *World Affairs* 115 (Summer 1952): 37.

man and Eisenhower administrations were not dealt with, in their most vital aspects, through the machinery of the NSC." [79] Here Bundy listed the United States' decisions on entering the Korean War, concluding the Korean truce, and determining specific major budgetary issues. Other incidents could be added; and then there are the occasions when strong NSC recommendations have been rejected, such as the Council's advice of intervention in Indo-China in 1954.[80]

The President, in addition, probably shared his brother's opinion that the NSC "has become so large and cumbersome that it is difficult to evolve and develop policy." [81] And among academic writers in general the Council had recently come under frequent attack, most commonly for its committee-like structure and operation.[82]

Yet these objections could hardly account for the President's decision. On this extraordinary occasion, superfluous aides could have been eliminated, and meetings made less formal and cumbersome. Also, once selected, the President's advisers acted very much like a committee, even to the point of being given the title of Executive Committee of the National Security Council. Moreover, all of the NSC's members were presidentially appointed, none—as was the case with the Cabinet—under pressure from political motives.[83] The answer, it would seem, lies deeper than any

---

[79] Letter of McGeorge Bundy to Senator Henry M. Jackson, U.S., Congress, Senate, Committee on Government Operations, Subcommittee on National Security Policy Machinery, *Organizing for National Security,* 87th Cong., 1st Sess., 1961, 1:1336-37.

[80] Ernest R. May, "Eisenhower, and After," *The Ultimate Decision: The President as Commander in Chief,* ed. May (New York: Braziller, 1960), pp. 220–21; Chalmers M. Roberts, "The Day We Didn't Go to War," *Reporter,* September 14, 1954, pp. 31–35. The NSC had had its successes, too, such as its decision in 1948 on the question of whether Trieste should be returned to Italy, a subject made highly urgent by Italian elections a week away. Joseph and Stewart Alsop, "How Our Foreign Policy Is Made," *Saturday Evening Post,* April 30, 1949, pp. 30–31, 113–15.

[81] U.S., Congress, Senate, Committee on Government Operations, Subcommittee on National Security and International Operations, *Hearings on the Conduct of National Security Policy,* Part 2, 89th Cong., 1st Sess, June 16, 1965, p. 94.

[82] See, e.g., Henry A. Kissinger, "The Policymaker and the Intellectual," *Reporter,* March 5, 1959, pp. 30–35; Hans J. Morgenthau, "Can We Entrust Defense to a Committee?" *New York Times Magazine,* June 7, 1959, pp. 62–66. A defense against the common criticisms of the NSC has been offered by a former Special Assistant to the President for National Security Affairs. Gordon Gray, "Role of the National Security Council in the Formulatrion of National Policy," *Organizing for National Security: Selected Materials Prepared for the Committee on Government Operations, United States Senate and Its Subcommittee on National Policy Machinery* (Washington: Government Printing Office, 1960), pp. 62–71 (see esp. pp. 67–71). For a good summary of the criticisms of the strategy-making process—and a criticism of the critics—see Samuel P. Huntington, *The Common Defense: Strategic Programs in National Politics* (New York: Columbia University Press, 1961), pp. 166–74.

[83] That from its inception the NSC had been designed as the President's personal instrument is suggested by Truman's remark to Defense Secretary James Forrestal at the NSC's first meeting. "Now Jimmy," said Truman, "this is going to be *my* Council," Harry S Truman to James V. Forrestal, September 26, 1947, quoted in John Osborn, "Nixon's Command Staff," *New Republic,* February 15, 1969, p. 12.

particular defect of the NSC. Probably, it can be found in those mental "habits" of the President which have already been mentioned—his distrust of formalism and his pervasive concern for pragmatism and flexibility.

A second striking fact about the President's advisers centers on their composition: none was a member of Congress. While one could not expect Congress to serve a meaningful role in a crisis such as this—it would act too slowly and inflexibly and without the necessary knowledge and training—it is surprising that not one member was chosen. President Eisenhower, for example, when deciding whether to intervene militarily on behalf of the French in Indo-China in 1954, seems to have given certain foreign affairs experts in Congress a virtual veto power.[84] Kennedy, of course, was much more interested and knowledgeable in foreign policy than was his predecessor;[85] yet, Kennedy, too, had expressed confidence in the judgment of a number of congressmen, most notably Senator Fulbright, who had demonstrated an impressive capacity for analysis and independence in deliberations prior to the Bay of Pigs invasion. Bringing a few congressmen in on the decision-making process concerning the missiles, in addition, might have been an astute political move, in that it might have reduced congressional pique at having been ignored and, by the participation of the legislators, have helped to commit Congress to the ultimate policy choice. Yet not only were congressional leaders excluded, but the President's special liaison aide to Congress, Lawrence O'Brien, was also passed over. In fact, not a single expert in the area of congressional relations was selected for the committee.

The President's neglect of Congress may have reflected a recognition that, as President Madison's biographer wrote in the context of the War of 1812,

deference to Congress in time of crisis will always appear not as sturdy republicanism, but as weakness. Since the time of Andrew Jackson, at least, the country has expected to follow its Presidents, and those who have not led have been deemed feeble.[86]

Certainly, an image of feebleness—whether from the vantage of the American public or the Soviet leaders—was the last thing President Kennedy wanted to construct.

---

[84] Eisenhower asked congressional leaders for their approval of the intervention, but they insisted that Britain and the other allies give their support. Britain, however, refused. See Roberts, *op. cit.*

[85] Yet clearly Kennedy's infatuation with counterinsurgency shows his foreign policy "instincts" to have been far inferior to Eisenhower's.

[86] Abbot E. Smith, *James Madison, Builder: A New Estimate of a Memorable Career* (New York: Wilson-Erickson, 1937), p. 286.

Also, it may have been that inasmuch as Congress—and internal politics generally—could neither significantly limit him nor aid him, the President, under the pressures of thermonuclear urgency, regarded it almost as a distraction. Moreover, to *include* some congressmen is to *exclude* others; hence, it may have appeared politically less risky, at least at this early stage of policy formation, to bypass this decision by excluding them all.

If questions of omission are difficult to answer, questions of selection seem relatively simple. For each man chosen commanded the personal confidence of the President, and all of the most influential advisers—with the exception of the Attorney General and Sorensen [87]—occupied formal positions of particular relevance to the crisis situation: five members, for example, were from the defense establishment, and three were from the State Department. Of those two chosen without formal qualifications, each possessed the complete confidence of the President; only the Attorney General played an important role in decision making, while Sorensen's duty was to write the President's crucial speech to the nation.

From the outset, "the President drew an absolute security curtain around the meetings." [88] Speaking at a news conference about a month later, he said, "I don't think that there's any doubt that it would have been a great mistake, and possibly a disaster, if this news had dribbled out when we were unsure of the extent of the Soviet build-up in Cuba and when we were unsure of our response and when we had not consulted with any of our allies who might themselves have been involved in great difficulties as a result of our action." [89] So as not to create suspicion, Kennedy insisted on carrying on his routine business throughout the crisis week. As a result of this conspiracy of silence, during the entire crisis period there was not one news leak. [90] "All of us knew," Sorensen recalled, "that, once the Soviets learned of our information and planning, our prospects for surprise and initiative would be greatly lessened." [91] Premature disclosures would have rendered impossible an American *fait accompli* and would have created alarm both at home and abroad that

---

[87] Dillon, as Treasury Secretary, was perhaps a third exception, although he had had considerable foreign affairs experience as Eisenhower's Undersecretary of State.

[88] Oulahan, *op. cit.,* p. 47. So effective were the administration's secrecy procedures that not until the President's Thursday meeting with Soviet foreign minister Gromyko did even Kennedy's personal secretary suspect that something was amiss; she did not learn of the nature of the crisis until Saturday. Evelyn Lincoln, *My Twelve Years with John F. Kennedy* (New York: David McKay, 1965), pp. 323–24.

[89] *New York Times,* November 21, 1962, p. 10. This is not to say, however, the meaningful consultation with the allies did in fact take place.

[90] But cf., John Hohenberg, *Foreign Correspondence: The Great Reporters and Their Times* (New York: Columbia University Press, 1964), p. 423.

[91] Sorensen, *Decision-Making,* p. 31; Hilsman, *op. cit.,* p. 198.

might have further limited the President's future range of choice. From such notification "we knew we could have gained nothing." [92]

Extraordinary steps were taken in order to maximize secrecy. Speaking of the policy makers, Secretary Rusk has recalled meeting "in a variety of places, so that we did not create too much traffic at any one place. Senior officers did their own typing; some of my own basic papers were done in my own handwriting, in order to limit the possibility of further spread of the utterly vital matters we were dealing with." [93] Former Assistant Secretary of State for Latin American Affairs, Edwin M. Martin, has reminisced about the evasive transportation tactics he pursued. On one occasion, he refused to drive to the White House in the limousine with the President's other advisers; for Martin noticed that he "was the only member of the group with an area connection—Latin America. If I had been entering the White House with the others, it would have clearly pointed to Cuba as the subject" all of Washington was beginning to buzz about.[94] All indications are that the participants reveled in the flattering melodrama of secrecy.[95] In addition to its strategic function, then, it seems to have raised adviser morale.

Closely related to the decision on secrecy was the policy to make news, as Assistant Secretary of Defense for Public Affairs Arthur Sylvester said, "part of . . . weaponry." [96] Sylvester, in fact, openly spoke of the government's "inherent . . . right . . . to lie" [97] in such circumstances. "In no

[92] Charles Burton Marshall, "Afterthoughts on the Cuban Blockade, "*New Republic,* November 10, 1962, p. 19.

[93] Dean Rusk, "Changing Patterns in World Affairs," *Department of State Bulletin* 47 (December 17, 1962): 910. (Interview by David Schoenbrun of Rusk on the television program, "CBS Reports: An Hour with the Secretary of State," November 28.)

[94] Edwin M. Martin, "Letter to the Editor: The Missile Crisis," *New York Times Book Review,* March 6, 1966, p. 53.

[95] Robert Kennedy recalled, for example, that on one occasion he and ten other persons piled into his car and drove from the State Department to the White House. Despite the crowding, it apparently occurred to no one that the officials could have had more room and been more comfortable had they dispensed with the chauffeur. That ten top officials seen emerging from a single car like circus clowns from a trick jalopy might itself arouse suspicions also was evidently never considered. This may have been due to a preoccupation with the excitement of the secrecy game. Robert F. Kennedy, "Thirteen Days," p. 148.

[96] *New York Times,* October 31, 1962. This is criticized in a *Times* editorial (*ibid.*), by Cater (*op. cit.,* p. 233), and by a series of Washington reporters. U.S., Congress, House, Committee on Government Operations, *Hearing, Government Information Plans and Policies,* 88th Cong., 1st Sess., 1963. For a discussion of "managed news" and the crisis, see Harry Howe Ransom, *Can American Democracy Survive Cold War?* Anchor Books (Garden City: Doubleday, 1964 [c. 1963]), chaps. 7 and 9. For a reporter's view, see Jack Raymond, *Power at the Pentagon* (New York: Harper and Row, 1964), pp. 322–28.

[97] Arthur Sylvester, quoted by E. W. Kenworthy, *New York Times,* August 31, 1966. This attitude was apparently carried over to the war in Vietnam, where Sylvester said that as a patriotic duty he expected "the American press to be handmaidens of Government." Still more bluntly, Sylvester declared to reporters, "Look, if you think any American official is going to tell you the truth, then you're stupid. Did you hear that—stupid." *Ibid.*

war or crisis," noted one observer, "was military news so controlled and managed at a single source as was the case in the Cuban emergency." [98] The President, of course, justified this control on grounds of national security and the need "to have the Government speak with one voice." [99] All this served to bear out James Reston's observation. "The first casualty of every international crisis," he said, "is truth. As official tension mounts, official accuracy declines and it becomes patriotic to mislead the enemy by evasion, distortion, and outright falsehood." [100]

From the very first meeting, the President rejected the alternative of silently assenting to the Soviet action, feeling that the "U.S. could not accept what the Russians had done." [101] Partly, this decision may be traced to some of his previous decisions with regard to Cuba, in particular, his numerous warnings delivered over the preceding six weeks. As Sorensen has described it:

President Kennedy, on the morning of the first of those seven [crisis] days, sent for copies of all his earlier statements on Cuba—on the presence of offensive, as distinguished from defensive, weapons—on threats to our vital interests—and on our armed intervention in that island. These earlier decisions made it unlikely that he would respond to the October crisis by doing nothing and unlikely that his first step would be an invasion.[102]

The comforting rigidity of consistency seems here to have been identified with strength. It was not simply that an American retreat entailed a national catastrophe. Plainly, this was not the case: accommodation could have been made. Europeans, as British Prime Minister Macmillan later observed, "had grown so accustomed to living under the nuclear gun that they might wonder what all the fuss was about." [103] Americans, too, had for some time been in range of Russian intercontinental ballistic missiles. But a Kennedy retreat may well have entailed a personal catastrophe, and this early emphasis on consistency which Sorensen noted, adds credence to the view that in some sense the crisis represented a rite of passage for the President, his international circumcision.

---

[98] "J & R Memo," *Army Navy Air Force Journal and Register,* November 3, 1962, p. 4.

[99] *New York Times,* November 21, 1962.

[100] *New York Times,* October 26, 1962. Reston himself apparently had been decisive in getting the *Times* to withhold exclusive news about the then pending Bay of Pigs invasion eighteen months earlier. Gay Talese, *The Kingdom and the Power* (Cleveland: World, 1969), p. 5. He also had softened the "news management" criticism of government as a witness at the Government Information hearing cited above. Yet shortly after the Bay of Pigs fiasco, Reston took the opportunity to chasten the press for having "had very little to say about the morality, legality, or practicality of the Cuban adventure, when there was still time to stop it." *New York Times,* May 10, 1961.

[101] Robert F. Kennedy, "Thirteen Days," p. 9.

[102] Sorensen, *Decision-Making,* pp. 34–35.

[103] Macmillan, paraphrased in Schlesinger, *op. cit.,* p. 816.

Kennedy's problem was how to react to the Soviet challenge. The situation seemed to present three general alternatives, of which in retrospect only one had a real chance of acceptance. First, the United States could do nothing. Initially, this seems to have been the position of McNamara[104] and Bundy.[105] McNamara, Hilsman recalls, pointed out that the Soviets already had intercontinental ballistic missiles that could reach the United States and would construct more in the future, regardless of the outcome of the Cuban crisis. The emplacement of medium and intermediate range missiles in Cuba would narrow the Soviets' missile gap, he conceded, but it would be narrowed in a few years anyway. "A missile is a missile," the Secretary argued. "It makes no great difference whether you are killed by a missile fired from the Soviet Union or from Cuba." Since the location of the missiles did not seem vital, no massive Soviet-American confrontation appeared called for. "The clear implication," Hilsman concludes, "was that the United States should do nothing, but simply accept the presence of Soviet missiles in Cuba and sit tight." This argument never won over the President or any of the other advisers, and was quietly dropped after two or three days.

Secondly, the United States could bomb the missile bases or invade Cuba, and, initially, the air strike alternative was favored by most of the participants,[106] especially General Taylor, Secretary Dillon, and Assistant Secretary Nitze,[107] a former Vice Chairman of the U.S. Strategic Bombing Survey during World War II.[108] To these men who viewed the crisis primarily in military terms, a military solution was quite alluring. Simply put, they felt that "we could beat Cuba and so why not fight them, without considering . . . the policies or the other aspects of the situation." [109] However, in addition to involving the greatest risk of general war, this "Pearl Harbor in reverse," as Sorensen later termed it, seemed to con-

---

[104] Hilsman, *op. cit.*, p. 195.

[105] Weintal and Bartlett, *op. cit.*, p. 66. Hilsman says, however, that "no one shared McNamara's view." Hilsman, *op. cit.*, p. 197. Robert Kennedy attributes that view to "a small minority." Robert F. Kennedy, "Thirteen Days," p. 8.

[106] *Loc. cit.*

[107] Abel, *op. cit.*, p. 52. The next day McCone adopted this view (*ibid.*, p. 53), and by Thursday, Acheson and Bundy had joined them (*ibid.*, p. 80).

[108] *The New Frontiersmen: Profiles of the Men Around Kennedy* (Washington: Public Affairs Press, 1961), p. 74. Yet among those favoring a milder response, Ball had served as Director of the U.S. Strategic Bombing Survey in London during World War II (*ibid.*, p. 25), and Stevenson had been a member of an Air Force Survey mission in London in 1944 (*ibid.*, p. 41).

[109] Richard E. Neustadt, U.S., Congress, Senate, Committee on Government Operations, Subcommittee on National Security and International Operations, *Hearings on the Conduct of National Security Policy*, Part 3, 89th Cong., 1st Sess., June 29, 1965, p. 136. Cf., the warning of a distinguished French analyst: ". . . beyond a certain point, violence becomes self-perpetuating. For war, as for fissionable matter, there is a critical volume." Raymond Aron, *Les Guerres en Chaîne*, 5th ed. (Paris: Gallimard, 1951), p. 36.

travene "the nation's basic commitment to tradition and principle." [110] America's "moral position in the world would be tarnished," and the Soviets would have been offered "an excuse for counteraction in Berlin or some other spot." [111] Moreover, it gradually came to be accepted that an air strike would bring in its train a dangerous dilemma: a "surgical" strike might provoke the Soviets to a nuclear exchange. The skepticism with which the metaphor "surgical strike" came to be greeted is illustrated—albeit in exaggerated form—by the remarks of one of Kennedy's diplomatic appointees:

The medical counterpart of a surgical air strike would be an operation by a surgeon with cataracts wearing skiing mittens who, in moving to excise a lung cancer, was fairly likely to make his first incision into the large intestine. [112]

Ultimately, even the Air Force's Tactical Air Command Chief told the President that "there was no way of making certain all the missiles would be removed by an air attack." [113]

The acknowledged unfeasibility was undoubtedly the key consideration in the air strike alternative's demise. And yet, as Allison has

---

[110] Sorensen, *Decision-Making, loc. cit.* Robert Kennedy recalls passing a cryptic note to his brother on this occasion: "I now know how Tojo felt when he was planning Pearl Harbor." Robert Kennedy, *loc. cit.* Dean Acheson was to dispute Robert Kennedy's analogy that an air strike against Cuba resembled the 1941 attack on Pearl Harbor, calling such a comparison "thoroughly false and pejorative. . . . [A]t Pearl Harbor, the Japanese without provocation or warning attacked our fleet thousands of miles from their shores. In the present situation the Soviet Union had installed ninety miles from our coast—while denying that they were doing so—offensive weapons that were capable of lethal injury to the United States. This they were doing a hundred and forty years after the warning given in President Monroe's time . . . . Moreover, within the last few months the Congress, and within the last few weeks the President, had reiterated this warning against the establishment of these very weapons in Cuba. How much warning was necessary to avoid the stigma of 'Pearl Harbor in reverse'?" Dean Acheson, "Dean Acheson's Version of Robert Kennedy's Version of the Cuban Missile Crisis," *Esquire,* February 1969, p. 76. Yet, of course, the United States had not warned Cuba that it would be attacked, and surely the Japanese felt that the destruction of the American Pacific fleet was as necessary to their national security as Acheson felt the destruction of the Soviet missiles was to America's. Further, to most of the world, an American attack on Cuba would *seem* analogous to Pearl Harbor—and, presumably a main reason for wanting to avoid "repeating Pearl Harbor" was the desire to avoid the opprobrium that would have inevitably accompanied it; Acheson's argument was unlikely to persuade many beyond his nation's borders, and perhaps might even leave many of his fellow citizens unconvinced. But the former Secretary of State, a man who had never been very solicitous about "world opinion," seems completely to have discounted the fact that even if an American attack were not truly analogous to the Japanese, for most people it would seem so.

[111] *New York Times,* November 3, 1962. For a sobering view of world opinion, see Hans J. Morgenthau, "Is World Opinion a Myth?" *New York Times Magazine,* March 25, 1962, pp. 23, 126–27.

[112] John Kenneth Galbraith, "Storm Over Havana: Who Were the Real Heroes? Book Review of *Thirteen Days* by Robert F. Kennedy," *Book World,* January 19, 1969, p. 16.

[113] Paraphrased in Sorensen, *Kennedy,* p. 697.

cogently argued, such a view was "false," for it was based on the assumption that "since the Soviet MRBM's [Medium Range Ballistic Missiles] were classified 'mobile' in U.S. manuals, extensive bombing was required." Actually, "the missiles were mobile in the sense that small houses are mobile; that is, they could be moved and reassembled in six days." [114]

A sixth consideration, in addition to nuclear war, morality, world opinion, retaliation in Berlin, and the "strike dilemma," was the President's insistence upon focusing his attention upon Khrushchev, and not permitting it to be deflected toward Castro. The official Cuban policy of the United States, stated a half year later, but in force at the time of the crisis, was expressed by Secretary Rusk:

The objective of the hemisphere and of the United States with respect to Cuba must be—and it is—the return of a free Cuba to this hemisphere. [115]

In accordance with this aim, some of the military urged that the crisis provided the United States with an opportunity to kill two birds with one air strike; that is, to get both Castro and Khrushchev out of Cuba.

But the President saw the official goal as secondary to the immediate problem. "From the very beginning of the crisis," noted one commentator, "the Kennedy Administration drew a sharp line between its attitude toward the Castro regime on the one hand, and Khrushchev's effort to extend the military front lines of the cold war in the Western Hemisphere on the other." [116] The United States could hardly invade Cuba to get at the Soviets without hopelessly diffusing the specificity of its aim. [117] The situation could no longer remain limited, and therefore, possibly manageable. Moreover, adequate preparation for an invasion would take more time than there seemed available; and even if it were successful, America would be faced with the awesome task of occupying a hostile country. Given the awareness of these factors, "no one was in favor of an immediate [full-scale] invasion." [118]

As a third general alternative, the United States could impose a blockade around Cuba. But this course, too, involved profound dangers, and

---

[114] Allison, *op. cit.*, p. 706.

[115] Dean Rusk, "Secretary Rusk Addresses Advertising Council," *Department of State Bulletin* 48 (April 1, 1963): 469. (Speech of March 12.)

[116] Dennis H. Wrong, "After the Cuban Crisis," *Commentary*, January 1963, p. 28.

[117] Portions of the military, however, favored the invasion alternative precisely because it would treat both the Khrushchev and Castro presences simultaneously. Speaking after the crisis, the President called an invasion "a mistake—a wrong use of our power. But," he added, "the military are mad. They wanted to do this. It's lucky for us that we have McNamara over there." John F. Kennedy, quoted in Schlesinger, *op. cit.*, p. 831.

[118] Unnamed participant, quoted in Oulahan, *loc. cit.*

for the first few days it attracted little support. For one thing, as Vice-President Johnson had warned on October 6, "Stopping a Russian ship is an act of war." [119] If Khrushchev were to defy the blockade, which did not seem unlikely, American forces would have to initiate action, possibly provoking Soviet action in Berlin or elsewhere. Psychologically, a blockade failed to offer the allure of a chance of success with a single blow. The embargo might become a drawn-out process, giving the Soviets time to recoup as the United States dissipated its initiative. And a blockade might not get at the missiles already in Cuba, but merely prevent an additional build-up.

Yet it appeared also to present some special advantages, and by Thursday they seemed overriding.[120] First, the blockade was consistent with the United States' policy of containment through deterrence.[121] And, being limited, it could more easily be controlled and would tend less to diffuse the President's intentions. Second, it "was a reversible action, causing no irremedial destruction." [122] The President was concerned, as he said later, to adopt a course which "had the advantage of permitting other steps if this one were unsuccessful. In other words, we were starting, in a sense, at a minimum place. Then, if that were unsuccessful, we could have gradually stepped it up until we had gone into a much more massive action which might have been necessary if the first step had been unsuccessful." [123] In this regard, Sorensen, writing of Kennedy's view on foreign affairs in general, has said, "Above all, he believed in retaining a choice—not a choice between 'Red and dead' or 'holocaust and humiliation,' but a variety of military options in the event of aggression, and opportunity for time and maneuver in the instruments of diplomacy, and a balanced approach to every crisis which combined both defense and diplomacy." [124] And, as one observer noted, "Between the embargo on aggressive weapons and atomic war there lies a wide range of reactions." [125] That the blockade, of all the alternatives, could be formulated and executed with the greatest precision and speed also served to increase the President's freedom of action.

---

[119] Lyndon B. Johnson, quoted in *New York Times*, November 3, 1962.

[120] McNamara, Ball, Gilpatric, Stevenson, and Bundy had opposed direct armed action from the outset. Abel, *op. cit.*, p. 53. On Thursday, these men—with the exception of Bundy—supported the blockade, by this time securing the support of the President's brother. *Ibid.*, p. 79.

[121] George Kateb has argued convincingly that containment became more "a universal and undiscriminating principle of foreign policy" under Kennedy than it had been under Eisenhower. Kateb, *op. cit.*, p. 55.

[122] Myres S. McDougal, "Editorial Comment: The Soviet-Cuban Quarantine and Self-Defense," *American Journal of International Law* 57 (July 1963): 603.

[123] "Conversation," p. 4. Hilsman advances a similar defense. *Op. cit.*, p. 205.

[124] Sorensen, *Kennedy*, p. 511.

[125] Nathan Glazer, "Letters from Readers," *Commentary*, May 1963, p. 443.

But, in "permitting other steps," the embargo had an advantage in addition to affording the decision makers greater room to maneuver. "in direct conflict situations," as Anthony Downs has pointed out, "you can improve your chances of winning by developing multiple capabilities even if you actually employ only one of them, since the threat of the others will force your opponent to prepare multiple lines of defense." [126]

Third, among all meaningful American reactions, the blockade seemed to hold the least chance of escalating into a thermonuclear war. One reason for this was that the action was to occur within the sphere of a third party, Cuba, thereby minimizing the actual contact of the antagonists. As Morton Halperin has explained, "As long as the United States and the Soviet Union confine a war to the territories of other countries, they cannot expect or demand the unconditional surrender of the other major power." [127] Other reasons were that a blockade would not hit Moscow with the same psychological shock as would an air strike, and that it offered Khrushchev time to withdraw and the opportunity to leave with less than a maximum loss of face.[128] In Sorensen's words:

The air strike or an invasion automatically meant a military attack upon a communist power and required almost certainly either a military response by the Soviet Union or an even more humiliating surrender.... The blockade, on the other hand, had the advantage of giving Mr. Khrushchev a choice, an option, so to speak, he did not have to have his ships approach the blockade and be stopped and searched. He could turn them around. So that was the first obvious advantage it had. It left a way open to Mr. Khrushchev. In this age of nuclear weapons that is very important.[129]

Additional reasons militating against a general war were that the blockade made full use of America's superiority in conventional forces

---

[126] Anthony Downs, *The Value of Unchosen Alternatives* (RAND Corporation, P-3017, November 1964), p. 8.

[127] Morton H. Halperin, *Limited War in the Nuclear Age* (New York: Wiley, 1963), p. 9.

[128] That Khrushchev was unconcerned with losing face—and in fact "probably regarded the conspicuous acceptance of humiliation as a virtue, since it proved he was a good Communist in the Leninist sense"—has been advanced unconvincingly by Bernard Brodie, *Morals and Strategy* (RAND Corporation, P-2915, June 1964), pp. 11–12. A less extreme version of this thesis—that "the prospect of humiliation ... did not have quite the same importance for Khrushchev"—has been put forth by Albert and Roberta Wohlstetter, *op. cit.*, p. 22. But cf., Nathan Leites, *The Kremlin Horizon* (RAND Corporation, RM-3506-ISA), who demonstrates that Khrushchev saw himself as "the citizen of a nation that ... has been despised and even despises itself. Khrushchev and other Bolshevik leaders just cannot forget this past contempt, nor do they perhaps feel, deep down, that it is entirely past: very little provocation is needed to arouse a sharp sense of being treated as inferior" (p. 24). Plainly, this second view coincided more with the President's perceptions, and constituted an assumption from which he acted.

[129] "Cuba: The Missile Crisis," NBC telecast, February 9, 1964, p. 22. (Mimeographed.) Hereinafter cited as "Cuba."

and its geographical position, and that its aim was plainly limited. "As each side recognizes the relatively limited objectives of the other," Halperin pointed out, "the danger of *explosion* into central war will be substantially reduced. However," he added, "even minor objectives may produce pressures to *expand* the war if one or both sides find that their limited objectives cannot be obtained at the level at which the battle is being fought";[130] hence, that the President could control the blockade more than he could other courses of action became an advantage difficult to overturn. Fourth, the blockade would adequately transmit the President's political message of America's firmness and resolve.

Virtually neglected as an alternative was any kind of significant non-unilateral action, e.g., calling for the aid of an international or a regional organization or of one or more of the United States' military allies. The United Nations' role in the crisis, for instance, was restricted to supplying a platform for propaganda. A year earlier, however, the President had declared to the General Assembly that "in the development of this Organization rests the only true alternative to war—and war appeals no longer as a rational alternative."[131] How can these words and the later decision of omission be reconciled? Hypocrisy is the obvious answer—hypocrisy, which in Mencken's words, "runs, like a hair in a hot dog, through the otherwise beautiful fabric of American life."[132] A more accurate summation of the President's views than his General Assembly speech was forthcoming a few weeks before the crisis. "For the next ten or twenty years," he said, "the burden will be placed completely upon our country for the preservation of freedom."[133]

The United States' determination to act "On our own if necessary"[134] stemmed from a number of factors. One of these was geography, which rendered the European allies' "immediate power at the point of contest . . . negligible."[135] While interallied consultation may be of great value if it "affirms the . . . equality and solidarity among allies," where one of these elements is absent—in this case, equality—"too great a concern with consultation may impede the military efficacy of the alliance and the political influence of individual members with outside pow-

[130] Halperin, *loc. cit.* (Emphasis in original.)

[131] John F. Kennedy, "Let Us Call a Truce to Terror," *Department of State Bulletin* 45 (October 16, 1961): 619. (Address of September 25.)

[132] H. L. Mencken, "Editorial," *American Mercury*, November 1926, p. 287.

[133] John F. Kennedy, quoted in the *New York Times*, August 29, 1962. Kennedy's treatment of the organization did not deter an admirer from concluding that "the manner in which he handled the Cuban Missile Crisis in 1962 . . . strengthened rather than weakened the United Nations." James P. Warburg, *The United States in the Postwar World* (New York: Atheneum, 1966), p. 227.

[134] John F. Kennedy, quoted in the *New York Times*, November 21, 1962; Harlan Cleveland, "Crisis Diplomacy," *Foreign Affairs* 41 (July 1963): 642.

[135] McGeorge Bundy, "The President and the Peace," *Foreign Affairs* 42 (April 1964): 36.

ers." [136] And where power was minimal, interest was also very small. Beyond a fondness for charging Americans with being "obsessed by Cuba" and advising them to "shrug off Cubanism," [137] Europeans had had little to say about Cuban–American relations. In fact, the Western European allies generally showed small concern for affairs outside their own continent, and were not viewed by Washington as partners in a world-wide operation. The President "understood quite clearly that NATO was an alliance by which the U.S.A. defended Europe—not an alliance by which Europe could be called upon to assist in the defense of the U.S.A." [138]

Geography also meant that the "United States, besides being custodian of a nuclear shield integral to the security of" Europe and the Western Hemisphere, was "the sole nation involved in both relevant security structures—the North Atlantic Treaty Organization and the Organization of American States. Its Government alone . . . had appreciation of the interaction between Cuba and, say, the Berlin situation." [139] In addition, also making for unilateralism was the insistence of McNamara, Acheson, and others upon the indispensability of "unity of planning and unity of command." [140] But beyond all these reasons stood a command too compelling to deny: for the President to forego claims of national sovereignty during a time of extreme crisis was immediately recognized as too quixotic to bear consideration. That, at such a moment, the United States would not be exercising maximum control over its own destiny was unthinkable. Doubtless, this conviction contributed to reducing the role of the Organization of American States [141] and of America's allies to the humbling ritual of ratification.[142] As one writer has noted, among all postwar attempts to influence American policy, "Allied pressure was

---

[136] George Liska, *Nations in Alliance: The Limits of Interpendence* (Baltimore: Johns Hopkins Press, 1962), p. 69. Harlan Cleveland, Assistant Secretary of State during the missile crisis, has argued, however, that interallied consultation "improves the quality of our decisions" by forcing the government "to think harder about what it is doing and why it is doing it . . . [I]t is comparatively easy for any government to kid itself; it is always much harder to kid foreigners." *Des Moines Register,* September 30, 1970.
[137] "Obsessed by Cuba," *Economist* 205 (October 6, 1962): 15–16; "Shrugging Off Cubanism," *ibid.,* pp. 16–17.
[138] Oscar Gass, "The World Politics of Responsibility," *Commentary,* December 1965, p. 87.
[139] Charles Burton Marshall, "Afterthoughts on the Cuban Blockade," *New Republic,* November 10, 1962, p. 20.
[140] Robert McNamara, cited with approval in Dean Acheson, "The Practice of Partnership," *Foreign Affairs,* 41 (January 1963): 258.
[141] The OAS could hardly have been involved in any meaningful sense—that is, its peacekeeping machinery could not have been used—inasmuch as neither Cuba nor the Soviet Union was a member.
[142] On the crisis relationship between the United States and its European allies, see H. A. DeWeerd, *British Attitudes in the Cuban Crisis* (RAND Corporation, P-2709, February 1963); "The Week of Cuba," *Encounter,* January 1963, pp. 84–95; Genêt, "Letter from Paris," *New Yorker,* November 17, 1962, pp. 170–72; Mollie Painter-Downes, "Letter from London," *ibid.,* pp. 223–25.

least important in the 1962 Cuban crisis when the United States was preparing to act alone." [143]

Another factor ruling out consultation is what Halperin has called the
"political-effects objective." [144] One of the President's main objectives was
to transmit to the Soviets the message that

> this latest Soviet threat—or any other threat which is made either independently
> or in response to our actions this week—must and will be met with determina-
> tion. Any hostile move anywhere in the world against the safety and freedom of
> peoples to whom we are committed—including, in particular, the brave people
> of West Berlin—will be met by whatever action is needed. [145]

Partially, in the words of one critic, this was "a test of nerve." [146] Hence,
any division of responsibility would have had to have been rejected as
self-defeating.

Yet because the United States would have acted alone is not to say
that it preferred the absence of support. Such a "narrow judgment," as
Bundy said afterwards, "neglects two great hazards. Immediately, a
serious division among the allies might have provoked action elsewhere,
most dangerously at Berlin"; and even if this were not to occur, America's leadership after the crisis in "the quest for peace" might be seriously
impaired. [147]

---

[143] Halperin, *op. cit.*, p. 8. While an American observer could declare triumphantly that
"The Cuban confrontation demonstrates . . . that the command of nuclear power is indivis-
ible" (Walter Lippmann, "Cuba and the Nuclear Risk," *Atlantic,* February 1963, p. 58),
Europeans tended to view the United States' actions from a different angle. Our allies,
wrote one social scientist, were reminded that "they stand to be exterminated without rep-
resentation, to be destroyed because of a war in a far and foreign territory." Amitai Etzioni,
Winning Without War, Anchor Books (Garden City: Doubleday, 1965), p. 46. "To the
French," as Brzezinski and Huntington have written, "the American response . . . was another proof that the alliance [NATO] meant the subordination of French interests. . . . To
them [the French] Cuba demonstrated that the United States had the capacity to defend *its*
own national interest, and that the United States was prepared to act unilaterally when necessary. Thus, while the episode served to reassure the French about the character of American leadership, it did not quite convince them that it was in the interest of France to accept
it." Zbigniew Brzezinski and Samuel P. Huntington, *Political Power: USA/USSR* (New
York: Viking Press, 1964), pp. 389, 396–97.
[144] Halperin, *op. cit.*, pp. 4–7.
[145] John F. Kennedy, "The Soviet Threat to the Americas," *Department of State Bulletin*
47 (November 12, 1962): 718. (Telecast of October 22.) Thus, Kissinger, for example, in as-
sessing Kennedy's action in Cuba, concluded that "it achieved far more than the immediate goal of dismantling Soviet missile bases in Cuba. It exploded the myth that in every situation the Russians were prepared to run greater risks than we. This myth had been the
basis of Soviet atomic blackmail and had transformed too many conferences into opportunities for the Soviets to set the terms of negotiations." Henry A. Kissinger, "Reflections on
Cuba," *Reporter,* November 22, 1962, p. 21. Kissinger thus appears to be suggesting that
the President's assumption of risk—for much of humanity as well as for himself—could be
justified in terms of considerations of oneupsmanship at international conferences.
[146] "Time for Plain Words," *I. F. Stone's Weekly,* October 29, 1962, p. 3.
[147] Bundy, *loc. cit.*

At the first meeting of the President's advisers no basic decision was taken regarding the United States' immediate course of action. It is perhaps not too much to call this turn away from haste an implicit decision in itself, in which the main elements were caution, preparation, and secrecy. Action was delayed pending receipt of further information, and to this end air surveillance of Cuba was intensified. This determination to wait should not be viewed as a temporary failure of nerve, for it was felt from the start that final action would have to follow as closely as possible the disclosure of the Russian installations—and this could not be put off for long. The importance of the President's refusal to be rushed or panicked should not be understated. Recalling the period, President Kennedy commented, "If we had had to act . . . in the first twenty-four hours, I don't think probably we would have chosen as prudently as we finally did. . . ." [148]

By the end of the meeting, some of the imposing problems of staff work were already evident. The Pentagon was charged with producing comprehensive estimates relating to each aspect of the several military alternatives. The State Department began examining Latin American and European allies, with an eye toward obtaining their support in the coming confrontation. That afternoon, Russian experts were consulted, in particular, Ambassador-at-Large Llewellyn E. Thompson and Ambassador to France Charles E. Bohlen, both former ambassadors to Moscow.

Ambassador Stevenson was also brought into the discussions. While favoring the blockade over the air strike, Stevenson in addition suggested a further exploration of the relevance of diplomatic instruments. Specifically, he mentioned the neutralization of Cuba, following America's departure from Guantanamo and the Soviets' withdrawal of missiles, and offering to bring home the United States' missiles from Turkey and Italy in exchange for Russia's removing its missiles from Cuba. The American missiles in Turkey and Italy, in Hilsman's words, were "obsolete, unreliable, inaccurate, and very vulnerable—they could be knocked out by a sniper with a rifle and telescopic sights." In fact, in August the President had ordered them withdrawn, and only the tardiness of the State and Defense Departments explained the presence of the missiles two months later.[149] Substantively, a smaller concession could hardly have been proposed. Yet the President was "surprised and displeased" [150] by the idea, and quickly rejected it. Why? Because although cheap, the concession might have increased Soviet prestige at American expense. "If the Soviets wanted to talk about the removal of American missiles in Europe," the official rationale was to be, "the United States would be

---

[148] "Conversation," pp. 2–3.
[149] Hilsman, *op. cit.*, pp. 202–3.
[150] Weintal and Bartlett, *op. cit.*, p. 66.

glad to do so—but only in the context of a disarmament agreement applying to both Eastern and Western Europe." [151] The President was confident he was holding the winning hand.

The following day, Wednesday, October 17, the President campaigned in Connecticut, fulfilling an earlier pledge that he could not avoid without arousing suspicions. In the words of an aide, "It would have been impossible to cancel without blowing the whole thing." [152] Kennedy did not return to Washington until nearly midnight. In his absence, top-level policy meetings continued, though with few traces of the formalities that had characterized the previous day's conferences. Again, invasion was dismissed as impractical. The air strike and blockade emerged as the two leading alternatives. Meanwhile, new aerial photographs—from which it was estimated that intermediate-range missile sites would be operational by December 1—heightened the sense of urgency. In the morning, Secretary Rusk had called in former Secretary of State Dean Acheson, a prestigious devotee of *Realpolitik* [153] and a powerful advocate of the centrality of the Atlantic Alliance in American policy.[154] Acheson, known as having "had a paramount influence over the President's long-range strategic views," [155] attended most of the day's meetings, arguing "strongly in favor of an air attack." [156] He expressed his belief that the missiles had increased American vulnerability by giving Soviet "short-range missiles the same bearing as intercontinental missiles," and that a passive United States reaction would cost the nation hemisphere and Western European confidence in its leadership.[157]

By Thursday, substantial American military deployments had begun, though the Defense Department took pains to emphasize the "normality" of the buildups. An increase in air power in the Southeastern states was explained as a normal reaction to the possession by Cuba of jet fighters. A long-scheduled Navy-Marine exercise in the Caribbean provided an excuse to transfer five thousand Marines and forty ships to the area. Consistent with this stress on secrecy, the President's day combined the ordinary mixture of the serious and the ceremonial.

Though the President managed to meet with his Cuban advisers twice

---

[151] Hilsman, *op. cit.,* p. 203. There seemed not the slightest chance, of course, that such an agreement would be concluded in the near future.

[152] Unnamed aide, quoted in Oulahan, *op. cit.,* p. 47.

[153] Oscar William Perlmetter, "The 'Neo-Realism' of Dean Acheson," *Review of Politics* 26 (January 1964): 100–23.

[154] See Dean Acheson, *Power and Diplomacy* (Cambridge: Harvard University Press, 1958), pp. 92–95.

[155] Sidney Hyman, "The Testing of Kennedy," *New Republic,* October 2, 1961, p. 12.

[156] Robert F. Kennedy, *Thirteen Days: A Memoir of the Cuban Missile Crisis* (New York: Norton, 1969), p. 9. Hereinafter cited as *Thirteen Days.*

[157] Dean Acheson, "Dean Acheson's Version of Robert Kennedy's Version of the Cuban Missile Crisis," *Esquire,* February 1969, p. 76.

that day, their meetings were for the most part among themselves. Secrecy was not the sole rationale for Kennedy's absence. Equally important was his conviction that the advisers would be most effective if given the most freedom; and, of course, he realized that they would most readily speak their minds when he was away.[158] For this reason, McNamara and Rusk also occasionally passed up meetings. Yet when he was present, the President emphasized discipline. "He held everything under tight control," one official said. "He issued orders like a military officer expecting to be obeyed immediately and to be challenged only on grounds of overriding disagreement." [159] In the afternoon the advisers' earlier preference for a blockade became more pronounced.

At five o'clock, the President, along with Secretary Rusk and Ambassador Thompson, met with the Soviet Foreign Secretary, Andrei A. Gromyko. The meeting, which had been set before the crisis, lasted over two hours, and has become one of the better-known episodes associated with that period. Insofar as the discussion touched on Cuba, it provided a further opportunity for the antagonists to restate their respective official positions: Gromyko assured the President that the Cuban buildup had "solely the purpose of contributing to the defense capabilities of Cuba," [160] while Kennedy reiterated his warning that, were he to learn differently, "we would take action. . . ." [161] The bulk of the talk, however, dealt with Berlin, on which issue Gromyko assumed a hardening stance. This served to underscore the President's view that Berlin loomed large in the entire crisis affair.

Why had the President sought to convey a false impression to Gromyko? This decision—while surely secondary, viewing the crisis as a whole—has aroused a fair amount of controversy. Some critics have argued that Gromyko should have been informed of American knowledge and intentions on the ground that this would have permitted the Soviet Union to retreat earlier and in a less tension-charged atmosphere.[162] The President, however, was guided by other considerations. First, as he subsequently explained, "our information was incomplete and we had not completely determined what our policy would be." Second, he wanted to "hold the initiative. . . ." [163] In addition, he was doubtless aware that the Soviet reaction might not have been retreat but, instead, the taking of

[158] Sorensen, *Decision-Making,* p. 60.

[159] Unnamed official, quoted in *New York Times,* November 3, 1962.

[160] Andrei A. Gromyko, quoted in Schlesinger, *op. cit.,* p. 805.

[161] "Conversation," p. 25. Hilsman argues that Moscow concluded from this meeting that the President had learned of the missiles, but would take no action, at least until the elections were over. *Op. cit.,* pp. 167, 199.

[162] See, e.g., Walter Lippmann, "Blockade Proclaimed," *New York Herald Tribune,* October 25, 1962.

[163] "Conversation," p. 26.

steps that would make the American response more difficult to frame and more dangerous to execute.

That evening the President met with his leading advisers. Secretary McNamara, who was known to favor conventional weapons and "the graduated application of military power," [164] related his plan for a pacific blockade—or quarantine—of Cuba, an alternative to which Kennedy had already been favorably disposed. This decision was crystallizing.

Following the meeting, the Attorney General instructed his deputy, Nicholas de B. Katzenbach, to study the legal ramifications of a blockade of Cuba. The relevance of law to a solution of the crisis had been stressed earlier that day by Ambassador Thompson. He had argued that "the Russians had a feeling for 'legality' and there was general agreement that a good legal case would help with world reaction." [165] Among those deemphasizing the role of law, former Secretary of State Acheson took the lead.[166] His position was that "the propriety of the Cuban quarantine is not a legal issue. . . . Survival is not a matter of law." [167] The President recognized that any basic contradictions between the two views were more apparent than real, and concluded that law had an important, albeit not decisive, part to play. "We were armed, necessarily, with something more substantial than a lawyer's brief," the State Department's legal adviser wrote later. "But though it would not have been enough merely to have the law on our side, it is not irrelevant which side the law is on." [168] While Katzenbach, himself a former professor of international law, was beginning his research at the Justice Department, at the State Department Leonard C. Meeker, the Department's Deputy Legal Ad-

---

[164] William W. Kaufmann, *The McNamara Strategy* (New York: Harper and Row, 1964), p. 294.

[165] *New York Times,* November 3, 1962; Sorensen, *Kennedy,* p. 706. A year and a half earlier, however, a social psychiatrist had advised the President: "Least of all does [Khrushchev] understand the principle of the rule of law, especially international law, in the constitutional sense. This applies especially to the obligations of nations; according to his doctrine, historical inevitability supersedes national commitments, and he has no concept of honor in regard to agreements that are only as good as their guarantees. There is no point whatsoever in operating from these assumptions in dealing with him, nor can he be educated to respect them." Bryant Wedge, "Khrushchev at a Distance—A Study of Public Personality," *Trans-action,* October 1968, p. 27. On the other hand, Tucker has argued that "in American doctrine, the just war is also the lawful war, the *bellum justum* is equated with the *bellum legale.*" Robert W. Tucker, *The Just War: A Study in Contemporary American Doctrine* (Baltimore: Johns Hopkins Press, 1960), p. 11, n. 1. This may suggest that the decision makers' concern for legality may have derived more from a desire to maximize domestic support and their own belief in the rightness of their actions than to appeal to Soviet sensibilities.

[166] Abel, *op. cit.,* p. 88.

[167] Dean Acheson, "Remarks," *American Society for International Law Proceedings* 57 (April 25, 1963): 14.

[168] Abram J. Chayes, "Law and the Quarantine of Cuba," *Foreign Affairs* 41 (April 1963): 550.

viser, was exploring the same problem. The task devolved to Meeker due to the absence of the Department's Legal Adviser, Abram J. Chayes, who was then in Paris on a mission to halt allied shipping to Cuba.

On Friday for the second time in the crisis week, the President spent the day fulfilling earlier promises of political campaigning. Again, the compelling reason for honoring these pledges was the maintenance of secrecy. Before leaving for the Midwest, he had expressed increasing interest in the blockade alternative, and later that morning Katzenbach and Meeker presented their views on its legality before a meeting of the planners. Each agreed that were the blockade to be based upon an OAS resolution, its legality would be assured; even a unilaterally imposed blockade could be legally justified, said Katzenbach, though in this conclusion Meeker was less sure. However, the reading of a "scenario" for the blockade prompted a reconsideration of an air attack. One decision that did come out of the morning meetings was that the President's disclosure of American intentions should be made on Monday night. This appeared to be the latest time by which the preparatory steps needed to effectuate these intentions could be taken.

In the afternoon, the advisers' recommendation of the blockade was finalized. Renewed interest had been shown in an air attack until Attorney General Kennedy reiterated the earlier objections on grounds of immorality and world opinion. "For the United States to attack a smaller country without warning," he declared, "would irreparably hurt our reputation in the world—and our conscience." [169] A more practical disadvantage of an unexpected air strike, as Llewellyn Thompson had told the President, was that "Khrushchev's reactions were apt to be particularly bad when faced with an ugly surprise." Thompson thus favored measures permitting Khrushchev time to regain his composure and view the situation realistically.[170] Yet a nonsurprise air strike was unthinkable, for the warning itself would make the United States "vulnerable to either endless discussion and delay (while work on the missiles went forward) or to a harsh indictment in the opinion and history of the world." [171] The quarantine, on the other hand, *was* a warning, in that it plainly marked the beginning of a military escalation, should it not be heeded; but the quarantine's warning seemed to contain fewer and smaller risks. With all the talk of national image, however, it almost seemed as if reflections were assuming the gloss of substance.

[169] Quoted in Hilsman, *op. cit.,* p. 203. There is no evidence of similar objections having been raised prior to the Bay of Pigs invasion eighteen months earlier. Perhaps, therefore, the Attorney General was bothered less by an American surprise attack on a small country than by the presence of its very large ally. Certainly, no one could have taken a United States' air strike on the missiles to be solely or even primarily an attack on Cuba.
[170] Thompson, paraphrased in Weintal and Bartlett, *op. cit.,* p. 67.
[171] Sorensen, *Decision-Making,* p. 35.

Though the advisers' choice seemed set, it was decided that staff work should thoroughly explore the other alternatives, so as not to limit unnecessarily the President's range of decision. Bundy, especially, was concerned that the President's choice of alternatives be as broad as possible.

With the announcement set for Monday night, time was running short. Saturday morning the President cancelled the rest of his political tour, claiming that a cold necessitated his return. Whether he in fact had a slight cold or not is a question that must be left to the ages,[172] but there is no doubt that the story served its purpose in permitting the President to resume his active role in policy making while arousing a minimum of suspicion. Yet even this "minimum" was becoming significant. Washington reporters began to sense the tension. One asked press secretary Pierre Salinger point blank if there were an emergency, which, of course, Salinger denied. Sizable troop movements were noticed in Florida. Vice-President Johnson returned from an Hawaiian campaign tour, also pleading a "cold." Former President Eisenhower was flown to Washington for a CIA briefing. "It would have been a dull reporter, indeed," recalled one journalist, "who could not see that there was extraordinary activity in the White House, Defense Department, and State Department."[173]

After a briefing by Bundy and a reading of Sorensen's first draft of his Monday speech, the President all but ratified his advisers' recommendation: he ordered blockade preparations to proceed, subject only to his final decision the following day. This, of course, was hardly unexpected; by October 18, the blockade had loomed first among the alternatives, both with the President and with the majority of his advisers. Yet, as we have seen, it would be quite untrue to suggest that the problem of how to react to the emplacement of Soviet missiles had been approached by so many closed minds. Decision making, instead, was a vital, almost living process. It was characterized first of all by a stress on the necessity of acting on adequate information. Probably, this can in part be traced back to the Bay of Pigs invasion attempt, an action based on grossly inadequate knowledge. Kennedy was deeply affected by his failure here, and a crisis a year and a half later and on the same stage must have served to underline all the lessons he had learned. His resistance to action, despite partisan pressure, until incontrovertible evidence of the missile sites was available, has already been noted.[174] And upon hearing the first in-

---

[172] Sorensen (*Kennedy*, p. 693) and Oulahan think that the President actually had a cold (*op. cit.*, p. 48), while the *New York Times* concludes that "the story was false." *New York Times*, November 3, 1962. The President's press secretary, Pierre Salinger, takes the middle ground, maintaining that the President had a cold but not a bad one. Pierre Salinger, *With Kennedy* (Garden City: Doubleday, 1966), pp. 251–52.

[173] John Hohenberg, *Foreign Correspondence: The Great Reporters and Their Times* (New York: Columbia University Press, 1964), p. 423.

[174] McGeorge Bundy recalled that, upon receiving the first news of the photographic evi-

telligence reports, for example, his earliest directive was for more photo-graphs.[175] As late as Friday, other courses were being considered.

This concentration on knowledge led to the setting up of candor as a subsidiary goal. Thus, while deliberations were going on, open discussion of alternatives was encouraged to the extent that everyone "spoke as equals," [176] and the President, Rusk, and McNamara occasionally absented themselves from debate in the interest of frankness. One factor making this possible was Kennedy's faith in his advisers. As Sorensen recalled, "The more he got into government the more he felt confident in using its machinery and relying on the men around him and determining which men he could rely on less. Each new idea could be tested. It wasn't enough that it came from one quarter. The opposing viewpoint within the Administration had to be heard . . . he treated us almost as associates rather than subordinates." [177] Other impulses toward candor were the "unprecedented nature of the Soviet move, the manner in which it cut across so many departmental jurisdictions, the limited amount of information available, and the security restrictions which inhibited staff work"—all of which "tended to have a levelling effect on the principals taking part in these discussions, so that each felt free to challenge the assumptions and assertions of all others." [178] Candor, in addition, had the advantage of fostering cohesion within the group. As an eminent English authority on communications has explained:

When "members" . . . are in communication with one another, they are associating, co-operating, forming an "organization," or sometimes an "organism." Communication is a social function. . . . By the possession of this structure the whole organization may be better adapted or better fitted for some goal-seeking activity.[179]

The President, recalling this frankness later, concluded that "though at the beginning there was a much sharper division . . . this was very valuable, because the people involved had particular responsibilities of their

dence, the President's "first reaction was that we must make sure, and were we making sure? And would there be evidence on which he could decide that this in fact really was the case?" "Cuba," p. 14.

[175] Sorensen, *Kennedy,* p. 675.
[176] Robert F. Kennedy, "Thirteen Days," p. 149.
[177] Theodore C. Sorensen, quoted, in Roberts, *op. cit.,* p. 168.
[178] Sorensen, *Decision-Making,* p. 59, and *Kennedy,* p. 679. Acheson concedes that "members of the group did all speak as equals," but adds that "in any sense of constitutional and legal responsibility they were not equal and should have been under the direction of the Head of Government or his chief Secretary of State for Foreign Affairs and his military advisers." Dean Acheson, "Dean Acheson's Version of Robert Kennedy's Version of the Cuban Missile Crisis, *Esquire,* February 1969, p. 46.
[179] Cherry, *op. cit.,* p. 6.

own. . . ." [180] In planning for the Bay of Pigs invasion, his advisers had spoken virtually with one voice; plainly, failure was too high a price for unanimity, especially when error might mean catastrophe. Hence, the requisite hammering out of differences demanded that free discussion itself be pursued as an instrumental goal. Thus, despite the pressure of time and the temptations to resolve issues simply by asserting authority,[181] the President's eventual decision on the missiles followed a process of relatively open debate. As one participant subsequently put it, "This was not a solomonic decision by the President. He was not choosing between sharply conflicting views. He was approving a view that his advisers had reached after exhaustive exploration of every possibility. The process was not a series of conflicts but an exchange of ideas developing a rolling consensus." [182]

As group interaction increases, social cohesion increases and the relevance of the task to the members grows. The importance of the issue, the group's homogeneity in social composition and personal status, the stability of membership which heightened morale, and the pressing time factor all appear to have served to heighten the members' allegiance to the group. In such cases, the group can constitute a potent force in setting behavior norms for those members firmly attached to it. Individuals who might earlier have disagreed, now feel increasing psychological cross-pressures. Typically, such conflicts are resolved in the direction of the strongest group tie,[183] and by the end of the week, it would be difficult to conceive of a group with greater influence upon its members than the President's advisers. With each new convert to the majority view, of

---

[180] "Conversation," p. 4.

[181] These temptations to make decision making the pulling of rank should not be discounted. "If I had only for five minutes the power to say: Thus it shall be, and not otherwise!" Bismarck sighed, as he struggled with Moltke, the General Staff, and the King during the siege of Paris. "That one need not have to bother with the Why and Wherefore, need not have to demonstrate and beg for the simplest things!" Otto Van Bismarck, quoted in Arnold Osker Mayer, *Bismarck, der Mensch und der Staatsmann* (Leipzig, 1944), p. 436, quoted in Vagts, *op. cit.,* p. 462. While Kennedy, unlike Bismarck, did not have to compete with others to have his basic decisions accepted, he may at times have shared the German's feeling of frustration and exasperation; that, despite ample opportunity, he refused to act from these sentiments, undoubtedly contributed to the success of his moves.

[182] Unnamed participant, quoted in *New York Times,* November 3, 1962.

[183] For background information, see George C. Homans, *The Human Group* (New York: Harcourt, Brace and World, 1950), pp. 119, 120, 133; Harold D. Lasswell and Abraham Kaplan, *Power and Society: A Framework for Political Inquiry* (New Haven: Yale University Press, 1950), p. 35; Leon Festinger, Stanley Schachter, and Kurt Back, *Social Pressures in Informal Groups* (New York: Harper and Row, 1950), p. 91; Harold H. Kelley and John W. Thibaut, "Experimental Studies in Group Problem Solving and Process," *Handbook of Social Psychology,* ed. Gardner Lindzey, 2 vols. (Cambridge: Addison-Wesley, 1954), 2:764; Ronald Freedman, Amos H. Hawley, Werner S. Landecker, Gerhard E. Lenski, and Horace M. Miner, *Principles of Sociology,* 2d ed. rev. (New York: Harcourt, Brace, & World, 1956), p. 178.

course, the pressure for unanimity grew; for "once some threshold degree of consensus is reached, there will be a snowballing of support as with increasing consensus the less and less confident members become convinced that the group will be able to mobilize sufficient power." [184] The behavior of the Executive Committee, then, tends to confirm Terence Hopkins' hypothesis regarding the exercise of influence in small groups.

On the one hand, interactions among participants are guided or regulated by the shared norms and, on the other, it is through the interaction sequences that normative consensus is maintained. [185]

But such pressure is not the only explanation for the phenomenon of the "rolling consensus." Deviate opinions often result from a member's vagueness as to the goal pursued [186] or simply from inadequate information. In highly cohesive groups, however, communication is likely to focus on dissenters,[187] and in this way, may "educate" them to the majority view. In either case, it is interesting to note that the Committee's consensus developed without formal coercion or even the threat of overt sanctions.

Another characteristic—substantive rather than procedural—of the decision-making process was a constant and acute awareness of the position of the adversary. In contrasting this with "some of the key decision-makers in the 1914 crisis," it has been said that "those in October 1962 thought in terms of linked interactions—closely tied reciprocations—rather than two sides, each acting independently, *in vacuo*." [188] Commenting on Kennedy's actions, Richard Neustadt has remarked, "For almost the first time in our foreign relations, the President displayed on that occasion both concern for the psychology of his opponent and insistence on a limited objective." [189] Thus, Sorensen, in describing the advisers' meetings, used these terms:

---

[184] John W. Thibaut and Harold H. Kelley, *The Social Psychology of Groups* (New York: Wiley, 1959), p. 261.

[185] Terence K. Hopkins, *The Exercise of Influence in Small Groups* (Totowa, N.J.: Bedminster Press, 1964), p. 22.

[186] Bertram H. Raven and Jan Rietsema, "The Effects of Varied Clarity of Group Goal and Group Path Upon the Individual and His Relation to This Group," *Human Relations* 10 (1957): 42.

[187] Stanley Schachter, "Deviation, Rejection and Communication," *Journal of Abnormal and Social Psychology* 46 (April 1951): 190–207.

[188] Ole R. Holsti, Richard A. Brody, and Robert C. North, "Measuring Affect and Action in International Reaction Models: Empirical Materials from the 1962 Cuban Crisis," paper delivered at the International Peace Research Society Conference at Ghent, Belgium, July 18 and 19, 1964, p. 40. (Mimeographed.)

[189] Richard E. Neustadt, "Kennedy in the Presidency: A Premature Appraisal," *Political Science Quarterly* 79 (September 1964): 328.

We discussed what the Soviet reaction would be to any possible move by the United States, what our reaction would have to be to that Soviet reaction, and so on, trying to follow each of those roads to their [*sic*] ultimate conclusion.[190]

Hence, the agreement to try not to rush Khrushchev into a precipitate, irreversible action, but to "slow down the escalation of the crisis to give Khrushchev time to consider his next move." [191] Hence, also, the concern to avoid presenting the Soviets with a choice of extremes, total surrender or all-out war. This was, of course, an important reason for the selection of the blockade.

While Sorensen was readying the President's speech, military preparations were proceeding apace. Admiral George W. Anderson, Chief of Naval Operations, acted as an "agent" of the Joint Chiefs in setting up the sea and air blockade. The magnitude of the preparations was such that, as Admiral Anderson later testified, "Some 180 ships were directly involved. . . . At the same time, our naval forces elsewhere were vigilant and prepared. Ten battalions of Marines were afloat in the vicinity of Cuba. Three more Marine battalions manned Guantanamo defenses, backed up by air and surface support from ships of the fleet. Our aircraft and ships were searching an area of some 3.5 million square miles for Russian merchant ships and submarines. They were engaged in the most extensive and . . . the most productive antisubmarine warfare operations since World War II." [192] The Army's arrangements were also massive. As General Earle D. Wheeler, Army Chief of Staff, subsequently reported, "The Army forces were altered, brought up to strength in personnel and equipment, moved and made ready for the operation as part of the largest U.S. invasion force prepared since World War II. The Cuba enterprise was the largest operation ever planned to be launched and supported direct from the United States." [193] In the event that the President decided to invade, Wheeler had "100,000 Army troops that would have gone ashore in Cuba, plus an additional 10,000 to 20,000 that would have been in support in the base area back at the United States." [194]

---

[190] "Cuba," p. 17. President Kennedy and others were aware that their motives might be misread by the Kremlin. "Well now," he said later, "if you look at the history of this century where World War I really came through a series of misjudgments of the intentions of others . . . it is very difficult to always make judgments here about what the effect will be of our decisions on other countries." "Conversation," pp. 23, 24. See also Sorensen, *Kennedy*, p. 513.
[191] "Cuba," p. 19.
[192] U.S., Congress, House, Committee on Armed Services, *Hearings on Military Posture*, 88th Cong., 1st Sess., 1963, p. 897.
[193] *Ibid.*, p. 692.
[194] U.S., Congress, Senate, Committee on Armed Services, *Military Procurement Authorization, Fiscal Year 1964*, 88th Cong., 1st Sess., 1963, p. 579. "Later information from Moscow indicates that the most impressive evidence from the Russian point of view was con-

Meanwhile, Katzenbach, Chayes, John T. McNaughton, general counsel to the Defense Department, and Adam Yarmolinsky, McNamara's special assistant, were finishing up the main points of the President's forthcoming blockade proclamation; State Department officials were organizing their approach to the OAS; Acheson was requested to inform General de Gaulle [195] and the NATO Council of the blockade; and U. Alexis Johnson produced a "master scenario" for the whole government, outlining each step that would have to be taken before the President's speech at seven o'clock Monday evening. The policy apparatus, in short, was in feverish movement.

On Sunday morning the President summoned his key advisers to the White House, asked certain factual questions, and, satisfied with their replies, confirmed his earlier orders on the blockade. Later, in the afternoon, Kennedy convened the National Security Council for the first time, briefed its members on the situation, and advised them of his decision. The essentially unilateral character of the blockade was retained: letters were prepared *informing* the allies of the coming action; the OAS was to be notified Tuesday, and a supporting resolution was drafted.

The formulations and preparations had been made. It remained now to execute them.

THE ACUTE CRISIS PHASE: OCTOBER 22-25

> *Tempers could sharpen knives, and do; we live*
> *In states provocative*
> *Where frowning headlines scare the coffee cream*
> *And doomsday is the eighth day of the week.*

Stanley Kunitz, "Foreign Affairs"

On Monday the first plateau was reached.

In the morning the President met with some of his planners, including Rusk, McNamara, Robert Kennedy, George Ball, and Alexis Johnson, whom he formally titled the Executive Committee of the National Security Council. Meanwhile, the President's chief aid for congressional affairs, Lawrence F. O'Brien, was instructed to summon twenty leaders from both parties to the White House. At noon Salinger announced to the press that the President would deliver a speech that evening on radio

---

firmation through their own intelligence channels that we had taken all measures consistent with serious military action." Weintal and Bartlett, *op. cit.,* p. 56.

[195] Acheson has reported that DeGaulle and Adenauer criticized the blockade as "a method of keeping things out, not getting things out, of a beleaguered spot." Dean Acheson, "Dean Acheson's Version of Robert Kennedy's Version of the Cuban Missile Crisis," *Esquire,* February 1969, p. 77.

and television "on a matter of the highest national urgency." [196] Military
forces were alerted, embassies were notified, allies were briefed, at three
the National Security Council was convened and an hour later the Cabinet met. At five o'clock, two hours before his speech, the President met
with about twenty congressional leaders. After their briefing by McNamara, Rusk, and McCone, Kennedy announced, "We have decided to
take action," [197] and told them of the proposed blockade. The congressmen, "visibly shocked," [198] found themselves confronted with a *fait accompli*. Senators Russell and Fulbright argued for an invasion, the latter
contending that "since blockade could lead to a forcible confrontation
with Russian ships, it was more likely to provoke a nuclear war than an
invasion pitting Americans only against Cubans." [199] Angered, the President replied, testily, that "it was easy to have such opinions when you
don't have the responsibility of acting. . . ." [200] In any event, it was too
late for anything but talk.

At six, Soviet Ambassador Anatoly F. Dobrynin, who had almost certainly been unaware not only of American moves but also of those of his
own government,[201] was briefed by Secretary Rusk. So effective were the
secrecy precautions that the Russians—as planned—were possibly the last
to know.[202]

At seven the President delivered his address to the nation. "His warnings on the presence of Soviet missiles in Cuba," Sorensen observed,
"had to be sufficiently somber to enlist support around the world without
creating panic here at home." [203] They also had to be firm. He began by
reviewing the evidence of a Soviet buildup of offensive weapons in
Cuba, emphasizing Russian duplicity,[204] and carefully putting the blame
for the crisis on the Soviet Union and not on Cuba. He continued:

---

[196] Pierre Salinger, quoted in Oulahan, *op. cit.,* p. 49.

[197] John F. Kennedy, quoted in James Reston, *New York Times,* October 26, 1962.

[198] Oulahan, *loc. cit.*

[199] Johnson and Gwertzman, *op. cit.,* p. 182.

[200] John F. Kennedy, quoted in Reston, *loc. cit.* It was also easy to have such opinions
when the senators lacked prior knowledge of events and had been omitted from the decision-making process. In fact, of course, several members of the Executive Committee had
offered advice similar to that of Russell and Fulbright.

[201] Abel, *op. cit.,* p. 50.

[202] The extent to which the Soviets were unprepared for the speech is suggested by the
fact that their "first official announcement of the blockades did not come until 5 p.m. on
Tuesday the 23rd, while the news had reached Moscow not later than 2 a.m." Michael
Tatu, *Power in the Kremlin: From Khrushchev to Kosygin,* trans. Helen Katel (New York:
Viking Press, 1968), p. 262.

[203] Sorensen, *Decision-Making,* p. 47.

[204] Bundy noted afterwards that the "clarity of the Presidential decision to insist on the
withdrawal of the missiles [was] reinforced in its power, and the Communist position corre-
spondingly weakened by the repeated Soviet assurances that no such weapons would or
should be placed in Cuba" (*op. cit.,* p. 360).

Nuclear weapons are so destructive and ballistic missiles are so swift that any substantially increased possibility of their use or any sudden change in their development may well be regarded as a definite threat to the peace. For many years both the Soviet Union and the United States, recognizing this fact, have deployed strategic nuclear weapons with great care, never upsetting the precarious *status quo* which insured that these weapons would not be used in the absence of some vital challenge. . . . But this secret, swift, and extraordinary buildup of Communist missiles—in an area well known to have a special and historical relationship to the United States and the nations of the Western Hemisphere, in violation of Soviet assurances, and in defiance of American and hemispheric policy—this sudden, clandestine decision to station strategic weapons for the first time outside of Soviet soil—is a deliberately provocative and unjustified change in the *status quo* which cannot be accepted by this country if our courage and our commitments are ever to be trusted again by either friend or foe. The 1930's taught us a clear lesson: Aggressive conduct, if allowed to grow unchecked and unchallenged, ultimately leads to war.[205]

Thus, though he seems to have viewed the missiles as threatening the political rather than the military balance of power, the President emphasized the military aspect in his public presentation. Presumably, such an interpretation would be more easily comprehended and supported. In such subtle ways, too, was "truth a casualty"—with the "national interest," of course, providing the justifying rationale.

The United States, said the President, would (1) impose a "strict quarantine" around Cuba in order to halt the importation of offensive Soviet armaments; (2) continue and increase its close surveillance of Cuba; (3) answer any nuclear missile attack launched from Cuba against any nation in the Western Hemisphere with "a full retaliatory response upon the Soviet Union"; (4) reinforce the naval base at Guantanamo; (5) call for a meeting of the OAS to invoke the Rio Treaty; and (6) ask for an emergency meeting of the United Nations Security Council "to take action against this latest Soviet threat to world peace." At the same time, Kennedy stated that additional military forces had been alerted for "any eventualities. . . ."

Following the speech, a number of diplomatic briefings were held. General support was expressed by the allies.[206] In the next two days, the crisis reached its most dangerous point.

---

[205] John F. Kennedy, "The Soviet Threat to the Americas," *Department of State Bulletin* 47 (November 12, 1962): 716. (Telecast of October 22.)

[206] A Labor M.P. has suggested that Rusk and Sorensen (and, presumably, possibly other advisers) saw this support as a facade, in which "if the United States took a strong action the allies would turn against her, and if she took a weak action they would turn from her." Letter of Christopher Roland to the editor of the London *Observer*, reprinted in "As Others See Us," *Saturday Review*, October 9, 1965, p. 47.

On October 23, the United States took action on several fronts; and, in each case, the execution of presidential decisions was so smooth that it resembled routine. Diplomatically, the State Department obtained unanimous support for resolutions calling for the withdrawal of the missiles from both collective security organizations involved, NATO and the OAS.[207] Had the OAS failed to provide the necessary vote authorizing the quarantine, Sorensen argued afterwards, "the Soviets and possibly others might have been emboldened to challenge the legality of our action, creating confusion and irresolution in the Western camp and giving rise to all kinds of cargo insurance and admiralty questions that this nation would not enjoy untangling."[208] Meanwhile, at the United Nations, Ambassador Stevenson asked for an emergency meeting of the Security Council, where he introduced a similar resolution.

Politically, the President issued a proclamation "to interdict . . . the delivery of offensive weapons and associated materiel to Cuba."[209] Vessels carrying missiles, bombs, rockets, and so forth would have either to turn back or, if they continued toward Cuba, to submit to search and seizure. Ships refusing to comply "shall be subject to being taken into custody." But "in any case," the proclamation concluded cautiously, "force shall be used only to the extent necessary." The blockade was to become effective at 10 A.M. Wednesday, October 24. This time lag between the President's televised speech and the beginning of the embargo was of significant importance. As Assistant Secretary of State Harlan Cleveland commented afterwards, "the advantage of naval quarantine over an air strike was that it put the option of starting violent action up to the Soviets, and gave them 48 hours (the time it would take the nearest Soviet freighter to reach the quarantine line) to think it over."[210]

Later that evening, the blockade plan was modified slightly in order to give Khrushchev more time to reconsider and act accordingly. The closer to Cuba the ships would be intercepted, noted British Ambassador Da-

---

[207] For the text of the OAS resolution, see *Department of State Bulletin* 47 (November 12, 1962): 722–23. Assistant Secretary of State Martin was especially important in securing the vote. Hilsman, *op. cit.*, p. 211; Martin, *loc. cit.* See, generally, John C. Drier, "The Organization of American States and United States Policy," *International Organization* 17 (Winter 1963): 36–53.

[208] Theodore C. Sorensen, quoted in *New York Times,* November 3, 1962. That the utility of the OAS had to be defended in terms of avoiding cargo insurance problems shows the prominent position it occupied in the minds of decision makers. During the missile crisis, as Ernst Haas notes, "the United States successfully used the political machinery of the OAS to legitimate its national measures against" a Communist threat. Ernst B. Haas, *Tangle of Hopes: American Commitments and World Order* (Englewood Cliffs: Prentice-Hall, 1969), p. 103. There is no reason to suppose that a challenge to the legality of the quarantine—whether in the OAS or elsewhere—would have dissuaded Kennedy in the least. Only the public rhetoric would have been altered.

[209] Proclamation No. 3504; 27 *Federal Register* 10403.

[210] Cleveland, *op. cit.*, p. 644.

vid Ormsby Gore, the longer Khrushchev would have to prepare his retreat, and, consequently, the less likely a war. The President agreed immediately, and, over Navy objections, issued the appropriate orders.[211]

Also on Tuesday evening, the President, acting in pursuance of a joint
congressional resolution passed three weeks earlier, issued an executive
order calling members of the ready reserve to active duty and extending
enlistments. With respect to this decision, it has been reported that some
of the President's aides advised him to place NATO forces on maximum
missile alert, which meant putting American-controlled nuclear warheads on the NATO-controlled missiles aimed at the Soviet Union. They
would in this way be prepared for immediate firing. But General Lauris
Norstad, Supreme Commander of NATO, is said to have objected successfully on this point, appealing to the President's desire for caution and
manageability of events. In the absence of secrecy, argued Norstad, plac-
ing the missiles on alert might precipitate a war—which neither side
wanted—by way of a "self-fulfilling prophecy." [212]

The Soviet reaction to the President's proclamation and executive order was more composed than it had been to his original televised speech.
At that time, "caught off guard . . . playing for time to think out its next
move," [213] the Kremlin had been "confronted [by] the immediate burden
of decision regarding the precipitation of violence." [214] Thus, content
analysis of available documents reveals the confused Soviets to be at
their highest level of potential violence on October 23.[215]

On Wednesday morning, the White House learned that Khrushchev
had rejected the blockade proclamation, terming it "piracy" and warning
that Soviet ships would not honor it. He also denied that offensive weapons had been installed in Cuba. Khrushchev maintained his firm stance
in an afternoon meeting with a visiting American industrialist, William
E. Knox, president of Westinghouse Electric International. Khrushchev
told Knox that "as the Soviet vessels were not armed, the United States
could undoubtedly stop one or two more but then he, Chairman Khrushchev, would give instructions to the Soviet submarines to sink the American vessels." [216] His position was that "he was not interested in the destruction of the world, but if we all wanted to meet in hell, it was up to
us." [217] Khrushchev closed the discussion of Cuba with a typically homely

[211] Schlesinger, *op. cit.*, p. 818; Robert Kennedy, "Thirteen Days," p. 152.
[212] Lauris Norstad, quoted in Ben H. Bagdikian, "Press Independence and the Cuban
Crisis," *Columbia Journalism Review*, Winter 1963, p. 6.
[213] *New York Times*, November 6, 1962.
[214] Horelick, *op. cit.*, p. 52.
[215] Holsti, Brody, and North, *op. cit.*, p. 19.
[216] "Cuba," p. 36.
[217] Nikita Khrushchev, quoted in W. E. Knox, "Close-up of Khrushchev During a
Crisis," *New York Times Magazine*, November 18, 1962, p. 128.

parable, whose point was, "You are not happy about it [missiles in Cuba] and you won't like it, but you'll learn to live with it." Later, it was reported that Defense Minister Malinovsky had been instructed to place all troops on alert.

The Soviet reaction, however, was not solely one of belligerence. In replying to an appeal for peace from the British philosopher Bertrand Russell, for example, Khrushchev had vaguely proposed a summit meeting. And to Knox, the Russian leader had not only acknowledged the presence of missiles in Cuba, but had taken pains to emphasize that the weapons were under Soviet control and would not be used unless Cuba were attacked—and then only on his personal orders. The President, interpreting these moves as delaying tactics designed to place the United States in an unfavorable light in world opinion and to permit completion of the installations, refused to answer Khrushchev's talk.

At this point, Acting UN Secretary General U Thant intervened, acting largely on his own but partly from the urgings of nonaligned nations.[218] Thant, in letters to Khrushchev and Kennedy, proposed that for two or three weeks the Soviets suspend their arms shipments to Cuba and the United States suspend its quarantine. Negotiations, he suggested, could be held during this period. Khrushchev, of course, accepted the proposal immediately; it would have robbed the United States of its diplomatic and military initiative, equated the installation of missiles with the American response, and permitted work to continue on those missiles already in Cuba. The President, therefore, while agreeing to talk with Thant on arranging negotiations with the Soviets, remained firm in his position that "the existing threat was created by the secret introduction of offensive weapons into Cuba and the answer lies in the removal of such weapons." [219] He would not lift the quarantine.

This incident reveals the dominant characteristics of Kennedy's decision making once the crisis had passed into its active phase: a considerable rigidity concerning his expectations about what constituted a successful solution to the problem, and an increasing conviction that he had made the proper choice of means. This firmness carried with it an important advantage; for, as Henry Kissinger has said, "We can negotiate with confidence if we know what we consider a just arrangement. If we lack a sense of direction, diplomacy at any level will be doomed." [220] Hence, in disposing of Thant's appeal, the President did not reject diplomacy as a

---

[218] On the Office of the Secretary-General as a "catalyst" in facilitating negotiations, see Thomas Hovet, Jr., "United Nations Diplomacy," *Journal of International Affairs* (No. 1, 1963), esp. pp. 34–35.

[219] *New York Times,* October 26, 1962.

[220] Henry A. Kissinger, *The Necessity for Choice: Prospects of American Foreign Policy,* Anchor Books (Garden City: Doubleday, 1962), p. 198.

means of settling the crisis, but rather indicated that it had to proceed within a certain—admittedly American-oriented—framework.

Meanwhile, the blockade had gone into effect. Secretary McNamara had announced that Soviet ships would enter the quarantine zone that evening, but Assistant Secretary Arthur Sylvester later declared that some of the Soviet ships had apparently altered their course. No contact was made that day.

American hopes were realized the next day, when twelve of twenty-five Soviet vessels turned back in mid-Atlantic. It was at this point that Secretary Rusk uttered his famous remark, "We're eyeball to eyeball and I think the other fellow just blinked." [221] Twelve other vessels apparently were awaiting further orders outside the quarantine zone. At 8 A.M. the first Soviet ship reached the blockade area, the oil tanker *Bucharest*.[222] Feeling certain that the ship contained no embargoed materiel and wanting to give Khrushchev more time and to spare him some humiliation, the President allowed the vessel to proceed to Cuba—once it had identified itself and satisfied the quarantine conditions—without boarding and search.

In the afternoon, tensions increased, as rumors of an American invasion of Cuba were strengthened by a statement of Representative Hale Boggs to his constituents. "Believe me," he said, "if these missiles are not dismantled, the United States has the power to destroy them, and I assure you that this will be done." The continued military buildup in Florida seemed to underscore the rumors.[223] At the same time, American intelligence revealed that work on the erection of the missile sites was proceeding at full speed.

That evening, as millions of Americans watched on television, Khrushchev's plan to use the Security Council "to place the United States on trial in the face of world opinion" [224] backfired, as Ambassador Stevenson vanquished Ambassador Zorin in a verbal encounter characterized by considerable melodrama.[225] As Schlesinger wrote later, "The Stevenson speech dealt a final blow to the Soviet case before world opinion." [226]

---

[221] Dean Rusk, quoted in Stewart Alsop and Charles Bartlett, "In Time of Crisis," *Saturday Evening Post,* December 8, 1962, p. 16.

[222] Allison, however, argues that on October 26 the Soviet tanker *Vinnitsa* successfully passed through the blockade, and docked in Havana, despite the official U.S. declaration concerning the *Bucharest*. "It seems probable," he concludes, "that the Navy's resistance to the President's order that the blockade be drawn in closer to Cuba forced him to allow one or several Soviet ships to pass through the blockade after it was officially operative." Allison, *op. cit.,* p. 707. If this is correct, Kennedy's vaunted "effective crisis authority" clearly was not as impressive as it seemed to observers at the time.

[223] About a month later, the Pentagon revealed that it had deployed over 300,000 men and 180 ships for action, and had "upgraded" alert on ICBM's aimed at the Soviet Union. *New York Times,* November 30, 1962.

[224] Fontaine, *op. cit.,* p. 67.

[225] That this dramatic confrontation possessed great significance has been argued unconvincingly by Alistair Cooke, "How the United States Heard the News," *Listener* 68 (November 1, 1962): 704.

[226] Schlesinger, *op. cit.,* p. 824.

From American public opinion, the President was faced with insignificant opposition, a fact which Sorensen regards as "essential." [227] In crisis situations, opinion formation tends in large part to be a product of the activation of previous experiences and attitudes,[228] and evidently the American background did not conduce to panic or even to widespread anxiety. James Reston, for example, saw the popular reaction as not one of disapproval or even of endorsement but simply of inertia. In his words, "on the whole people went along about as before, unprepared and unafraid." [229] And even those few newspaper articles that related how residents of Washington and Los Angeles had bought up bottled water, food concentrates, transistor radios, and other emergency supplies, hastened to add that these actions did not indicate panic.[230] In any event, the President was less impressed by these reports than by the 48,000 telegrams he received, which supported him by a ratio of ten to one.[231]

Among public figures, backing for the President was, if anything, even stronger. Besides the expected response from the Democrats, Kennedy heard his actions supported by former Presidents Eisenhower and Hoover, Republican leaders Nixon, Dirksen, Rockefeller, Keating, and Miller, the AFL-CIO, the National Council of Churches, and even Governor Ross Barnett of Mississippi. To all but maverick groups and individuals,[232] in short, public support seemed virtually obligatory.

By Thursday evening the President was convinced that, as Averell Harriman had argued, Khrushchev's reactions were "not the behavior of a man who wanted war." Intelligence indicated that "the Russians appeared to be engaged in a studied effort to disassociate Berlin from Cuba," and "the essence of the emerging [Soviet] pattern seemed to be concern for a peaceful settlement." [233] Realizing the full strength of his hand, Kennedy sent a confidential message to Khrushchev that night in which he said that, "were the dismantling of the bases not ordered within forty-eight hours, the United States would feel compelled to adopt new

---

[227] Sorensen, *Kennedy*, p. 707.

[228] S. M. Lipset, "Opinion Formation in a Crisis Situation," *Public Opinion Quarterly* 17 (Spring 1953): 43.

[229] *New York Times*, November 4, 1962.

[230] *New York Times*, October 26, 1962. New York City called for 49,000 fire volunteers for use in emergency "in the event of an attack." *New York Times*, October 27, 1962.

[231] Hugh Sidey, *John F. Kennedy, President*, new ed. (New York: Atheneum, 1964), p. 344.

[232] Most protesters did so in the name of peace. They included Linus Pauling, Norman Thomas, Protestant Episcopal Bishop Lichtenberger, the Women's International League for Peace and Freedom, and the Communist Party. The most vehement spokesman for the "harder" line was former World War I air ace Eddie Rickenbacker, who viewed the President's settlement as a renunciation of the Monroe Doctrine.

[233] Schlesinger, *op. cit.*, pp. 821, 823.

measures." It was thought that the letter, in its emphasis on American resolve, would act to crystallize Khrushchev's apparent decision to retreat.
And to underline this threat, American authorities "launched a campaign of alarmist excitement without precedent. This was not without
foundation: it seemed that the order to bomb the bases had been issued
for Monday morning." [234]

Though work still continued on the sites, by the end of the acute crisis
phase each side had grasped the other's position and foresaw the episode's outcome. The problem then became largely one of working within
the broad outlines in attempting to obtain the best possible results for
one's side.

THE BARGAINING PHASE: OCTOBER 26-NOVEMBER 20

> *The air is full of after-thunder freshness*
> *And everything rejoices and revives.*
>
> Pasternak, "After the Storm"

With the turning point plainly past, Friday saw tensions receding somewhat, though the United States continued firm in its application of pressure. In the morning a Soviet-chartered Lebanese freighter, *Marucla*—
ironically, a former American Liberty Ship—was searched without incident, and, when no embargoed materiel was found, was cleared and
permitted to proceed to Cuba. Pressure was applied in other ways: Ambassador Stevenson was instructed to reiterate to Thant America's absolute insistence on the withdrawal of the missiles; State Department press
officer Lincoln White called special attention to the President's Monday
night warning that, were work on offensive weapons to be continued,
"further action will be justified"; [235] the Army moved antiaircraft missiles
to Key West, and the Commander of the Atlantic Fleet pronounced
Guantanamo "defensible"; Representative Clement Zablocki, a Democrat from Wisconsin, declared that the United States might soon have to
resort to "pin-point bombing" of the missile sites, and the Pentagon ominously refused to comment on these remarks; the late editions of many
newspapers featured headlines on a possible invasion or bombing.

That night, after consultations with Ambassadors Stevenson and Zorin, Thant made public the replies of Kennedy and Khrushchev to a new
appeal. The Soviets agreed to keep their ships away from the blockade

---

[234] Fontaine, *op. cit.,* p. 68.
[235] This threat had not been authorized by the President, who reprimanded White for his
slip. Hilsman, *op. cit.,* pp. 213–14.

zone for the time being, and the President answered that he would try to avoid any direct confrontation "in the next few days." At the same time, however, he repeated that the removal of the missiles was "a matter of great urgency." Meanwhile, the White House issued a statement that "the development of ballistic missile sites in Cuba continues at a rapid pace. . . . The activity at these sites apparently is directed at achieving a full operational capacity as soon as possible." [236] Photographic evidence indicated that the work speed-up would enable the missiles to be operational by the end of the month. At the White House, officials told newsmen that "the choice was between expansion of the blockade and some form of air action." [237]

Beneath the cover of these movements and reports the bargaining phase began. Its opening could hardly have been more theatrical. That afternoon Alexander Fomin, a counselor at the Soviet Embassy, contacted John Scali, the State Department correspondent for the American Broadcasting Company, relaying Khrushchev's proposal that he withdraw the missiles from Cuba in exchange for the President's public declaration not to invade Cuba.[238] Scali delivered the message to the State Department, and it was discussed by the Executive Committee. It was decided to encourage negotiations by replying that the proposal had "real possibilities" but that time was short. Scali conveyed this message, and two hours later, a long letter from Khrushchev to the President began to arrive. The President and his advisers were called, and when the letter had been assembled and translated, they found it more conciliatory in tone than they had expected. The letter "pulsated with a passion to avoid nuclear war and gave the impression of having been written in deep emotion. . . ." [239] In it, Khrushchev admitted the presence of Soviet missiles in Cuba, and though insisting on their defensive character, said that he understood the President's feelings about them. Almost coyly, a deal was proposed: "If assurances were given that the President of the United States would not participate in an attack on Cuba and the blockade lifted, then the question of the removal or the destruction of the missile sites in Cuba would then be an entirely different question." [240] And in New York, it was learned that Zorin had presented an identical offer to Thant.

The following morning, another communication was received from Premier Khrushchev. He now proposed a trade of Soviet missiles in

---

[236] John F. Kennedy, quoted in "White House Notes Continuation of Missile Buildup on October 25," *Department of State Bulletin* 47 (November 12, 1962): 740. (Press release of October 26.)

[237] *New York Times,* November 3, 1962.

[238] Abel, *op. cit.,* pp. 175–77; Hilsman, *op. cit.,* pp. 217–19 and 221–22; and Hilsman, "The Cuban Crisis: How Close We Were to War," *Look,* August 25, 1964, pp. 17–21.

[239] Schlesinger, *op. cit.,* p. 827.

[240] Robert F. Kennedy, *Thirteen Days,* pp. 88–89.

Cuba for NATO missile bases in Turkey, with the UN Security Council
to verify fulfillment of each side of the deal.[241] This letter, so different in
tone and substance from the first, provoked a number of questions
among members of the Executive Committee: had Khrushchev been
overruled by "harder" elements in the Kremlin? Was he applying pressure in order to insure American acceptance of his earlier proposal? In
any event, this alternative had been discussed several times during the
early and acute crisis phases, and each time rejected. One key adviser
counselling against acceptance of the deal that Saturday was Assistant
Secretary of Defense Paul Nitze.[242] The crucial argument is said to have
been that to agree to such a barter would have transformed the encounter into an American defeat: though the missiles in Turkey were "anti-
quated and valueless," [243] they were not lacking in symbolic meaning:
their removal, the President is said to have felt, "could break up the alliance [NATO] by confirming European suspicions that we would sacrifice their security to protect our interests in an area of no concern to
them." [244]

But how seriously ought one to take this view? Might not one argue, in
fact, that the President's actions did "confirm" these "suspicions," for
Cuba was "an area of no concern" to Europeans, and their security was,
if not sacrificed, certainly imperiled by the blockade. As Etzioni has
pointed out:

The Russians had, by 1962, a comparatively small number of long-range missiles and bombers capable of striking in United States, but a large number of
medium—and intermediate—range missiles and bombers. . . . Western Europe
served as the major hostage for the Russians, with the Soviets capable of striking
America's allies with much greater facility than could be directed against the
United States itself.[245]

If the President had actually been so concerned about the allies' security,
why had he not consulted with them on policy or at least advised them of
the facts at an early stage? Does risking the NATO countries' decimation
on an issue which they plainly did not perceive as decisive, without permitting them any role in policy formulation or execution, bespeak undue
vigilance with regard to their security? Standing up for the allies' security
by refusing to remove the Turkish missiles becomes an especially odd

[241] "Chairman Khrushchev's Message of October 27," *Department of State Bulletin* 47
(November 12, 1962): 741–43.
[242] "J & R Memo," *Army Navy Air Force Journal and Register*, November 3, 1962, p. 4.
[243] Robert F. Kennedy, "Thirteen Days," p. 168.
[244] Sorensen, *Kennedy*, p. 696. This feeling was echoed in Henry A. Kissinger, "Reflections on Cuba," *Reporter*, November 22, 1962, p. 22.
[245] Etzioni, *op. cit.*, p. 45.

posture in view of the fact that one committee member told Kennedy that they had been "practically forced on" Turkey "by the previous administration." [246] Thus, it is not surprising that even Robert Kennedy confessed later in his memoirs, "The fact was that the proposal the Russians made was not unreasonable and did not amount to a loss to the U.S. or to our NATO allies." [247]

Why, then, did the President reject the bargain? His brother has suggested that it was less the substance of the Russian proposal Kennedy objected to than the way it was offered—as a "threat." [248] If this were true, then the President's rejection signaled his readiness to transform the conflict from a "chicken" game (i.e., one in which "the penalties for mutual non-cooperation"—mutual destruction—"are clearly much higher than the penalties to either side for giving in"—humiliation) to a "prisoner's dilemma," at least for Kennedy, in which the penalty for unilateral concession has come to appear greater than his share of the penalty for mutual noncooperation.[249] Since the Soviets were to abandon this approach, the implications of the President's willingness to change the nature of the conflict were never made clear. Speculation, however, is not encouraging, for a careful reading of the Soviet letter[250] discloses no threatening words whatever. When mere proposals are seen as threats, the prognosis for future communications does not inspire confidence.

In one sense, of course, the Soviet communiqué did constitute a "threat." For the offer, and the concession that acceptance would entail, clearly threatened the victory within reach, a victory national but mostly personal. Such a concession at this stage was unthinkable. Thus, in a statement responding to Khrushchev's proposal, the White House emphasized that there could be no worthwhile negotiations until work on the missile installations had ceased. "Several inconsistent and conflicting proposals have been made by the U.S.S.R. within the last twenty-four hours," the statement said, "including the one just made public in Moscow. . . . The first imperative must be to deal with this immediate [Cuban] threat, under which no sensible negotiations can proceed." [251]

---

[246] Sorensen, *Kennedy,* p. 696. It is a tribute to Sorensen's capacity for critical judgment that, "to the President's great interest" an adviser minimizes the importance of the Turkish missiles and the Turks' desire for them in one paragraph, while Kennedy decides that their removal would threaten allied security in the next. There is no indication that Sorensen considered this an anomaly worth explaining.

[247] Robert F. Kennedy, *Thirteen Days,* p. 94.

[248] *Ibid.,* p. 95.

[249] Karl W. Deutsch, *The Analysis of International Relations* (Englewood Cliffs: Prentice-Hall, 1968), p. 130.

[250] It is reprinted at Robert F. Kennedy, *op. cit.,* pp. 196–201.

[251] "White House Statement of October 27," *Department of State Bulletin* 47 (November 12, 1962): 741. (Press release of October 27.)

Tensions rose still higher when it was learned that a U-2 reconnaissance plane was missing over Cuba and presumed lost. This was the first time that American planes had been shot at, and, to some, this seemed to indicate "that the confrontation was entering its military phase." [252] The sites were becoming operational, it was argued, and extensive air strikes would be needed to eliminate them. Again, the President refused to be harried into precipitate and irreversible action, insisting that "the Russians be given time to consider what they were doing before action and counteraction became irrevocable." [253] In addition, if the plane had been shot down by Cubans, the military implications of the incident would diminish—because the Cubans lacked authority over the missiles—and American waiting could be justified as giving Khrushchev time to reassert his control over Castro. Consequently, the United States' response was limited to "insure that such missions are effective and protected." At the same time, it was announced that 14,000 air reservists—twenty-four troop carrier squadrons—were being recalled to active duty.

In the evening, the planners, recognizing that the situation was deteriorating and seeing their earlier note to Moscow as projecting an essentially negative image of the United States to the world, decided to draft a second reply. Khrushchev's first letter was obviously more favorable to American interests, but what was to be done about the second letter? Following the Attorney General's ingenious suggestion that the second message simply be ignored, the President interpreted the first letter as a bid for an acceptable settlement.[254]

As I read your letter [wrote the President], the key elements of your proposal—which seem generally acceptable as I understood them—are as follows:

---

[252] Schlesinger, *op. cit.,* p. 827.

[253] *Ibid.,* p. 828.

[254] Alsop and Bartlett, *op. cit.,* p. 18. Michael Tatu, at the time *Le Monde's* correspondent in Moscow, argues that Robert Kennedy's ploy was appropriate, though for reasons that none of the Americans recognized. Tatu contends that Khrushchev's colleagues "outvoted [him] on Saturday, that he did not approve of anything that was done that day, not even the Turkish proposal, and chose subsequently to regard the events of the day as an interlude of no significance." Tatu, *op. cit.,* p. 270. Pachter, noting that the "Turkish proposal" vote was much more formal, maintains that it was a conventional Foreign Ministry message, while the first telegram was a personal message, Khrushchev being responsible for both. The confusion resulted, he says, over the fact that the "note first received had been written last; the slow note of the Foreign Ministry had been overtaken by Khrushchev's panicky telegram." Henry A. Pachter, *Collision Course: The Cuban Missile Crisis and Coexistence* (New York: Praeger, 1963), p. 68. Sorensen considers Pachter's interpretation "highly doubtful." Sorensen, *Kennedy,* p. 712. Although Robert Kennedy obviously was a key figure in the rejection of Khrushchev's offer—which would have permitted him to save face at virtually no military cost to the United States and thereby have terminated the threat of thermonuclear destruction—McNamara later said of the Attorney General's crisis performance: "He understood . . . that, above all else, a United States President must, while defending our vital interests, prevent the confrontation between nuclear powers which can lead to nuclear

(1) You would agree to remove these weapons systems from Cuba under appropriate United Nations observation and supervision; and undertake, with suitable safeguards, to halt the further introduction of such weapons systems into Cuba.

(2) We, on our part, would agree—upon the establishment of adequate arrangements through the United Nations to ensure the carrying out and continuation of these commitments—(a) to remove promptly the quarantine measures now in effect and (b) to give assurance against an invasion of Cuba.

The President reiterated, however, that

... the first ingredient ... is the cessation of work on missile sites in Cuba and measures to render such weapons inoperable under effective international guarantees. The continuation of this threat, or a prolonging of the discussion concerning Cuba by linking these problems to the broader question of European and world security, would surely lead to an intensification of the Cuban crisis and a grave risk to the peace of the world.[255]

In this letter is the same firmness, the same reasonableness, the same insistence on narrow objectives and a step-by-step approach that had characterized earlier presidential decisions. But in one respect, this message points up a jarring feature of the Kennedy diplomacy, for the President's decision to publish it immediately appears self-defeating: while carefully framing his strategy and wording his letters in order to maintain and increase his control over events, he insisted at the same time on conducting much of the negotiations in public—a tactic which has been widely criticized for diminishing the decision maker's control. This contradiction becomes even more baffling when one considers that the critics come from the "classical realist" school of foreign policy analysts,[256] a school represented among the President's advisers by Acheson, Thompson, and others, and from which he had been said to draw many of his more basic foreign policy notions.[257] Sorensen's explanation that the letter was released to the public "in the interests of both speed and psychology"[258] is both incomplete and unconvincing. For one thing, had speed been para-

holocaust." *New York Times,* April 14, 1968.

[255] John F. Kennedy, "President Kennedy's Message of October 27," *Department of State Bulletin* 47 (November 12, 1962): 743. (Press release of October 27.)

[256] See, e.g., Hans J. Morgenthau, *Politics Among Nations: The Struggle for Power and Peace,* 2d ed. (New York: Knopf, 1958), pp. 519–21; Walter Lippmann, *Essays in the Public Philosophy* (Boston: Little, Brown, 1955), *passim;* Harold Nicolson, *The Evolution of the Diplomatic Method* (London: Constable and Co., 1954), pp. 84–91.

[257] Reston argued that "The new Kennedy style of diplomacy ... is power diplomacy in the old classical European sense. ..." *New York Times,* October 26, 1962.

[258] Sorensen, *Kennedy,* p. 714.

mount, the note could have been delivered by hand, and, in fact, "At the private request of the President, a copy of the letter was delivered to the Soviet Ambassador by Robert Kennedy with a strong verbal message...." [259] As for "psychology," open diplomacy frequently degenerates into propaganda battles whose psychological force actually *inhibits* negotiations. "Once the diplomats state their national demands in public," writes Joseph Frankel, "they generally cannot agree to a compromise without loss of face; in other words, they cannot negotiate." [260] In addition, the urgency of secrecy would appear to be directly proportional to the gravity of the issues involved. Perhaps the President saw world opinion as too potent an ally to ignore. Or, possibly, success seemed certain enough to permit a risk that would bring his nation an unexcelled propaganda victory. And as a politician, Kennedy doubtless felt that publicity would aid the Democrats in the coming election; certainly, any retreat or indication of gullibility or weakness was viewed as entailing a party disaster at the polls. Former President Eisenhower, in fact, when informed of Kennedy's plans apparently "took a skeptical view, suspecting perhaps that Kennedy might be playing politics with Cuba on the eve of congressional elections." [261] And Sorensen revealed coyly that, during the early policy debates, an unnamed advocate of the airstrike passed him a note reading:

Have you considered the very real possibility that if we allow Cuba to complete installation and operational readiness of missile bases, the next House of Representatives is likely to have a Republican majority? [262]

Sorensen, of course, deals with the aspect of party politics with great delicacy. He is careful to point out that the writer of the note was a Republican and that his rationale was nonpartisan and patriotic: a Republican victory, he wrote, "would completely paralyze our ability to react sensibly and coherently to further Soviet advances." Yet the facts are, first, that the President is a party leader; second, that Kennedy was a mediocre party leader with an undistinguished legislative record; and third, that a Republican House would probably render the remainder of his term an exercise in frustration.

[259] *Ibid.,* p. 715. Khrushchev, in his memoirs, writes of an exhausted Robert Kennedy pleading on his brother's behalf for Khrushchev's "help in liquidating this conflict. If the situation continues much longer," the Attorney General is alleged to have said," the President is not sure that the military will not overthrow him and seize power. The American army could get out of control." Nikita Khrushchev, "Khrushchev Remembers: Part IV," *Life,* December 18, 1970, p. 50. This version of the Robert Kennedy-Dobryin meeting seems, to say the least, highly dubious.
[260] Joseph Frankel, *International Relations,* Galaxy Books (New York: Oxford University Press, 1964), p. 128.
[261] Abel, *op. cit.,* p. 78.
[262] Unnamed Republican, quoted in Sorensen, *Kennedy,* p. 688.

Probably more important, that a crisis triumph would cover the President with glory and earn him an immortality not only in history books but in the popular imagination was a fact of which he could hardly have been unaware.[263] The Kennedys had always been preoccupied with Success; and now that the greatest victory of all seemed so near at hand, the temptation of publicity was perhaps too great.

The letter having been published and delivered to the Soviets, the group felt, as one participant recalled later, "a strong sense that we were coming right down to the wire of another decision—probably more than the public realized." [264] Sorensen, speaking of the events of October 27, explained, "Obviously these developments could not be tolerated very long, and we were preparing for a meeting on Sunday which would have been the most serious meeting ever to take place at the White House." [265] No decision was made on the next step, "but we were pretty close," one official reported, indicating possible expansion of the embargo or firing on antiaircraft batteries. While none of the planners expected the confrontation to involve nuclear weapons, they felt that large-scale fighting in Cuba would probably provoke the Soviets into counteraction elsewhere. As the President said a few weeks later, "If we had invaded Cuba . . . I am sure the Soviets would have acted. They would have to, just as we would have to. I think there are certain compulsions on any major power." [266]

---

[263] In fact, however, the crisis appears to have affected his popularity in an odd way. When put in general terms, his postcrisis popularity was the highest since the preceding April. The Gallup poll asked a national sample of the adult population, "Do you approve of the way Kennedy is handling his job as President?" The results were:

	Approve	Disapprove	No Opinion
October, 1962	61%	24%	15%
November, 1962	74	15	11

Yet, paradoxically, public support for the administration's Cuban policy was *lower* after the crisis success than after the disastrous Bay of Pigs failure. Gallup asked his sample, "In general, would you say that you are satisfied or dissatisfied with the way the Kennedy Administration has been handling the Cuban situation in recent weeks?" The results were:

	Satisfied	Dissatisfied	No Opinion
May 5, 1961	61%	15%	24%
February 24, 1963	56	28	16

Moreover, satisfaction *decreased* for the remainder of his administration. Hazel Gaudet Erskine, "The Polls: Kennedy as President," *Public Opinion Quarterly* 28 (Summer 1964): 334, 338. In line with this, George Gallup commented after the election, "The Cuban crisis did not have any real effect in changing votes. A Gallup Poll in early October—before the President's decision to quarantine Cuba—showed that an election at that time would have produced much the same results as actually did occur." *New York Herald Tribune,* November 12, 1962. None of this, of course, implies that Kennedy and his advisers had foreseen the crisis' odd effect on public opinion.

[264] Unnamed participant, quoted in *New York Times,* November 3, 1962.

[265] "Cuba," p. 42.

[266] John F. Kennedy, quoted in Schlesinger, *op. cit.,* p. 830.

Early Sunday morning, Moscow Radio announced that Premier Khrushchev would shortly make an important statement. In this, another letter to Kennedy, Khrushchev said:

> I regard with great understanding your concern and the concern of the United States people in connection with the fact that the weapons you describe as offensive are formidable indeed . . . the Soviet Government, in addition to earlier instruction on the discontinuation of further work on weapons construction sites, has given a new order to dismantle the arms which you describe as offensive, and to crate and return them to the Soviet Union.[267]

In return, Khrushchev trusted the President's assurance that there would be no invasion of Cuba, extending it to include attacks "not only on the part of the United States, but also on the part of other nations in the Western Hemisphere."

The President and his advisers quickly framed a reply. In a message broadcast to Moscow over the Voice of America, Kennedy spoke of the Soviet Premier's "statesmanlike decision," and termed it a "welcome and constructive contribution to peace." [268] The President added that the quarantine would be lifted as soon as the UN had taken the "necessary measures," and further, that the United States would not attack Cuba. Kennedy said that he attached great importance to a rapid settlement of the Cuban crisis because "developments were approaching a point where events could have become unmanageable." It was reported later that both the President and his advisers had agreed that the Soviet missiles had to be removed or destroyed before becoming operational, and, consequently, had planned an airstrike against the installations not later than Tuesday.[269]

Though the sense of relief must have been immense, the President was careful to insure that there be no exulting over a Soviet defeat. As a correspondent of the *Economist* noted, "Mr. Kennedy . . . showed that he knew not only how far to go but precisely where to stop. His acceptance of Mr. Khrushchev's retreat was unreserved and handsome. . . . There was not a touch of the intoxication that confuses success with victory. . . . The Russian retreat from the Western Hemisphere was made as easy as it could, in the circumstances of an essentially brutal confrontation of material force, be made." [270]

---

[267] Nikita Khrushchev, "Chairman Khrushchev's Message of October 28," *Department of State Bulletin* 47 (November 12, 1962): 743–44.

[268] John F. Kennedy, "President Kennedy's Statement of October 28," *Department of State Bulletin* 47 (November 12, 1962): 745. (Press release of October 27.)

[269] Alsop and Bartlett, *loc. cit.*

[270] "After Cuba," *Economist* 205 (November 3, 1962): 431.

By agreeing to UN inspection, the Soviets, "for the first time, conceded the principle of on-the-spot verification of measures of disarmament within the territory of a satellite." [271] And, in ignoring Castro, "Khrushchev had not even treated him politely." [272] At the peak of the crisis, "no Cuban voice was heard or listened for. The island's identity vanished behind the storm." [273] In his letter offering to withdraw the missiles, the Soviet premier had not even mentioned the necessity of obtaining Cuban agreement to the settlement.[274] Consequently, "Castro made no attempt to conceal his grievances and wounded pride," [275] and announced on the same day that Cuba would not accept the Kennedy-Khrushchev accord unless the United States met further conditions, including the evacuation of the naval base at Guantanamo.

Into this breach moved Secretary General Thant. First, he prevailed upon President Kennedy to lift the blockade for two days, apparently as a face-saving gesture for Castro, and on Wednesday he got the United States to suspend its aerial surveillance for two days. However, the mission failed, and though on his return he reported that the dismantling of the bases would be completed within two days, the President decided to resume the air surveillance and the quarantine. Castro continued to reject any form of international inspection, even by the International Red Cross. Yet American reconnaissance flights ascertained that the bases were being removed, and the Soviets confirmed this to Thant. Finally, on November 2, the United States and the Soviet Union announced their agreement to have the Red Cross inspect Cuban-bound ships at sea to assure that they were not carrying offensive arms, although the President continued to withhold his guarantee against invasion pending an agreement on international inspection of the sites. That evening in a televised speech to the nation, the President revealed that aerial photographs showed that the Soviet missiles were being dismantled, and that progress toward peace was being made. Meanwhile, Soviet Foreign Minister Mikoyan had arrived in Havana to "discuss the situation with the Cubans calmly," [276] but his attempts at reaching a settlement were no more successful than Thant's. Yet it was obvious, as the *Times* editorialized, that because of pressing economic factors, "Castro cannot afford to go too far in defiance of Moscow." [277]

---

[271] Thomas Borman, "Cuba: An International Milestone," *Listener* 48 (November 8, 1962): 744.

[272] Panatela, "Some Misunderstanding!" *Reporter,* December 6, 1962, p. 34.

[273] "Castro's Morning After," *Economist* 205 (November 3, 1962): 434.

[274] Both in Moscow and in the West, observers concluded that Khrushchev accepted Kennedy's settlement without even consulting Castro. *New York Times,* October 30, 1962.

[275] Theodore Draper, "Castro, Khrushchev, and Mao," *Reporter,* August 15, 1963, p. 27.

[276] Nikita Khrushchev, "Khrushchev Remembers: Part IV," *Life,* December 18, 1970, p. 52.

[277] *New York Times,* November 3, 1962.

The major antagonists would not permit Cuba to sabotage the solution in the name of saving face. "Unlike German leaders in 1941, Premier Khrushchev did not irrevocably tie his policy to that of a weaker—and perhaps less responsible—ally." [278] Almost from the outset, he made it clear that he conceived of the crisis in exclusively Soviet-American terms and, therefore, took steps to insure the viability of the accord. On November 6, for example, Vasily V. Kuznetsov, Khrushchev's special representative for the Cuban negotiations, gave John McCloy private assurances to the effect that the Soviet Union would honor its inspection pledge, despite Kennedy's refusal to make guarantees against an invasion unless Castro accepted inspection. Three days later, the United States announced that all known offensive missile sites had been dismantled and that the missiles were being shipped out. The next day, the Navy intercepted five ships leaving Cuba to verify that missiles were being removed, though in keeping with the new spirit of relaxation, the ships were not boarded. Thus, despite the inability to carry out on-site inspection due to Castro's intransigence, aerial and naval surveillance were considered adequate to confirm that the bases had in fact been removed. On November 20 the Pentagon announced that the missiles had left Cuba aboard Soviet ships and at his first news conference in over two months, the President declared the quarantine lifted.

APPEARANCES AND REALITY IN THE MISSILE CRISIS

*Peace hath her victories
No less renown'd than war.*

Milton,
"To the Lord General Cromwell"

The President's success in the missile crisis was doubtless aided by his having perceived reality with the accuracy of a draftsman. [279] The situation in Cuba, the situation in the Soviet Union, the situation at home in the United States—in none was he significantly misled by appearances. To what can this remarkable achievement be attributed? Several factors deserve mention.

---

[278] Holsti, Brody, and North, *op. cit.*, p. 35.
[279] This is not to say, however, that successful policies necessarily presuppose accurate perceptions. See Ole R. Holsti, "Comparative 'Operational Codes' of Recent U.S. Secretaries of State," paper delivered at the meeting of the American Political Science Association, New York, September 1969.

First, institutionally. the environment was most propitious. Kennedy had learned—academically, from Richard Neustadt[280] and experientially, from nearly two years in office—that the President must be wary of institutional competitors for his power. Lowering his guard would be inviting their domination, as the Bay of Pigs fiasco made clear. "It's a hell of a way to learn things," he said after that disaster, "but I have learned one thing from this business—that is, that we will have to deal with the CIA." [281] Which is to say, more broadly, that he had learned that institutions, as part of their challenge to the President's leadership, might attempt to convince him of the reality of appearances in order to win his support for their views—and they might do this with the best of intentions. But in the missile crisis, his institutional leadership emerged intact. Thus, while the CIA and Joint Chiefs of Staff might have provided him with faulty information at the Bay of Pigs and while the military and State Department officials might have provided Johnson with faulty information before the Tet offensive, the CIA and the Defense Department provided Kennedy with accurate information during the missile crisis. Although the tardiness of their original discovery of the missiles certainly exacerbated crisis tensions, the agencies recovered quickly, and thereafter adequately informed decision makers of the nature of the Soviet threat. The agencies also played important parts in the scrutinization and interpretation of feedback from the Soviets and Cubans.

Second, organizationally, the Executive Committee was important in helping to plumb the reality of the situation. The President, through his selection and leadership of the Committee, deserves much of the credit for this. The men chosen were calm, rational, and frank. That they were able to function well together, however, was due not only to their own qualities, but also to the kind of leadership Kennedy chose to exercise.[282] Leaders of small groups most often are spoken of as "task leaders" or "social leaders." [283] Task leaders provide intellectual initiative and direction, while social leaders promote harmony, mutual respect, and dedica-

---

[280] Richard E. Neustadt expounded this view as an early adviser to Kennedy and in his influential book, *Presidential Power: The Politics of Leadership* (New York: Wiley, 1960).

[281] Quoted in Hilsman, *op. cit.,* p. 63.

[282] That role-taking can be spoken of an entailing a choice is contended by a leading sociological analyst of leadership: "Role-taking is in effect a decision by the individual—not always consciously arrived at—regarding how he ought to work. And this involves an estimate of his own place among others, including the demands made upon him and his own capabilities." Philip Selznick, *Leadership in Administration: A Sociological Interpretation* (New York: Harper and Row, 1957), p. 83.

[283] See Robert F. Bales, "Task Roles and Social Roles in Problem-Solving Groups," *Readings in Social Psychology,* ed. Eleanor E. Maccoby, Theodore M. Newcomb, and Eugene L. Hartley, 3d ed. (New York: Holt, Rinehart and Winston, 1958), pp. 437–47, and Bales, "The Equilibrium Problem in Small Groups," *Working Papers in the Theory of Action,* ed. Talcott Parsons, Bales, and Edward A. Shils (Glencoe: Free Press, 1953), p. 349.

tion to the group's purpose. Ordinarily, it is difficult to combine these two roles in a single individual, for task leadership generally necessitates an emotional detachment from others that precludes social leadership.[284] In the missile crisis, however, there was no need for a full-time social leader because most of the social maintenance functions were performed by the members themselves. The President's selection, in other words, insured that from the outset, there would be agreement on norms, on values, on the task to be faced; and there was friendship and reciprocal esteem, too. Above all, as one member later recalled, "There was a deep sense of the sharing of danger." [285] In such an atmosphere, a wholly socially-oriented leader would have been superfluous, if not actually dysfunctional.[286]

At this point, the question arises as to what kind of leader the President was, if his social functions were few and if he frequently absented himself when his advisers were considering the problem at hand.[287] The answer is that Kennedy's leadership constituted what has been termed "democratic leadership." Closer to the "social" end of the continuum, the

democratic leader encourages the members to influence one another in their work on the task, thereby avoiding the risk of antagonizing them by personal and direct pressures. By group decision and participation procedures, he attempts to distribute many of the task functions among the membership at large, and in this manner is enabled to perform a [social] maintenance role himself.[288]

Here it must be recalled that the President chose all of his own advisers, virtually without outside restraint: all of them shared, or at least were sympathetic to, his values. The relinquishing of direct control, therefore, could hardly have been thought to result in significant deviation from the decision they would have taken had he been present.

---

[284] Fred E. Fiedler, *Leader Attitudes and Group Effectiveness* (Urbana: University of Illinois Press, 1958), p. 44; Robert F. Bales and Phillip E. Slater, "Role Differentiation in Small Decision Making Groups," *Family, Socialization, and Interaction Process,* ed. Talcott Parsons and Bales (Glencoe: Free Press, 1955), chap. 5; Robert F. Bales, "Task Status and Likeability as a Function of Talking and Listening to Decision-Making Groups," *The State of the Social Sciences,* ed. Leonard D. White (Chicago: University of Chicago Press, 1956), pp. 148–61.

[285] Unnamed Committee member, quoted in Sidey, *op. cit.,* p. 349.

[286] Of course, the price for all this harmony was the exclusion from the Committee of individuals who might have differed from the consensus in basic and persistent ways. Thus, with this selection, the range of alternatives seriously considered by the Committee and by the President was limited more than would otherwise have been the case.

[287] One member had, in fact, concluded that the Committee meetings were "repetitive, leaderless, and a waste of time." Dean Acheson, "Dean Acheson's Version of Robert Kennedy's Version of the Cuban Missile Crisis," *Esquire,* February 1969, p. 77.

[288] John W. Thibaut and Harold H. Kelley, *The Social Psychology of Groups* (New York: Wiley, 1959), p. 282.

But not only was there little to lose from democratic leadership; the working procedures it fostered contributed importantly to the President's decision. For in small groups, this approach has repeatedly been found to be more effective than authoritarianism, in terms of promoting group cohesion, facilitating its work, and improving the members' satisfaction with what is produced.[289]

Yet the group "brainstorming" procedure followed in the beginning of the early phase in Kennedy's absence is a technique currently out of fashion. Its rationale consists in the beliefs that:

(1) the larger the number of uninhibited ideas produced, the more likely that new and inventive thinking will occur, and (2) brainstorming by several persons working together is more effective than by individuals working alone.[290]

But if the general question of the utility of brainstorming for group problem solving remains undecided,[291] in the specific instance of the Executive Committee it seems to have worked quite adequately. One reason for its success—and, indeed, of the success of the Committee in general—lay in the nature of its intragroup conflict. Characterized by "substantive" and not "affective" struggles, the Committee was the scene of intellectual conflict over the subject at hand and not emotional quarreling arising primarily from interpersonal friction.[292] Had this situation been reversed, the Committee might have proved itself dysfunctional in a disastrous way; for its recommendations might have been so personality-oriented as effectively to have subverted attempts at solving the problem ostensibly responsible for their birth.

The President's utilization of his organization, then, appears to have been shrewdly adapted to the conditions at hand. It permitted his advisers the freedom essential for effective discussion, yet maintained the

---

[289] The group procedures also seem to have fostered a sense of membership interdependence, a trait which has been found to contribute to an enlarged sense of responsibility toward the group and a greater willingness to work in its behalf. E. J. Thomas, "Effects of Facilitation and Interdependence on Group Functioning," *Human Relations* 10 (1957): 347–66.

[290] Fremont J. Lyden, "Brainstorming and Group Problem Solving: The Same Thing?" *Public Administration Review* 25 (December 1965): 333.

[291] For criticisms of brainstorming, see Donald W. Taylor, Paul C. Berry, and Clifford H. Block, "Does Group Participation When Using Brainstorming Facilitate or Inhibit Creative Thinking?" *Administrative Science Quarterly* 3 (June 1958): 23–47; Bernard S. Benson, "Let's Toss This Idea Up . . . ," *Fortune,* October 1957, pp. 145–46; M. Dunnette, "Are Meetings Any Good for Solving Problems?" *Personnel Administration* 27 (March–April 1964): 16. This view is disputed by Abram R. Solem, "Almost Anything I Can Do, We Can Do Better," *Personnel Administration* 28 (November–December 1965): 6–15; and by the popularizer of this technique, advertising executive Alex F. Osborn, *Applied Imagination* (New York: Scribner's, 1957).

[292] Harold Guetzkow and John Gyr, "An Analysis of Conflict in Decision-Making Groups," *Human Relations* 7 (1954): 367–81.

presidential control essential for effective task leadership; and it made the best use of the available time.

Moreover, that the President relied so extensively upon group decision making may itself have improved the quality of the final product. First of all, as Sidney Verba has pointed out, while group decision making does not guarantee sound results, it does militate against a decision's performing a strictly personality-oriented function.[293] Were only one decision maker to have assumed any importance in the crisis, the decisional process probably would have proceeded in this fashion: the decision maker, once he had reached preliminary conclusions, would have been reluctant to give them up. Feeling relatively—and increasingly—certain of the wisdom of his choices, he would have tended not to see what did not harmonize with them. With this natural tendency heightened by the tensions of a crisis situation, final acceptance of the original solution would have been virtually inevitable. Decision making, thus, might have degenerated to a solemn ratification of impulse. Now, to some extent this was true in the case of the Cuban missiles, for the early choice of the blockade was in fact never overturned. But that there existed a group composed of advocates of different points of view kept these alternatives alive, and made the President's final selection less a reiteration of a position than a decision. The blockade was selected, then, *not* because it was the only choice to receive significant attention, but because it won out in the market place of ideas that, for a week, was called the Executive Committee of the National Security Council.

There were further advantages to collective decision making. First, the presence of an audience tends to moderate the opinions offered, stripping them of extreme judgments and idiosyncratic associations.[294] But when a "free-wheeling" attitude obtains—as it did during the early crisis talks—this moderation seems to militate against neither novelty[295] nor creativity[296] in ideas. Second, since uniformity did not exist at the outset, a group-oriented approach necessitated consideration of more alternatives than would have appeared to an individual; and as a greater number of alternatives are perceived, a greater chance of making the correct choice results.[297] Third, the information and skills brought to bear upon

---

[293] Sidney Verba, "Assumptions of Rationality in Models of the International System," *World Politics* 14 (October 1961): 103. Holsti, Brody, and North contrast this with the case of the German Kaiser who in 1914 "underwent an almost total collapse at the time he made a series of key decisions. . . ." *Op. cit.,* p. 37, n. 14.

[294] Floyd H. Allport, *Social Psychology* (Boston: Houghton Mifflin, 1924).

[295] Irving Lorge, Joel Davitz, David Fox, and K. Herrold, *Evaluation in Instruction in Staff Action and Decision Making,* Technical Report No. 16 Prepared by the Air Research and Development Command of Maxwell Air Force Base (Maxwell Air Force Base, Alabama: Human Resources Research Institute, 1953).

[296] Osborn, *op. cit.*

[297] J. F. Dashiell, "Experimental Studies of the Influence of Social Situations on the Be-

the task were additive: as opposed to an individual, a group tends to gather and retain more information,[298] to exercise a greater memory capacity,[299] and, in general, to possess a larger pool of available knowledge relevant to the problem.[300] Both in terms of scope and depth, the President's advisers had a decisive edge over the President alone. Fourth, "discussion leads to the improvement of individual judgments," whose "combination . . . is advantageous." [301] As a process, group decision making performs a cleansing and objectifying function.

This is not to say that collective decisions are without their drawbacks. Conformity pressures, as was earlier noted, may be so intense that considerations of the merits of the issue may be sublimated. Groups may also be used as buck-passing organizations, or, in Harold Leavitt's words, "as psychological defense devices to protect superiors' weaknesses from being exposed to subordinates, and vice versa." [302] And this buck-passing may result in the adoption of a dangerous decision. Emphasizing the importance of diffusion of responsibility, Kogan and Wallach have concluded that "the effect of asking a group of individuals to reach a consensus about the level of risk to accept in decision making results in a strong move toward greater risk taking." [303] This, in fact, is what may have taken place during the Bay of Pigs deliberations a year and a half earlier. "Nobody in the White House wanted to be soft," one White House aide recalled. "Everybody wanted to show they [*sic*] were just as daring and bold as anyone else. They didn't look at the plan closely enough." [304] In the missile crisis discussions, this tendency might help to explain the advisers' rejection of mild plans of action, but what is one to

---

havior of Individual Human Adults," *Handbook of Social Psychology,* ed. C. Murchison (Worcester: Clark University Press, 1935), pp. 1097–1158; Arthur Jenness, "The Role of Discussion in Changing Opinion Regarding a Matter of Fact," *Journal of Abnormal and Social Psychology* 37 (October–December 1932): 279–96.

[298] Irving Lorge, Jacob Tuckman, Louis Aikman, Joseph Spiegel, and Gilda Moss, "Solutions by Teams and by Individuals to a Field Problem at Different Levels of Reality," *Journal of Educational Psychology* 46 (January 1955): 17–24.

[299] Herbert Gurnee, "Maze Learning in the Collective Situation," *Journal of Psychology* 3 (1937): 437–43; H. V. Perlmutter and Germaine de Montmollin, "Group Learning of Nonsense Syllables," *Journal of Abnormal and Social Psychology* 47 (October 1952): 762–69.

[300] Donald W. Taylor and William L. Faust, "Twenty Questions: Efficiency in Problem Solving as a Function of Size of Group," *Journal of Experimental Psychology* 44 (November 1952): 360–68.

[301] Michael Argyle, *The Scientific Study of Social Behavior* (London: Methuen, 1957), p. 119. However, "the product of the 'best' individual [may be] superior to that of the 'best' group." Irving Lorge, David Fox, Joel Davitz, and Marlin Brenner, "A Survey of Studies Contrasting the Quality of Group Performance and Individual Performance, 1920–1957," *Psychological Bulletin* 55 (September 1958): 369.

[302] Harold J. Leavitt, *Managerial Psychology* (Chicago: University of Chicago Press, 1958), p. 205.

[303] Nathan Kogan and Michael A. Wallach, "Risks and Deterrents: Individual Determinants and Group Effects," *American Journal of Orthopsychiatry* 33 (March 1963): 223.

[304] Unnamed White House aide, quoted in Sidey, *op. cit.,* p. 127.

make of their later refusals to bomb or invade Cuba? The answer may be that the men of the Executive Committee were strong and accustomed to wielding authority, and consequently, not given to buck-passing to the degree necessary to yield truly risky decisions.

It has also been said about collective decisions that if two heads are better than one, too many cooks spoil the broth: the result may be so wide-ranging as to be without value or so compromised as to be simply an "average" opinion.[305] And in matters of strategy, compromise may prove disastrous.[306]

While several of the defects of the group approach were in evidence during the missile crisis, on balance there can be little doubt that the stress placed upon collectivity reduced the incidence of misleading appearances.

A third basic check upon the influence of appearances was the President's cool, almost detached, personality, which helped to prevent the growth of an emotionalism that could distort perceptions. The importance of accurate perceptions can hardly be overstated, for in the last analysis one's behavior is necessarily dependent upon what W. I. Thomas called one's "definition of the situation." [307] Perception may be friendly or hostile, constant or changing; but in any case it will be selective, and consequently a distortion and a simplification of objective reality. "As a rule," said Lowell, "men see what they look for, and observe the things they expect to see," [308] and especially in political matters, "information and arguments . . . will 'register' only if they link up with the citizen's preconceived ideas." [309]

There are several major sources of misperception: the individual's psychological needs; the element of surprise; and the felt necessity for a speedy response. The first of these sources will be examined later; the

---

[305] Daniel M. Johnson, *The Psychology of Thought and Judgment* (New York: Harper and Row, 1955), p. 471.

[306] Arthur I. Waskow, for example, argued that the American compromise between the Air Force's counterforce theory of deterrence and the Army's theory of balanced deterrence resulted in a policy which "would nullify the advantages claimed for the two pure theories, would combine all the worst disadvantages of each, and would possess major disadvantages of its own." *The Limits of Defense* (Garden City: Doubleday, 1962), p. 54.

[307] Quoted in E. P. Hollander and Raymond G. Hunt, eds., *Current Perspectives in Social Psychology* (New York: Oxford University Press, 1963), p. 255. Cf., the more specific conclusion of a distinguished British psychiatrist: "So the stressful situation . . . is not given by events but by the organism's interpretation of events in relation to itself." Geoffrey Vickers, "The Concept of Stress in Relation to the Disorganization of Human Behavior," *Modern Systems Research for the Behavioral Scientist: A Sourcebook*, ed. Walter Buckley (Chicago: Aldine Publishing Co., 1968 [c. 1959]), p. 355.

[308] A. Lawrence Lowell, *Public Opinion in War and Peace* (Cambridge: Harvard University Press, 1923), p. 22; Walter Lippmann, *Public Opinion* (New York: Macmillan, 1922), p. 21.

[309] Joseph Schumpeter, *Capitalism, Socialism, and Democracy* (New York: Harper and Brothers, 1942), p. 263.

second was of minor significance; and the third was not as potent as one might have supposed. Instead, it was a fourth source, cultural bias, which posed the greatest threat, and seems to hold the most importance for the future: the President inevitably was anchored in the American national experience. Having undergone a particular kind of political socialization, he became a part of a society—and, to narrow the terms further, a social and economic class, and a governing elite—held together by a number of specific psychological tendencies giving it a bias in its dealings with external forces. This socialization, moreover, differed in critical ways from that of his adversary, making difficult not only perception but also communication; for in the words of a famous linguistic analyst, "the concepts a culture lives by [cannot] be grafted into another language as easily as the technicalities of the missile." [310] This fact had been explicitly brought to the President's attention a year earlier in a social psychiatrist's personality assessment of Khrushchev prepared for the Vienna summit meeting.[311]

This tendency to distort communications by filtering them through "national perspectives" is heightened during periods of crisis.[312] It is sobering to consider the possible consequences had Kennedy fallen victim to such misperception: blinded with hostility and ethnocentric preconceptions, the President's perception of the emplacement of Soviet missiles could have resulted in intense frustration; this feeling, in turn, could have aroused aggressive impulses; since aggression itself is "a frustration to its object," [313] counteraggression might have been provoked; with thermonuclear weapons at the ready, catastrophe might have followed.[314]

---

[310] I. A. Richards, "Growing Pains: Book Review of *General Linguistics: An Introductory Survey* by R. H. Robins and *The Linguistic Sciences and Language Teaching* by M. A. K. Holliday, Angus McIntosh, and Peter Stevens," *New York Review of Books*, April 14, 1966, p. 24.

[311] Bryant Wedge, "Khrushchev at a Distance—A Study of Public Personality," *Trans-action*, October 1968, p. 27. In this study, Wedge not only analyzed Khrushchev as "a stable hypomanic character (chronic optimist opportunist)," but also outlined what were considered to be the most effective ways of dealing with such a personality. Although there is no reason to believe that Kennedy consciously followed these management principles or even referred to Wedge's study, the President's adherence to its lessons is uncannily consistent.

[312] Bryant M. Wedge, "National Perspectives and International Communications," *American Journal of Orthopsychiatry* 33 (March 1963): 209–10.

[313] Robert R. Sears, Eleanor E. Maccoby, and Harry Levin, "The Socialization of Aggression," Maccoby, Newcomb, and Hartley, *op. cit.,* p. 352.

[314] This interpretation follows the famous Dollard hypothesis that aggression is a function of frustration; which is to say, that aggressive behavior is a common instrument used in dealing with interferences with ongoing goal-oriented activities. See John Dollard, *et al., Frustration and Aggression* (New Haven: Yale University Press, 1939); Elton B. McNeil, "Psychology and Aggression," *Journal of Conflict Resolution* 3 (September 1959): 202–3; Leonard Berkowitz, *Aggression: A Social Psychological Analysis* (New York: McGraw-Hill, 1962).

It must certainly be ruled fortunate, then, that President Kennedy was not given to emotionalism or lacking in discipline.[315] "I've never seen a man so fully engaged," [316] Bundy recalled of the President during the crisis. Yet at its peak, Kennedy's secretary remembers his pausing to check with his tailor on the fit of a new suit, and inspecting the grass on the White House lawn.[317] The President's "engagement" plainly was a peculiar kind, embodying at once a most intense involvement and a surprisingly detached perspective. Though in charge of "a gate to a thousand wastelands mute and cold!" [318] he revealed no hint of panic or even of undue haste, no hypernationalism, no loss of self-mastery. His perception of the information gathered by the institutional apparatus, therefore, appears to have been remarkably clear and accurate, given the extraordinary circumstances.[319]

Implicit in all this is the recognition that President Kennedy—and indeed all Presidents in similar situations—reacted not only as a President, but also as a specific man. This suggests, first, that Kennedy saw the Soviets' emplacement of missiles not merely in national terms, but in personal terms, as well. As he had told James Wechsler of the *New York Post* a year earlier, "If Khrushchev wants to rub my nose in the dirt, it's all over." [320] Hence, the Soviet action in Cuba, in an important sense, constituted an individual affront. "It was the courage of John F. Kennedy which was in question," wrote one correspondent, "the credibility

---

[315] Vickers has observed that "Animal experimentalists have demonstrated the genetic basis for differential immunity and vulnerability to stress in animals." *Op. cit.*, p. 356. This suggests a provocative—though, of course, untestable—hypothesis to the effect that the famous coolness of the President's parents may have been transmitted to him through biological inheritance, as well as through ordinary social learning.

[316] McGeorge Bundy, quoted in Sidey, *op. cit.*, p. 335.

[317] Lincoln, *op. cit.*, pp. 326, 327.

[318] Friedrich Nietzsche, "Lonesome," *Twentieth-Century German Verse,* ed. Patrick Bridgwater (Baltimore: Penguin Books, 1963), p. 1.

[319] This was true despite the considerable anxiety that must have accompanied his role. As Max Bruck has noted, "The cumulative effect of an individual's anxiety may be to narrow his perceptions and prevent him from achieving a dispassionate assessment of the nature of the problem-solving task." Max Bruck, "A Review of Social and Psychological Factors Associated with Creativity and Innovation," *Empathy and Ideology: Aspects of Administrative Innovation,* ed. Charles Press and Alan Arian (Chicago: Rand McNally, 1966), p. 40.

[320] John F. Kennedy, quoted in Schlesinger, *op. cit.*, p. 391. The occasion of this remark was the Berlin crisis of 1961. If one can believe former ambassador to the Soviet Union, George F. Kennan, Kennedy had clearly been bested at an earlier 1961 summit meeting with Khrushchev at Vienna. "I think they thought this is a tongue-tied young man who's not forceful and who doesn't have any ideas of his own," Kennan recalled, "they felt they could get away with something," He speculated that this impression may have encouraged Khrushchev to send missiles to Cuba. *New York Daily News,* August 31, 1970. Perhaps, the memory of the meeting also encouraged Kennedy to take a harder line at the missile confrontation.

of his willingness to go all the way if the missiles were not removed." [321]
In fact, with its extraordinary mixture of the problematic and the consequential, the crisis was perhaps the quintessence of Goffman's "fateful" event, providing a "central opportunity to show strong character" through the "voluntary taking of serious chances. . . ." The Kennedy-Khrushchev battle, however else it might be described, was clearly from the President's vantage a "character contest," in which he was "concerned with establishing evidence of strong character at the expense of the character of his opponent." [322] Thus, the crisis followed Goffman's scenario with remarkable fidelity. Beginning with "one player offending against a moral rule"—i.e., Khrushchev's secretly sneaking the missiles into Cuba—the contest soon became one concerning a "matter of principle," involving "the system itself"—i.e., the President's refusal to acquiese in an alteration of the international balance of power, whatever the price of that refusal and even if the alteration were not decisive. "Full of dramatic risk," the fateful event requires that the individual

arrange to be in a position to let go and then let go. . . . He must expose himself to time, to seconds and minutes ticking off outside his control; he must give himself up to the certain rapid resolution of an uncertain outcome. And he must give himself up to fate in this way when he could avoid it at reasonable cost. [323]

This, surely, is an apt description of Kennedy's behavior, waiting for the Soviet ships to encounter his blockade after having rejected the Cuban missile-Turkish missile trade-off, a deal whose military cost to the United States was comparatively very small. [324]

Kennedy's concern, however, was not only his self-image, but also his public image, and here he could not have been unaware of the immense prestige that would be accorded the victor in such an epic character contest. Certainly, as an avid reader of James Bond mysteries, the President

---

[321] I. F. Stone, "The Brink: Book Review of *The Missile Crisis* by Elie Abel," *New York Review of Books*, April 14, 1966, p. 13.

[322] Erving Goffman, "Where the Action Is," *Interaction Ritual: Essays on Face-to-Face Behavior*, Anchor Books (Garden City: Doubleday, 1967), pp. 164, 260, 236, 240. "Strong character" includes the very qualitites which the President sought to exemplify: courage, gameness, ability to resist temptation, gallantry, and above all, composure. *Ibid.*, pp. 218–22. Kennedy, of course, did not want to humiliate Khrushchev to the point of compelling him to respond to the crisis militarily. Yet this does not mean that Kennedy was not engaged in a Goffmanesque character contest; for an unlimited effort to humiliate Khrushchevwas perceived as suicidal for the United States, and the contest requires assumption of a *risk* of disaster, and not of the disaster itself. In the missile crisis, in other words, words, maximization of Kennedy's strong character at Khrushchev's expense necessitated restraint.

[323] *Ibid.*, pp. 242, 241, 260, 261.

[324] The risk, as will be argues shortly, was not as great as it has often been portrayed, but in fateful events, "chance taking is embraced but not fondled." *Ibid.*, p. 172, n. 23.

must have noted and experienced the huge appeal of commercialized vicarious fatefulness,[325] and his preoccupation with Success and public relations suggests that he appreciated its potential for generating respect and popularity: would he otherwise have conducted so much of his crisis diplomacy in full view of the American and, indeed, world publics? Thus, from the beginning, the crisis issue was not simply America's prestige, but, perhaps more importantly, Kennedy's prestige. Though impressive speeches, a polished style, and a retinue that had "swamped the national consciousness" [326] had hidden most of the administration's inadequacies from public view, a spectacular diplomatic defeat would be seen as truly damaging, and a failure to utilize the contest for maximum public opinion effect, as foolish in the extreme. It would be unkind to say that the Kennedy statue had feet of clay. Rather, they were merely press releases.

Yet, as was said earlier, psychological needs are less important in decision making than are the habits developed to deal with them. And the President's style clearly suited the crisis problem perfectly, for the virtues required were caution, reason, and magnanimity. Certainly, an important decisional input was the President's aim, as he had remarked in another context, "to do things well, and to do them with precision and with modesty. . . ." [327]

The President's explicit goal—the maintenance of America's world position—remained constant from the outset. Conflict, then, both within himself and among his advisers, was always severely circumscribed. Differences between opposing sides were less profound than they would have been had conflict centered upon aims; and the response to the problem was more stable.[328] Hence, Kennedy never wavered in his determination to oust the Soviet missiles from Cuba, refusing to narrow his objective to a token success or to broaden it to include the related question of Castro. This constancy of purpose plainly influenced the decision to blockade Cuba, for the President and his advisers were agreed that this approach best combined the nation's interest in security and status with that in peace. The rationale for this strategy was that it afforded the President the greatest freedom of movement, the widest choice of means toward his explicit end.

Once this decision had been taken, however, and Soviet-American interaction had begun—which is to say, once the decisional output had begun to produce feedback, which itself became an input—an odd situation

[325] *Ibid.,* pp. 262–66.

[326] Midge Decter, "Kennedyism," *Commentary,* January 1970, p. 19. She notes that the President and his family, as well as his retinue, were involved in the "swamping."

[327] John F. Kennedy, quoted in Wicker, *op. cit.,* p. 23.

[328] Patricia Kendall, *Conflict and Mood: Factors Affecting Stability of Response* (Glencoe: Free Press, 1954), pp. 16–19.

began to develop. That flexibility which had characterized the President's leadership of the Executive Committee, that willingness to bend which had permeated the whole substance of collective decision making, that recognition of the importance of freedom of action which had seemed so vital in the choice of strategies—that capacity for change which had appeared so essential—had vanished. And nobody seemed to notice or care that it had gone. The rigidity which had attached to the explicit goal of maintaining the American position had now been attached to the specific policy as well.

One may speculate as to the reasons behind the President's turn to relative intransigence. First, after struggling with the problem of how to react for a number of days, the temptations to consider the decisions reached as final must have been potent, and the thought of reopening deliberations must have seemed foolish and indecisive to the extreme; and seeing his adversary now wrestling with the same problem must have been gratifying. If one views Kennedy's crisis behavior as in some sense a rite of passage, this explanation becomes even more attractive. In any event, that the decision and the rigidity following it served some personality functions would be difficult to deny.

Second, the President realized that it was planning that had given him the initiative, and that a turn to improvisation once interaction had begun might reduce him to the level of irresolute fumbling, as it apparently had done to his opponent. Third, both Kennedy's advisers and, more importantly, passing events reassured him that he had indeed made the best selection. The significance of reinforcement, however, should not be overstated; for strategy adoption and maintenance is not simply a function of rewarded stimuli.[329] Yet presidential conservatism was certainly a factor contributing to strategic rigidity. As the President was fond of saying, "When it is not necessary to change, it is necessary not to change." [330]

At this juncture, it becomes clear that one useful way of regarding Kennedy's strategic rigidity is as a learned pattern of responses. Although originally stressing flexibility, he quickly saw that the feedback from the interaction revealed the utility of intransigence. From this angle, the interaction period can be viewed as evidence tending to confirm Kenneth Boulding's maxim: "Conflict management is essentially a

---

[329] Thus, shifts in strategy may occur even when *all* strategic alternatives are fully rewarded. Isadore Krechevsky, "The Genesis of 'Hypotheses' in Rats," *University of California Publications in Psychology* 6 (1932): 45–64.

[330] Lord Falkland, quoted approvingly by Kennedy in Tom Wicker, *Kennedy Without Tears: The Man Behind the Myth* (New York: William Morrow, 1964), p. 35. In this vein, the President's favorite book was said to be David Cecil's *Life of Melbourne,* who is remembered for remarking, "If it was not absolutely necessary, it was the foolishest thing ever done." Quoted in *loc. cit.*

learning process." [331] Presidents, in this context, face two primary problems. First, they must learn to control themselves, their immediate advisers, and their bureaucracies in general. For President Kennedy, possessing broad self-discipline, able and dedicated aides, and a bureaucracy content to follow orders, this first problem did not brook large. Yet other Presidents in other crises may not find themselves so fortunately situated, and if this capacity for internal control cannot be developed, success in dealing with international conflict may become difficult, indeed.

Second, Presidents must learn to manage the behavior of their international adversaries in order to secure from them some degree of "psychological surrender. . . ." [332] Since in the foreseeable future, no third parties—the UN, for example, or the International Court of Justice—seem capable of arbitrating disputes among the great powers and enforcing conditions of settlement, this problem likely will characterize foreign policy crises under a number of succeeding Presidents.

Management of the adversary appears dependent upon the President's learning ability in three related areas.[333] First, he must learn to perceive with sufficient accuracy the nature of his adversary; second, he must learn to anticipate the reactions of his adversary; and, third, he must learn to empathize with his adversary. Thus, accuracy in the interpretation of information becomes a *sine qua non* of success, and the President's perceptual and memory capacities take on added importance in his battle with misleading appearances. Kennedy, it need merely be mentioned, meticulously scrutinized the feedback from the Soviets as a means of learning of Khrushchev's situation, his pressures, and his needs; and the President carefully formulated his international communications so as to minimize the chances of their being critically distorted by his opponent's national perspective. In all these areas, of course, President Kennedy received important assistance from competent advisers and intelligence agents. But inasmuch as he insisted upon making the final decisions, this aid did not obviate the necessity of his learning how to manage the conflict. To the extent that future Presidents demand ultimate crisis authority, they, too, would seem faced with learning international conflict management; and experience appears to be the only teacher. Thus, it may be that in some future crisis, an American President may not prove as adept as Kennedy in learning

[331] Kenneth E. Boulding, "Conflict Management as a Key to Survival," *American Journal of Orthopsychiatry* 33 (March 1963): 230.
[332] André Beaufre, *An Introduction to Strategy with Particular Reference to Problems of Defense, Politics, Economics, and Diplomacy in the Nuclear Age*, trans. R. H. Barry (New York: Praeger, 1965), p. 134.
[333] Boulding, *loc. cit.*

> ... games that call for patience,
> foresight, maneuver,
> like war. . . .[334]

By this point, it is evident that despite the enormous bureaucratization of government and the famous "institutionalization of the presidency," Kennedy took a profoundly personal view of crisis diplomacy. From the choosing of advisers to the controlling of blockade operations to the correspondence with Premier Khrushchev, the crisis revolved like a satellite around the President. Illustrative is an incident which took place during the acute crisis phase. As Robert Kennedy relates it:

When it was reported to [the President] that our photography showed that the Russians and Cubans had inexplicably lined up their planes wing tip to wing tip on Cuban airfields, making them perfect targets, he requested General Taylor to have a U-2 fly a photographic mission over our fields in Florida. "It would be interesting if we have done the same thing," he remarked. We had. He examined the pictures the next day and ordered the Air Force to disperse our planes.[335]

All of this suggests that crisis management was a personal presidential *tour de force.* In some sense this was true, though the importance of competent staff assistance should not be neglected in an enthusiasm for the heroic. There are a number of limitations inherent in such a personal approach, the most obvious being its inordinate dependence upon the capabilities of a single man at a given time. Yet perhaps so long as crises are viewed as sufficiently extraordinary to warrant wholesale departures from established techniques, this method probably is inescapable.

If President Kennedy's appreciation of the realities of the missile crisis were obviously satisfactory, the same could not be said of the press and the general public. In the nuclear age, it is hard to quarrel with Twiggy's observation that "wars frighten me more than spiders, I swear," [336] and so it is hardly surprising that among those writing on the President's crisis success, it has become almost commonplace to aver "to the fact that the results were attained by leaning far over the brink, a brink a hundred megatons deep. . . ." [337] The President himself, in his televised speech of October 22, talked of a "worldwide nuclear war in which the fruits of victory would be ashes in my mouth." [338] And in descriptions of the events,

---

[334] W. H. Auden, "Fairground," *New Yorker,* August 20, 1966, p. 32.

[335] Robert F. Kennedy, "Thirteen Days," p. 151.

[336] Twiggy, quoted in Oriana Fallaci, "My Name Is Twiggy," *Saturday Evening Post,* August 12, 1967, p. 61.

[337] Etzioni, *op. cit.,* p. 159.

[338] John F. Kennedy, "The Soviet Threat to the Americas," *Department of State Bulletin* 47 (November 12, 1962): 716.

"abyss" [339] and "precipice" [340] are recurring terms. The question arises, however, as to what degree these remarks can be written off to rhetoric, to a sense of the dramatic, to a desire to use the crisis as an episode from which the proper lessons can be extracted or the proper figures praised. In retrospect, it appears difficult to dispute the *Economist's* judgment that once the Soviets had "been found out, their position was irretrievably weak." [341] Here was a situation in which America's military superiority—both nuclear and conventional—was overwhelming, in which America's purpose was sharply focused and widely known, and in which these two elements were aligned in a truly impressive fashion. Equally important, the Soviet Union was being guided by sane men, who recognized the intractibility of their dilemma. On the one hand, they could withdraw the missiles, and suffer "a terrible humiliation." [342] On the the the other hand, they could refuse to withdraw the missiles, and then be confronted with still more disagreeable alternatives: to witness idly the American invasion of Cuba, and destruction of the Castro regime—an act of overwhelming self-abasement—or to counter with thermonuclear retaliation—an act of simple self-annihilation. Intermediate responses plainly would have been too ineffective to consider seriously.

Thus aware of the hopelessness of their stance, they realized that they "had to cut [their] losses quickly, before they mounted." [343] And the President, as his brother later recalled, fully appreciated the overriding importance of this fact.[344] Given all this, how significant was the possibility that the crisis could have developed into a general war? As the Wohlstetters argue, "the main risks were of a local, non-nuclear action," and, because of Cuba's insular status, "possibilities of isolating a limited conflict have seldom been clearer." [345] Local actions can escalate into major affairs, of course, but in this case the principals' desire to control events and to avoid general war seems to have greatly reduced the probability of an all-out nuclear exchange. In fact, it was probably more the pres-

---

[339] See e.g., Steel, *op. cit.,* p. 42; Karl E. Meyer, "Back from the Abyss," *New Statesman* 64 (November 2, 1962): 606; Robert F. Kennedy, "Thirteen Days," p. 7. Kennedy's article is subtitled, "The Story about How the World Almost Ended."

[340] *Washington Post* quoted in *New York Times,* November 4, 1962; Robert F. Kennedy, "Thirteen Days," p. 164.

[341] "After Cuba," *Economist* 205 (November 3, 1962): 431.

[342] According to an East European diplomat, "By initiative, Kennedy inflicted on the Soviets a terrible humiliation, from which they have yet to recover fully." Anonymous East European diplomat, quoted in Philip Ben, "How the Czechs Got a U.S. Brush-off," *New Republic,* August 31, 1968, p. 8.

[343] "Soviet Brinksmanship: Why Did the Russians Do It?" *Economist* 205 (November 3, 1962): 433.

[344] Robert F. Kennedy, "Thirteen Days," p. 173. The implicit contradiction between this recognition and Robert Kennedy's otherwise breathless account of "how the world almost ended" is, of course, never brought out.

[345] Albert and Roberta Wohlstetter, *op. cit.,* p. 6.

ence of nuclear weapons that was responsible for the prudent exercise of power than any other factor.

"Let us not forget," wrote the sculptor Rodin, "that power produces grace. . . ." [346] But grace, like beauty, is in the eyes of the beholder; hence, it is the *appearance* of power that "produces grace"; and, conversely, grace that produces the appearance of power. Can it be, then, that the magnitude of the success is, in some sense, a function of the famous Kennedy style? (Had the President been Truman and not Kennedy would the accolades have been comparable?) Can it be said that the crisis, under the attention of the mass media, swelled into a kind of instant folk tale, which time has served only further to distend? Are Americans so pleased with themselves and so enamored of their dead President that a limited though famous triumph has come to be viewed as the most important success in human history? [347] Is one justified in concluding, as Tallulah Bankhead used to say, that there is less to this than meets the eye? Suspicions persist, and they persist because hindsight makes every event inevitable. From a distance of several years, the crisis appears to have been folded up by fate, neatly and simply, like a discarded coat donated to a rummage sale. Yet the truly relevant question must be: how great did the chance of a nuclear holocaust seem to be to the participants *at the time?* I am inclined to think that *past the early stages of interaction,* it never loomed very large to the President. While he clearly saw the need for the caution, and managed events superbly, he was fully aware that he held an unbeatable hand and that his opponent knew it and would have to concede. It was because he was certain of the outcome that the President could afford to permit Khrushchev extra room to maneuver an exit; and this feeling helps to explain Kennedy's embrace of open diplomacy and his increasing rigidity, too.

It would be disingenuous not to include a reply to this view, and fortunately, Richard Neustadt has offered an eloquent response. In contrasting the decision makers with their academic critics, he writes:

If you are sitting on top you know how uncertain is your own judgment. You know how limited it is. You know how partial are your facts. You know how tired you can get. You know how many mistakes human beings can make. And you have to assume that the men at the top on the other side are in the same situation. In that perspective there was every justification for uncertainty, concern, care displayed by the White House in the Cuban missile crisis. [348]

---

[346] Auguste Rodin, *Les Cathedrales de France* (Paris: Librairie Armand Colin, 1921), p. 3.

[347] For an example of this kind of view, see Max Ascoli, "Editorial: Escalation from the Bay of Pigs," *Reporter,* November 8, 1962, p. 25.

[348] U.S., Congress, Senate, Committee on Government Operations, Subcommittee on National Security and International Operations, *Hearing on the Conduct of National Secur-*

To say that the disagreement on the possibility of disaster concerns a matter of degree is not to resolve it with a platitude. Though lacking a standard to measure that degree leaves the debate with a taint of futility, the question of relative risk is simply too important to ignore.

All this is not added to deprecate the President or to minimize his achievement. Quite the contrary. That the possibility of general war, once the quarantine had been established, was small, constitutes a very powerful argument for the rightness of his decision. It is lacquering the events with romance that one objects to; it is transforming the episode into a kind of prettified plastic rose, at which one is to gaze and emit the appropriate murmurs, that one finds so repulsive. The primary decision concerned the blockade, and, while the subsequent moves were important and were executed in a near-flawless manner, once this point was passed, one must agree with Air Marshal Sir John Slessor: "The real, breath-taking decision will be that which President Kennedy would have had to make in October 1962, if Khrushchev had not bowed to the inevitable when he did—namely, when and in what way to break off negotiations and accept the inevitability of war." [349] And after October 22 this did not seem very likely because it was not very likely.

"The only infallible criterion of wisdom to vulgar minds," said Burke, is "success." Maybe. For all attempts to prove such a causal relationship seem to smack of a disagreeable latter-day Calvinism. Yet if a policy works and does no violence to a nation's values, what else can one call it? And because it might not work again with other men in other places hardly affects this judgment. When, looking back, the President spoke of an American people who had "neither dissolved in panic nor rushed headlong into reckless belligerence," [350] he could more accurately have been describing himself. A bit over a year after the crisis, the hero was dead. Of all the weeks of his life, perhaps none were more impressive than the last two in October 1962, when events crowded upon one another as if in a scene from Brueghel, and from the center he seemed almost to manage the world.

Nothing perhaps is more closely associated with modernity than nuclear weapons. But if the missile crisis were the preeminent *modern* crisis, it was not due to its potential destructiveness alone, for this is not only the atomic age but also the public relations age. Politicians talk and of-

ity Policy, Part 3, 89th Congress, 1st Sess., June 29, 1965, p. 136.
[349] Air Marshal Sir John Slessor, "Atlantic Policy: Control of Nuclear Strategy," *Foreign Affairs* 42 (October 1963): 100–1.
[350] John F. Kennedy, "Strength for Peace and Strength for War," *Department of State Bulletin* 49 (November 4, 1963): 694. (Address of October 19.)

ten think like advertising men, and a concern with appearances is so pervasive as to make governing almost a branch of cosmetology. As the ultimate modern crisis, the missile crisis was dominated by appearances from beginning to end—and even beyond. From the outset, the threat posed by the Soviet missiles was perceived mainly as one to images—America's and, possibly more importantly, Kennedy's. The response, as a consequence, was pursued and conceived in similar terms. Thus, the Turkish missiles-Cuban missiles trade was ruled out as making the United States *appear* weak, and a significant reason for rejecting an attack on Cuba was that it would make America *appear* pernicious; open diplomacy was utilized, presumably to heighten the magnitude and dissemination of the *propaganda* victory. Given the concern with images and the success of the crisis' resolution, it is hardly surprising that the missile episode became the greatest of public relations triumphs for the President and his nation. Its apocalyptic grandeur endures to this day, like confetti which has not yet settled to the ground. Even the decision-making process has been mythologized. This is not to say, however, that everything was mere appearance; for the possibility of disaster, while small, was as real as death.

7

Some Conclusions

"My money affairs are in a bad way. You remember before the wedding, Anisim brought me some new rubles and half rubles? I hid one packet, the rest I mixed with my own ... [N]ow I can't make out which is real money and which is counterfeit, it seems to me that they are all false coins ... &when I take a ticket at the station, I hand three rubles, then I think to myself: Are they false? And I'm frightened. I can't be well."

Chekhov, *The Hollow*

At the beginning of this study, a tripartite thesis was stated, whose repetition at this concluding stage may be germane. Decision makers, it was suggested, tend to define a given situation as a "crisis" if they see it as constituting a serious and immediate threat to national or presidential appearances of strength, competence, and resolve. Further, it was contended, factors tending to distort the President's perceptions of reality are found everywhere, are powerful in affecting his decisions, and to a significant extent probably cannot be overcome. Also, it was maintained that Presidents are willing and, at least in the short run, generally able to mislead the public regarding the nature of the presidential response to crises, if Presidents feel that national or personal interests make such deceptions desirable.

   Five case studies of presidential crisis decision making were presented. By their nature, such studies cannot establish the ultimate validity of a thesis, but merely can provide concrete illustrations of it. Nonetheless, enough information was offered to permit at least tentative generalizations.

I

Expectations regarding the decision makers' definitions of "crisis" were confirmed. The problem of appearance and reality in foreign policy crisis decision making, thus, in the last analysis becomes one partly of metaphysics: what *is* a crisis? The simplest answer would seem to be: a crisis is any situation which decision makers perceive as a crisis. And what kind of situations are these? The case studies suggest that often—maybe invariably—the main identifying characteristic is a threat seen as posed to certain desirable appearances, chiefly the appearances of national and presidential strength and resolve. Maintaining and enhancing that image for the nation seemed to entail the execution of the Bay of Pigs invasion, for which preparations had already begun. A concern with the appearance of national strength and resolve was in evidence not only in Kennedy's determination to expel Castro from Cuba, but also in Johnson's decision to intervene early and decisively in the Dominican Republic in order to prevent the establishment of another national embarrassment in the Caribbean. The policy decision underlying the pseudocrisis at the Gulf of Tonkin—that the United States should escalate its military activities in South Vietnam in order to forestall that government's collapse—reflects a concern with the image of national strength and resolve, too. For if the Saigon government were to fall after having been given well-publicized pledges of support by the United States, American power and will, it was felt, would have been called into question. Even the response to the Gulf of Tonkin attacks was framed in similar form: for the United States to tolerate North Vietnamese attacks on American ships without responding quickly and powerfully would be to cast doubt on its strength and will, and thereby to encourage the enemy in its action. By the same token, Kennedy's actions during the missile crisis—his determination not to acquiesce in the emplacement of Soviet missiles in the hemisphere, his rejection of the Turkish missiles-Cuban missiles trade, and so on—also partly reflected a concern with the national appearance of strength and resolve. At the Tet offensive—where the United States was surprised and on the defensive but had to react rhetorically almost immediately—the concern with an image of national strength and resolve was perhaps superseded by that with one of competence and preparedness. Hence, not only was America portrayed as powerful enough to withstand the attacks and dedicated enough to continue, but also as so highly skilled that the offensive had not been even a tactical surprise.

To say that an essential attribute of these crises was that the American image seemed to be threatened is not to minimize the issue; for doubtless Kennedy and Johnson agreed with a leading student of foreign affairs that "prestige is the faculty enabling a great power to avoid final, miserable choices between surrender and war." [1] A distinguished strategic analyst has provided the rationale for this position:

It is not enough to say that nations should have the greatness to ignore loss of face, to disown their reputations, to turn away from a challenge. A main constraint on the use of force in the world today is the expectation of a violent response. . . . Forgiveness has its limits if we want to preserve a set of expectations to constrain behavior, particularly in a world in which the main adversaries do not acknowledge each other's claims as rightful and in which each side may have strong defensive motives for exploiting offensive opportunities. [2]

This leads to the paradoxical conclusion that international confrontations over issues of national prestige may serve peace more than the postponing of such confrontations until more "substantial" matters are in dispute. And this, in turn, assumes that these more "substantial" matters are also more explosive. Yet, arguably, the opposite may be the case. In the first place, concern with intangibles like national images inevitably introduces greater vagueness into the business of goal setting and implementation, for such psychological objectives may be impossible to define adequately. Suppose, for example, a President aspires to a national image of strength. How strong does he want the nation to appear? How can he be sure that he is not projecting arrogance, instead of strength? How, at the same time, can he make his government appear prudent, yet not irresolute? The lines demarcating one image from another are shadowy and constantly changing, and making matters still more difficult and uncertain is the fact that the intended audience is composed of foreigners of widely differing viewpoints, interests, and cultural backgrounds. Thus, while President Johnson may have interpreted his Dominican Republic intervention as a sign of national strength, others looked on it as an act of arrogance. And though President Kennedy may have seen his refusal to commit Americans to a massive invasion at the Bay of Pigs as an indication of his government's prudence, others viewed it as evidence of weakness, indecisiveness, perhaps even cowardice.

The obvious difficulty of getting other (often hostile) countries to view a nation in the "proper" light, in addition, may consume so much of the decision makers' attention that more important considerations are neglected. Nor is this blindness to reality in the pursuit of appearances restricted to the United States alone. One English expert on the Middle

[1] Charles Burton Marshall, "Cuba—Why the Russians Are There," *New Republic*, October 1, 1962, p. 9.
[2] Thomas C. Schelling, speaking before the fifty-seventh annual meeting of the American Society of International Law on April 26, 1963, quoted in Kahn, *op. cit.,* p. 226.

East, for example, seems to suggest that an important force behind Britain's disastrous 1956 Suez attack was Britain's desire to reassert itself as a great power after a long series of humbling reverses, including the pulling out from India and Palestine and the relinquishing of naval supremacy to the United States. Thus, hegemony in the Middle East perhaps came to be valued more as a symbol than for its substantive benefits. Prime Minister Anthony Eden, as a consequence, was determined not to acquiesce in the affront to Britain contained in Nasser's nationalization of the Suez Canal, despite the facts that Egyptians had been operating the Canal competently, and the Canal concession was due to expire in a few years anyway. His resulting decision to join with France and Israel in an attack on Egypt produced an international fiasco, and forced him to exchange his office for the demeaning role of the writer of self-pitying memoirs.[3]

If the repairing of national prestige is fraught with peril, the decision makers' concern with their own appearances may be even more dangerous. For though Schelling ignores domestic politics, prestige may be the currency in this realm as much as in the international one, and may be no less sought after merely because it might be counterfeit. Certainly all five case studies reveal an intense presidential concern with their own images as perceived by their own people.

Partly, the appearances pursued can be described in terms of the traits expected of the traditional masculine leader: strength and resolve. But another trait often sought was the appearance of prudence. If in the last century Cardinal Newman could declare that "calculation never made a hero,"[4] few could say that now; in the nuclear age, coolness and caution have supplanted impulsive fearlessness as an attribute of the public hero. At the Bay Pigs, for example, Kennedy was plainly aware that a refusal to approve the invasion would deface his desired public appearance of strength and resolve. But he felt, too, that a decision to involve the nation massively and more directly in the action would have damaged his appearance of prudence and moderation.[5] Later, at the missile crisis, his inflexible determination to oust the Soviet missiles from Cuba, and his cautious and methodical approach to that end enhanced a similar public image. President Johnson also was concerned with these two facets of his image, strength-resolve and prudence. His rapid intervention in the Dominican Republic, for instance, showed him to be a man of action whose

---

[3] Elizabeth Monroe, *Britain's Moment in the Middle East* (Baltimore: Johns Hopkins Press, 1963), chap. 8.

[4] J. H. Newman, quoted in Søren Kierkegaard, *The Living Thoughts of Kierkegaard,* ed. W. H. Auden (New York: David McKay, 1952), p. 25.

[5] Some portions of the public, of course, interpreted this decision less as an act of prudence than of weakness, indecisiveness, or cowardice.

action was founded on the most cautious and foresighted of platitudes: "An ounce of prevention is worth a pound of cure." The quick and potent yet limited response to the Gulf of Tonkin attacks also served the Johnson image of strength and prudence. At the Tet offensive, however, he seems to have been most concerned with the traits of strength and competence, although some interest in prudence is suggested by his unwillingness to respond with a great military or even verbal escalation of the American war effort, such as by invading the North or mining the port of Haiphong.

Why did Presidents Kennedy and Johnson pursue such desirable public images as part of their efforts to define and handle crises? Electoral ambition may have been a factor. Both Vietnam crises preceded presidential elections, and the missile crisis arose less than two weeks before a congressional election. Certainly, both Presidents felt that in such circumstances the public wants and expects leadership, and rewards those in control for the appearance of satisfactory performance. A more important spur to image seeking, however, may have been the normal demand issuing from the individuals themselves for public respect and approval. Also present may have been a desire on the part of the Presidents to fortify not only their public images, but their self-images, as well. Kennedy during the missile crisis, for instance, seems to have wanted to atone for past failures in the Berlin and Bay of Pigs crises; and Johnson during Tet may have tried to reinforce and reassert a sense of mastery damaged by the surprise and ferocity of the enemy offensive.

The five crises suggest, then, that "proper" appearances may be sought for reasons quite unrelated to the traditional diplomatic goals of stabilizing or improving one's national position in the web of international power relations. For these "proper" appearances would seem to be critical elements in the domestic political life of any modern nation, particularly democracies, where favorable images may be translated into votes. The image of strength, resolve, prudence, and competence constitutes an essential prop underpinning the legitimacy and authority of governments of major powers: national prestige is demanded by the public, by associates and rivals of those in political control, and by those in control themselves. Thus, while it may sometimes be possible to resolve "substantive" disputes by resorting to expediency, issues of prestige by raising the specter of personal or national humiliation may call into question the very right of the losing government to continue in power. And, in fact, Khrushchev's Cuban retreat contributed importantly to his fall from power two years later,[6] and Johnson's setback during Tet helped to set in motion a chain of events which culminated in his renunciation of renom-

---

[6] Robert Conquest, *Russia After Khrushchev* (New York: Praeger, 1965), pp. 114, 180; Kenneth R. Whiting, *The Soviet Union Today*, rev. ed. (New York: Praeger, 1966), p. 88.

ination. Plainly, if there is one thing for which governments will fight above all else, it is to maintain themselves in control or to prevent drastic loss of power. Confrontation over issues of prestige, then, may not put off confrontations over more explosive matters because prestige may *itself* be the most explosive matter. Appearances cannot adequately be considered solely in antiseptic impersonal terms, despite what Schelling has said.

All this is not to say, of course, that a nation's image has no relation to its real power. If "power" be its capacity to influence the behavior of other nations, clearly a nation will be more influential if they perceive it as strong and resolute. In other words, "power" may be scarcely less subjective than "crisis," if, by a "powerful nation," we mean one which other nations perceive to be powerful. Thus, a nation's image before the world might be of considerable practical significance. Moreover, a nation's self-image, too, may affect its power. A populace confident in its government's strength and purpose may be a definite asset to its leaders; and the leaders' own self-images certainly will affect their relations with decision makers of other nations.

II

Expectations concerning the decision makers' capacity to perceive reality also were supported. The problem of appearance and reality in foreign policy crisis decision making, in other words, may be partly a problem of metaphysics, but it is also partly a problem of information: the information decision makers and the public possess regarding the crisis and each other. As such, it suggests no simple or obvious solutions, and for certain of its aspects, perhaps no satisfactory solutions at all. This is less a counsel of despair than a realistic reminder that in this area, as in so many other areas of life, the desirable is not always attainable or even theoretically identifiable.

Consider, first, the solubility of the decision makers' appearance and reality problem. Approaches to this problem must take into account three stages: information requirements must be determined in the light of prescribed purposes or goals; [7] next, the information must be gathered, analyzed, and transmitted to the decision maker; finally, he must receive and evaluate this information. There can be no question that present data gathering and analyzing facilities far exceed the capabilities of any existing in the past. Merely enumerating some of the more noteworthy developments since the Second World War is impressive: intelligence agencies have increased swiftly in size and efficiency; nonprofit advisory corporations like RAND or the Hudson Institute have

---

[7] Some information is necessary, too, in order to select these goals, and be aware that there is a decision to be made.

sprung up to meet a need for expert independent advice and criticism; a stunning growth in postgraduate university education has provided large numbers of specialists on almost every topic, and many of these specialists either are employed by the government directly or serve it in a consultative capacity; and technological advances in communication and transportation have vastly enlarged the opportunities for speed, precision, and reliability in the acquiring, interpreting, and sending of data.

It would be a mistake to conclude, however, that these dramatic developments have conquered the decision makers' appearance and reality problem, as if it were a jungle disease that could be eradicated easily by the administration of a vaccine. The problem persists, and many of the newer developments have proved to be either mixed blessings or simply irrelevant.

Take, for example, the growth of intelligence agencies, specifically the CIA. This has permitted the assembling of much more information than had been possible under the haphazard prewar system, when "the President and his principal policy-making associates received bits and pieces of foreign information from many sources, principally State Department offices in foreign countries, but also military attachés, friends, and associates, or the press." [8] Today, like a diligent myopic squirrel examining a pile of nuts, the CIA scrutinizes a vast array of overt and covert information sources: rows of experts analyze Soviet propaganda, U-2 pilots take reconnaisance photographs a dozen miles above the ground, trenchcoated secret agents sneak their microfilm back to the home office.

Yet like any other large, relatively healthy organization, as the CIA has grown it has enthusiastically taken on new functions. Thus, in addition to assembling and evaluating intelligence, it has occasionally planned and executed major foreign policy maneuvers. As the Bay of Pigs and (to a lesser extent) the Dominican experiences make clear, this operational function may pollute the intelligence function by destroying the indispensable quality of disinterestedness. By "disinterestedness" is not meant a completely open mind, for the only completely open mind is a blank one. The prospect of intelligence agents compulsively laboring over a gigantic cake of disparate facts in the hope that somehow Truth will pop out, pristine and pure, is not reassuring. Agents require preconceived notions in order to guide them to areas worthy of study, and to organize the data that they find. [9] As a practical matter, then, agents approach their investigations with certain hypotheses in mind. The decisive question is whether the agents are relatively free of emotional attach-

---

[8] Ransom, *op. cit.*, p. 134.

[9] Since there is no reason to assume that the selected facts are perfectly representative of the entire universe of facts, selection itself implies bias. Thus, the very process making facts useful makes them, to some extent, misleading. Moreover, selection implies bias whether the process follows well thought out principles or mere whim.

ments to their hypotheses. If not, a truly critical testing will be impossible, and the agents' conclusions concerning their hypotheses will simply be more or less artful masks hiding preset judgments. As a result of this kind of emotional attachment, President Kennedy was informed that the invading Cuban exiles would be supported by local resistance efforts; similarly, President Johnson was told that the Dominican rebels were dominated, or were in the process of becoming dominated, by Communists. The first of these conclusions was false, and the second highly dubious.

As for the large numbers of specialists and the prestigious advisory corporations, they obviously constitute a rich potential source of information. What is truly striking during crisis periods, however, is how little they are used. In ordinary times, expert reports and recommendations may be digested and absorbed by the regular governmental structure, often with far-reaching policy effects. Albert Wohlstetter's famous RAND study on the vulnerability of Strategic Air Command forces to a Soviet first strike, for example, had a profound impact upon American strategic theory and practice. But in times of crises, these experts rarely get the President's ear. This practice does not result from a belief that there is insufficient time to utilize the experts' services; for, plainly, the fact that these men already are knowledgeable concerning the topic would save time by decreasing the quantity of information the advisers would have to learn, and by providing the President with an expert teacher and counselor on technical matters. It is not the time factor which excludes these experts, then, but perhaps the psychological factor. Which is to say, Presidents often seem almost to regress under the pressure of crisis, reverting to reliance upon a few trusted associates whose familiar presence probably promotes feelings of security and reduces feelings of anxiety. At the missile crisis, for instance, Kennedy's most influential adviser was not an acknowledged expert in international relations or national security, but his brother, the Attorney General, with whom the President was very close. Aside from Llewellyn Thompson and Averell Harriman, former ambassadors who were present at only a few of the meetings, no specialists on Soviet affairs were even brought into the discussions. No academicians or RAND-type analysts were consulted at all.[10] That this crisis had a happy ending does not necessarily obviate the desirability of fully utilizing expert advice, as the Bay of Pigs fiasco illustrates. In this case, expert judgment was significantly excluded not only by the President—only one of his main Latin American advisers was an expert of the first

---

[10] It is hardly surprising, then, that a miffed associate of the RAND Corporation later deplored the President's neglect of scholarly "Kremlinologists or Sovietologists." Bernard Brodie, *The Communist Reach for Empire* (RAND Corporation, P-2-16, June 1964), p. 3.

order, and none was a full-time specialist in the area [11]—but by the CIA and State Department as well. The results, of course, were disastrous.[12]

The utilization of experts by itself does not guarantee that appearances will not be mistaken for reality. In order to be of maximum beneficial effect, the specialists must be properly chosen. That is, they must have the President's personal confidence or they will be paid little attention; they must be frank, outspoken, and lucid or their knowledge will not be adequately communicated; they must be able to appreciate the political realities circumscribing their recommendations or they will be dismissed as unrealistic and irrelevant; and, of course, they must possess a competence commensurate with their position. This last requirement, for all its obviousness, is often overlooked, perhaps because to the non-expert all experts often look alike. The results of such an error, however, may be quite costly. Herbert Feis has shown, for example, that many experts were selected for use in carrying on America's relations with war-time China. For the most part, though, they tended to be learned in Oriental cultures and languages, but "almost none [was] well-schooled about either Communist dogma or methods." [13] Their expertise, then, did not adequately fit them for their role in making judgments about the nature and goals of the Communist movement in China, and so it is not surprising that their reports to Washington on the revolution frequently reflected more appearance than reality.

When faced with crises, Presidents tend to surround themselves with men whose influence seems significantly related to their capacity to play a psychologically supportive role. This does not mean, of course, that Presidents necessarily turn to sycophants, yes-men, or favorite story-tellers. But it does mean that the President's advisers very likely share his values and assumptions regarding means and ends. This suggests that criticism or examination of the framework within which the policy makers are proceeding is rare indeed. No one seems to have questioned the assumptions of President Johnson's Dominican intervention, for example, and only Senator Fulbright challenged those of President Kennedy prior to the Bay of Pigs—and *then*, without success.[14]

---

[11] Kennedy's top expert was Adolf A. Berle, a lawyer and economist better known as an old New Deal figure. Of the other experts, Arthur Schlesinger was primarily an American historian, social critic, and presidential speech writer, and Richard Goodwin, a lawyer and speech writer. Thomas Mann, who had greater expertise than any of the three, appears to have had little influence.

[12] Another illustration of the failure to use expert advice was General Douglas Mac-Arthur's refusal, during the Korean conflict, to grant the relevance of expert advice on Soviet intentions in Europe. See Richard P. Stebbing, *The United States in World Affairs, 1951* (New York: Harper and Bros. for the Council on Foreign Relations, 1952), pp. 107–9.

[13] Herbert Feis, *The China Tangle* (Princeton: Princeton University Press, 1953), p. 184.

[14] As was pointed out earlier, none of the critics of the Bay of Pigs operation was consulted during the missile crisis deliberations.

The desire to avoid this kind of fundamental conflict is easily under-
standable: Presidents do not want to be faced with basic challenges while
under duress; they do not want to be forced to rethink elemental goals
and values when time is short; they do not want to risk a disharmony
that could prevent their advisers from making significant contributions.
And yet the fact remains that the basic premises may, after all, be contradictory, obsolete, or simply erroneous; and if these flaws are not exposed, the whole project is bound to fail. The very process of examination and the conflicts it may produce, in fact, are often valuable, for
they may supply the pressure for a creative or innovative solution to the
problem or at least enlarge the range of possible presidential choice.

Some conflict, then, is clearly desirable from the point of view of maximizing rationality in decision making, and penetrating to the reality of
the problem to be solved. But how much? On the one hand, if only one
or two dissenters are included among the policy makers, the dissenters'
influence is likely to be nil: probably, either they will buckle under the
pressure to conform and acquiesce to the majority's view, or they will
simply be written off early by the majority as irritating and irrelevant.
Effective dissent ordinarily would seem to require a larger number of
dissenters. Yet on the other hand, the greater the number of dissenters,
the better the chance that they will produce a conflict potent enough to
immobilize the whole group. It is exceedingly difficult, therefore, to obtain sufficient conflict to be useful, but not so much as to be destructive.
Whatever the pros and cons of promoting intragroup conflict, however, it
is plain that from the President's vantage, it can serve only to make an
unpleasant situation even more so. Consequently, he is unlikely to culti-
vate it, regardless of its merits.

But if Presidents do not want to be faced with basic challenges, neither
do advisers want to offer them. "The presidential assistant," as one former Johnson aide recalls, "depends entirely upon his capacity to please
one man, and he either succeeds in doing so or leaves." Clearly, this recognition is incompatible with offering basic challenges to that man's policies during time of stress. Nor can one embolden advisers by gathering
them in a group; for all would recognize that "it comes together not to
reach an agreement but to help one man make up his mind [and] he is
the only person in the room whose opinion really matters." [15]

Yet it is as true today as in the infancy of the nation that "key policy
decisions are still made by the President aided by a small group of ad-

---

[15] Reedy, *op. cit.*, This recalls "the time-honored anecdote about Lincoln's decision which
was taken contrary to the unanimous vote of his Cabinet (seven noes, one aye—the ayes
have it). . . . " Richard F. Fenno, Jr., *The President's Cabinet* (Cambridge: Harvard University Press, 1959), p. 29.

visers" [16] and that these advisers are chosen less for their expertise than for their ability to provide psychological support; it is also true that competent staff work has become of major importance. In fact, to the extent that decisions may be conceived as relationships "between knowledge and action," [17] staff work may be decisive. Yet in only the missile crisis was the staff work adequate. One reason for this may be that while the Executive Committee reflected the President's belief in the flexibility of organizations, it was far more tightly run than was the earlier group of advisers working on the Bay of Pigs plans. This is revealed not only in the obvious facts that meetings were held more frequently during the missile crisis, and that Kennedy's personal control was greater when he was in attendance, but in more subtle ways as well. At one point, for example, when the Executive Committee was unable to agree on a recommendation and "the strain and the hours without sleep were beginning to take their toll," [18] an organizational ploy was followed to prevent the Committee from degenerating to a state of unfruitful bickering. The Committee split itself into subgroups, each of which wrote a paper defending its proposed recommendation. The papers were then handed to other subgroups for analysis and criticism, and later given back to the original subgroup for additional reviews. From this process emerged two "definitive plans" [19]—one calling for a blockade and the other for military action—each considering the tactics and contingencies in some detail. The belief in the value of precise organizational staffing was implicit, too, in the meetings of top intelligence officials chaired by McCone and held before every Executive Committee session. [20] All of this mitigates the force of a judgment of one analyst, who after noting the dearth of experts present on Soviet affairs, concluded that there was "limited staffing for so grave a crisis." [21] This judgment appears even more exaggerated when the staff work of the missile crisis is contrasted with those of the other crises under consideration: at the Bay of Pigs, a poorly organized and noncritical staff produced self-indulgent fantasy; during the Dominican revolt, the staff was caught unprepared and (at the lower levels) inexperienced; and at Tet, the staff's evaluations of trends and capabilities were simply incorrect.

Why has competent crisis staff work so rarely been achieved? Part of

---

[16] Doris A. Graber, *Public Opinion, the President, and Foreign Policy: Four Case Studies from the Formative Years* (New York: Holt, Rinehart and Winston, 1968), p. 329.

[17] Harry Howe Ransom, *Central Intelligence and National Security* (Cambridge: Harvard University Press, 1959), p. 2.

[18] Robert F. Kennedy, "Thirteen Days," p. 148.

[19] *Ibid.*, p. 149.

[20] Kirkpatrick, *op. cit.*, p. 262.

[21] Brodie, *loc. cit.*

the difficulty stems from problems inherent in predicting human behavior. Social scientists cannot forecast events with the accuracy of a chemist predicting the results of boiling a test tube full of sulphuric acid or even, probably, of a weatherman announcing that it will rain tomorrow. The student of human behavior is confronted with far more variables—many of which are unknown to him—and a far more limited capacity to replicate occurrences. Considerations of this nature have led one sociologist to complain that "in social science as in the courtroom, the more significant the events we are interested in, the less we can reproduce them"; [22] and an eminent philosopher has suggested that the intrinsic interest of a subject is inversely related to our ability for "accurate observation and systematic study." [23] The difficulties of predicting human behavior may be even greater for intelligence analysts, despite the fact that they doubtless are supported by a vastly larger financial commitment. The nature of politics, in the first place, makes the possibility of biased information gathering and reporting larger[24] and the relevance of experiments smaller. Second, intelligence predictions, if they become known to the enemy, may themselves alter events, becoming self-falsifying prophecies. Third, probably the greater likelihood of practical consequences, flowing from intelligence work as contrasted with most academic social science operates as an impediment to maximizing the usefulness of a forecast. This usefulness may partly be a function of precision and clarity, but practical significance may promote vagueness and ambiguity in predictions by increasing the cost to the analyst of making a mistake. Vagueness and ambiguity, in other words, may constitute one of the analyst's means of self-defense, in that they lend themselves less than precision and clarity to *post facto* determinations of error and consequent placings of blame. These theoretical and practical limitations on the predictive capacity of the intelligence analyst suggest that it would be unrealistic to expect a consistently high quantity and quality of high-probability forecasts. Nonetheless, prediction supplies the *raison d'être* for much of the intelligence effort; thus, analysts excuse their limited abilities in this regard at the price of making a good deal of their work appear to be activity in search of a goal. If high probability predictions are difficult, they are rarely impossible, and remain the key to the policy-making utility of the intelligence function.

Another obstacle to competent crisis staff work may be that the top

[22] Helmut Schoeck, "Truth in the Social Sciences," *Truth, Myth, and Symbol,* ed. Thomas J. J. Altizer *et al.* (Englewood Cliffs: Prentice-Hall, 1962), p. 20.
[23] Michael Polanyi, *Personal Knowledge: Toward a Post-Critical Philosophy,* rev. ed. (Chicago: University of Chicago Press, 1962), p. 139.
[24] Increasing the possibility of bias still further is the fact that intelligence analysts are not disinterested observers, but are employed by and committed to one side of a conflict. See, *supra,* chap. 2.

staff is necessarily limited by the work of subordinate technical staff and line personnel, and their work is not always satisfactory.[25] Tet and the Dominican intervention illustrate this. Also, the President himself may not adequately appreciate the importance of staff work or be able to improve it. This seems to have been one of the lessons Kennedy learned from the abortive Bay of Pigs operation. Neither the nation nor the President paid an unacceptable price for this lesson, but there is no reason to suppose that the future necessarily will unfold in such a fortuitous manner. The desirability of a smooth-functioning preexisting staff to deal with unexpected crises, therefore, is quite obvious. This may not, however, be a realizable goal, for presidential crisis management is critically dependent upon the peculiar nature of the crisis and the values, attitudes, and perceptions of particular Presidents. And with such wide variations in this regard, "it is pointless to try to develop some ideal organization of the presidency." [26] Similarly, the working procedures followed within the organization must be geared to the President—not the other way round; hence, it would be naive to declare *a priori* one set of procedures as best adapted to *all* crises, and thus worthy of being established on a continuing basis. Group decision making and democratic leadership, for example, may have fitted Kennedy's psychological make-up, but other Presidents may be too authoritarian or too easily influenced by others for these techniques to be suitable for them.

Finally, if technological advances in communication and transportation have made it easier and quicker to assemble and analyze information, they have not solved the problem of insuring that the information is accurate or its significance is appreciated. Certainly, the quantity of information passing from Vietnam to Washington prior to the Tet offensive was impressive, but the various sophisticated transmitting devices did nothing to improve its inadequate quality. By the same token, American officials were aware of enough facts in April 1965, to lead them to suspect that a Dominican coup was imminent, but they failed to grasp their significance.[27]

At this juncture, it is useful to point out that "all large organizations are not teams, but coalitions." [28] Which is to say, all members do not

---

[25] There is also the possibility that the top staff may limit the subordinate technical staff and line personnel with disastrous results similar to those that occurred during the Bay of Pigs.

[26] Burton M. Sapin, *The Making of United States Foreign Policy* (New York: Praeger, 1966), p. 65.

[27] This is related to what Roberta Wohlstetter has termed a security organization's "noise" problem. Its communications system is frequently so filled with alarm signals—of which most are unwarranted by the facts—that it becomes exceedingly difficult for higher level officials to distinguish a true crisis from a false alarm. Instead of standing out, then, an alarm signal may be lost in the "noise" of other communications. *Op. cit.*

[28] Anthony Downs, *Inside Bureaucracy* (Boston: Little, Brown, 1967), p. 76.

work toward the same goals, although they do have some goals in common. Thus, while each official may be devoted to the organization's goals, his first loyalty is almost certainly to himself; probably even his own bureaucratic subunit has a claim on his allegiance exceeding that of the larger organization. The information he passes up to his superiors, consciously or unconsciously, tends to reflect this fact. From the superior's point of view, the primary function of the information flow may be to give him an accurate view of the environment with which he has to deal; but from the subordinate's point of view its primary function is apt to be the maximizing of rewards and minimizing of punishments due him and his bureaucratic subunit. He may desire praise, for example, or promotion, greater authority for his subunit, or larger appropriations. And he may want to avoid condemnations, restricted authority for his subunit, and smaller appropriations. Even if he is responsible only for reporting events and not for their occurrence, probably he recognizes that the ancient practice of executing bearers of bad news has not been abolished but merely "civilized." His most obvious strategy, then (again, consciously or unconsciously), is to tell his superiors what they expect to hear. Apparently, this was the strategy adopted by American officials in Vietnam before Tet: Washington obviously wanted and expected to be told that things were going well; probably officials on the scene wanted to believe this and, therefore, did believe it; and consequently, this was what President Johnson and other top policy makers were told. The same kind of process seems to have preceded the abortive invasion at the Bay of Pigs.

There is no reason to suppose that technology can banish completely this kind of informational problem. But new developments or managerial techniques may reduce its effect somewhat.[29] If different and fairly evenly matched organizations are charged with gathering and evaluating the same information, it may be that each will correct many of the distortions of the other, resulting in a more accurate product. And the use of direct communications systems, such as the "hot line" from Washington to Moscow, can effectively eliminate distortion attributable to middle men. It would be misleading, however, to exaggerate the importance of these devices. Competitive sources of information did not provide President Johnson with an accurate picture of reality during the Dominican revolt or prior to the Tet offensive; nor did the decentralized intelligence apparatus existing before the CIA's creation in 1947 prove more effective than the present system of coordination.[30] There is, in any case, the possibility that the least valid interpretation might prove the most per-

---

[29] This was suggested by Downs, *ibid.,* pp. 118–26.
[30] See Harry Howe Ransom, *Central Intelligence and National Security* (Cambridge:

suasive or that the competition might cause officials to falsify or exaggerate reports in order to win.[31] The costs—financial and otherwise—of having different organizations performing essentially the same task are also bound to be substantial. As for the "hot line," probably it has proved of greater value to writers of melodrama than to Presidents, for it has rarely been used.

Even if all the President's subordinates were to perform their functions exactly according to instructions and without human bias, the problem of appearance and reality would not disappear because the President's limitations and biases would intrude upon their information. His time, energy, and interest are confined within narrow boundaries, of which the pressure of crisis makes him well aware. He can absorb only a small amount of data, assess only a few values and assumptions, weigh only a handful of alternatives. He knows—rightly—that he cannot be certain about the future, that his predictions may fail, but that he cannot afford to be indecisive and that few will care later to hear his excuses.

Atop these limitations lie the biases with their numerous and immense opportunities for distortion. One need only enumerate some of the forces for error mentioned in earlier pages: selective attention and perception, national perspective, misapplying analogies from history or personal experience, personal cravings for success and security. The President, in short, unavoidably confronts the information less as a *tabula rasa* than as a wall of graffiti. And this must be so, if he is to be able to function at all. For these inherent tendencies and preexisting knowledge and attitudes are indispensable to his effort to organize events, and thereby extract meaning from the chaos of available stimuli. But the biases also, in the last analysis, render insoluble to some important extent his problem of appearance and reality. Organizations, advisers, technology—none of these ultimately can nullify the fact that the President is a man, and as such, is subject to the limiting and distorting pressures inherent in the species.[32]

Harvard University Press), chap. 3, where there is a discussion of the fears, dissatisfactions, and ambitions leading to the establishment of the CIA. It is also pertinent to note the caveat of a distinguished student of industrial organization: "Meaningful decentralization is probably impossible without a resolution of the goals into nonconflicting, operative subgoals so that these can be placed under independent control," Chadwick J. Haberstroh, "Control as an Organizational Process," *Management Science* 6 (January 1960): 171.

[31] Thus, revelations concerning rivalry, distrust, and suspicion characterizing relations between various American intelligence agencies in Vietnam indicate that such competition may often be dysfunctional. As one middle-level State Department official who served there put it, "If I had some good agents in one area of the country and you had one that was getting a lot of good stuff, I might try to blow his cover and put him out of action. Same government, same objectives, different teams. Sometimes three or four agencies in Vietnam employ the same Vietnamese agent. The agencies won't open their personnel registries to one another so there is just no way of checking." *New York Times*, October 1, 1969.

[32] Put differently, the President repeatedly faces situations where the acquisition and assi-

III

Finally, expectations relating to the President's desire and ability to mislead public opinion were also confirmed. Each of the five crises represents an attempt by an administration to convince the mass public and attentive public of the reality of certain appearances—of the wholly Cuban nature of the Bay of Pigs invasion, of the unassailably humanitarian goal of the Dominican intervention, of the decisive failure of the Vietcong's Tet offensive, of the unprovocative innocence of American ships in the Gulf of Tonkin incidents, and of a normal "business as usual" atmosphere in the White House during the formulation of plans to deal with the emplacement of Soviet missiles in Cuba. Except for the missile crisis, these attempts at deceiving the public seem to have been accompanied by a certain amount of self-deception on the part of the decision makers: at the Bay of Pigs and the Gulf of Tonkin, they persuaded themselves that appearances could successfully be dispensed as reality, in the manner of sugared placebos; during the Dominican revolt after the anti-Communist rationale surfaced and again before the Tet offensive, decision makers believed in the reality of the appearances they purveyed.

In comparing these crises and trying to determine what factors tend to lead to deception, it may be useful first to visualize a spectrum: at one end, appearance manipulation is practiced solely because it is necessary for the situation to be handled effectively; at the opposite end, it is practiced solely for the benefit of the persons, organizations, and parties concerned. Most crises, of course, fall between the two endpoints, and probably the closer one gets to the center, the greater the controversy over the justification of the deception.

Of the crises discussed here, the place nearest the first endpoint of instrumental justification must be reserved for the news management surrounding the missile crisis. Secrecy was so obviously essential to proper decision making, in fact, that it has drawn virtually no criticism. In the face of its exorbitant costs, few have spoken out dogmatically for the "people's right to know." If attempts to manipulate public appearances during the missile crisis have sparked little controversy, the same cannot be said of attempts relating to the Bay of Pigs affair. Primarily because it failed, the entire operation has come under intense attack, but *if one grants the plan's assumptions,* its claims to appearance manipulation seem nearly as justified instrumentally as do those of the missile crisis. If the invasion's preparations were hidden from view, it could benefit from

---

milation of information is very costly in terms of time, effort, money, other opportunities foregone, and so forth. Great progress has been made in permitting him to cut his information-acquiring costs by the development of specialized institutions serving this function. But in cutting his information-assimilation costs, he relies, as did his predecessors, on ideology, preexisting beliefs, and other crude and often inadequate tools.

the element of surprise, and thus have a greater chance of succeeding; if American involvement were concealed, Cuban antagonism to the post-Castro government would be reduced and the American image in Latin America and the underdeveloped world generally would be spared a disfiguring blemish. That the possibility of keeping either secret was remote did not diminish its desirability. Yet another purpose the secrecy served—and one with fatally counterproductive effects—was to shield the CIA leadership from challenge by protecting the plan from independent scrutiny. This personal and organizational reason for secrecy may in some sense have actually been more important than the instrumental reason; for when the personal demand for secrecy collided with the instrumental demand for further investigation, it was the latter which gave way.

The deception concerning the Dominican intervention probably features roughly the same mixture of instrumental and self-serving justifications. The early reliance upon the wholly humanitarian rationale of saving American lives reduced the initial criticism of the United States from abroad, and made the Marines' job easier. But an important purpose of this story—and especially of the later emphasis upon the Communist danger—was to earn support for the decision at home. That support was desired not primarily for tactical reasons—the military commitment was so small that it hardly required the widespread approval necessary for a major war—but in order to ward off criticisms of the President, and retain public support to be used for other purposes.

Nearer still to the self-serving end of the spectrum are the administration's efforts at the time of the Tet offensive. Tactically, the attempts to convince the public that the Vietcong failed may be justified as having been necessary to avert a deterioration of the will to fight on the home front, a deterioration that could have reduced the government's capacity to prosecute the war, especially in a presidential election year. The fact that after the public refused to be misled, domestic support for the war did in fact decline merely underlines the importance of appearance manipulation. In this crisis, however, it is even clearer that pesonal, organizational, and partisan motivations were at least as strong in dictating the deception. It was not simply that failure had to be concealed to help the war effort; more importantly, a major setback after several months of official optimism would damage the prestige and mock the claims of competence of President Johnson, General Westmoreland, and virtually all the other civilian and military figures connected with the war; it would also subject the organizations involved—the Defense and State Departments, the Army, the CIA, and so forth—to criticism and in some cases possibly to a loss of authority or funds; and failure would hurt the Democratic party and its President in an election year by turning public sentiment against them and promoting intraparty conflicts over the war's management.

The pseudocrisis concerning the Gulf of Tonkin incident presents a special case. On the one hand, propaganda about "aggressive" North Vietnam and "innocent" America bore no reasonable relation to dealing with the attacks. On the other hand, aside from making the President more attractive to "hawks" prior to an election, the deceptions were not especially self-serving. The point here is that the incidents did not constitute a true crisis, and so their main justification cannot be sought in the short-run, but rather in the long-run. From this point of view, the President's response in seeking a supporting congressional resolution had instrumental and self-serving justifications: militarily, the resolution permitted the President to forestall the collapse of the South Vietnamese regime the following year by escalating American participation in the war; personally, the resolution reduced criticism of the President from members of Congress and the public in general by legitimating his decision.[33]

Crises, of course, are subjectively defined by the President and his advisers. And in determining to what extent they see the situation as giving them license to lie or withhold relevant facts, their justifications inevitably are a mixture of the instrumental and the self-serving. Moreover, it is a safe assumption that any borderline information will be kept secret, its very existence being vociferously denied. The Gulf of Tonkin incidents even suggest that crises themselves may sometimes be only appearances, artfully constructed like phony storefronts in a Hollywood western.

It is easy to become indignant about a good deal of official behavior in crises and pseudocrises. It is easy to declare platitudinously that "in the United States foreign policy is the expression of the will of the people," [34] and to conclude, therefore, that the administrations should have been frank with the public and followed its will.

This approach, however, raises two troublesome questions. First, is it useful to speak of the public's "willing" anything? If the public is simply the sum of the individuals in the society, then the "public will" must refer to that which everyone "wills." But it is exceedingly rare to find that everyone wills the same thing. In fact, many persons know and care so little about politics that it hardly makes sense to say that they will anything at all. Among the attentive public—the persons who are fairly well informed—typically there is no unanimity, and often not even a majority.

---

[33] The reduction of congressional and other criticism could also be justified instrumentally in terms of warding off internal differences, which might hurt the war effort.

[34] Henry M. Wriston, *Diplomacy in a Democracy* (New York: Harper and Bros., 1965), p. 72.

With respect to the Vietnam war, for example, portions of the attentive public could be found favoring every alternative from an all-out military effort to immediate withdrawal.[35] Which public's "will" should prevail? The most numerous? The most knowledgeable? The most intense?

The second question is: how can one deny the President the right to try to manipulate public opinion in support of the national interest as he sees it, while at the same time time demand that he provide leadership? And that the public demands leadership in foreign affairs is difficult to deny. This was borne out by the results of a 1960 poll of 1,342 residents of Detroit. The respondents were asked:

Now, suppose that fighting is breaking out somewhere abroad, and the President thinks it's *important* to send American troops there. He knows, however, that most Americans are *opposed* to sending our troops there. Now, what do you think: Should he send these troops, which he may *legally* do as President, or should he *follow* public opinion and keep them home?

Seventy-five percent of the respondents replied that the President should send the troops.[36] Presidential leadership, in other words, was overwhelmingly supported, even at the expense of mass public opinion.

And yet when Americans disagree with specific presidential foreign policies, they often attack the President for not following public opinion. Critics of the war in Vietnam, for example, often interpret the 1964 election as a referendum defeating the escalation alternative, and attack President Johnson for failing to contain the war. What is one man's politics of leadership, in other words, may be another's politics of deception or manipulation.

Regardless of terminology, it can hardly be questioned that leadership is essential to the effective running of government. This is not, of course, a recent development, for the need for leadership flows from two permanent conditions: first, the widespread public ignorance and/or apathy in the face of the need for expertise in the making of decisions; and sec-

---

[35] See e.g., Howard Schuman and Edward O. Laumann, "Do Most Professors *Support the War?*" *Trans-action,* November 1967, pp. 32–35, which emphasizes the lack of consensus among University of Michigan professors on the desirability of halting American bombing of North Vietnam.

[36] Roberta S. Sigel, "Image of the American Presidency—Part II of an Exploration into Popular Views of Presidential Power," *Midwest Journal of Political Science* 10 (February 1966): 126. President Nixon's dispatching of American troops to Cambodia provided an occasion for a true-to-life replication of Sigel's finding. A Gallup poll disclosed that, though fifty-eight percent of those who said they had heard of read of the Cambodian situation opposed sending American troops, fifty-one percent approved of the way Nixon was handling the situation. Whether this constitutes support for Sigel's finding or merely evidence of public ignorance (i.e., respondents whose answers placed them among both majorities because they were unaware that Nixon had in fact dispatched the troops) must remain moot. *Washington Post,* May 5, 1970.

ond, the myriad publics making conflicting demands upon government in the face of limited social and economic resources. In complex modern industrial societies, these ancient needs are especially pressing; for expertise is more indispensable than ever, and the number of publics making claims on government has grown enormously. Today, moreover, the American public demands that its leaders actually lead—or at least give the appearance of doing so. Any concept of democracy that depends upon the people's deciding issues and rejects opinion leadership in their name, therefore, applies only to a world of fantasy.

And yet democracy cannot be identified with the *Führerprinzip.* The core of democracy, instead, is the notion that the leaders be responsible to the nonleaders. Thus, it is obvious that leadership and opinion manipulation can coexist with democracy only up to a point, beyond which democracy simply ceases to exist. Without indulging in Orwellian nightmares, one must admit that the increasing knowledge of communications and the application of this knowledge for political purposes has added a very modern urgency to this traditional tension between leadership and democracy. How, then, is this leadership—in the sense of entailing the creation of a permissive consensus—to be controlled?

In ordinary times, there are a number of important limitations on the leader's capacity to create a permissive consensus. If the President initially has unlimited access to the mass media and often can manage news for his own purposes, still he does not enjoy the monopoly over the means of mass communications that is found in a totalitarian state. It is, of course, easy to overstate the diligence of a critical press, for most of its "scoops" and exposés result from deliberate official "leaks" or from information simply handed to reporters by interested congressmen or bureaucrats. But if the media usually are not especially active in their criticism, neither are they willing to lend themselves to the single purpose of glorifying the President and his policies. In any case, the availability of the media may be as much a liability as an asset, for constant and close exposure may exaggerate unpleasant mannerisms or call attention to unflattering personality traits that would otherwise go unnoticed.

By the same token, if the President is able to make use of the values and assumptions inculcated into Americans by the school system,[37] still he is denied the manipulative possibilities of the vast educational indoctrination and youth training programs of a Nazi Germany or a Soviet Union. And if he can avail himself of the FBI to attempt to remove cer-

---

[37] On the importance of the public school in political socialization, see Robert D. Hess and Judith V. Torney, *The Development of Basic Attitudes and Values Toward Government and Citizenship During the Elementary School Years,* Part I, Cooperative Research Project No. 1078 (Washington: Government Printing Office for the United States Office of Education, 1965).

tain kinds of opponents from society, still he can benefit from no ubiqui-
tous secret police or the freedom to silence masses of dissenters by extra-
legal means.[38]

The differences in the ability of democratic and totalitarian leaders to
mobilize consent, then, though they may be essentially differences in degree and not in kind, are very great indeed. In the one case, they permit
effective opposition; in the other, they deny it. This opposition may be
vocal, and in fact open criticism of the President is one of the few con-
stants in the swiftly changing American political scene. Almost everything he does, from working for open housing legislation to lifting
beagles by their ears, is subjected to attack from elements of both political parties inside and outside Congress, from interested groups and private individuals, from portions of the press, and probably *sub rosa* from
units within his own bureaucracy. Most opposition, however, is not open
in the sense that it is made available to the entire society, but instead
consists of conversations between ordinary citizens, and unvoiced but
deeply held beliefs. This private or silent opposition should not be min-
imized, for it may constitute a major obstacle to opinion change, and
thus to policy leadership. White racism, for example, is surely a barrier
to the passage and enforcement of civil rights legislation; and this feeling, plus the Protestant Ethic and the American Dream, reduces the
chance of short-run success for antipoverty programs.

In brief periods of crisis, the long list of limitations on presidential
opinion leadership ceases to be impressive. Once the crisis begins—and
the administration's ability to define crises is a great asset, as the Gulf of
Tonkin episode indicates—criticism becomes muted. The felt necessity to
join together and support the nation and the President in their time of
need is so strong that opposition appears unseemly, if not actually unpatriotic. Even when a small amount of criticism of forthcoming, as it
was during the passage of the Gulf of Tonkin resolution or during the
Dominican Republic intervention, the mass public pays these verbal attacks little attention. This is because, by and large, neither the public nor
governmental officials want the President to be restricted at these crucial
times. Ultimately, then, the decision makers' decisive crisis limitations
are *internal:* their own sense of right and wrong and fair play, and their
own calculations of the postcrisis effects of their actions on the nation
and on their own careers. Formal checks are too easily swept aside by the
urgency of the moment to be of much value. Both houses of Congress
had to pass the Gulf of Tonkin resolution in order for the "crisis" to have
had the desired result, for example, but this barrier was very easily

---

[38] These distinctions between democratic and totalitarian systems were suggested by Carl
J. Friedrich and Zbigniew K. Brzezinski, *Totalitarian Dictatorship and Autocracy,* 2d ed.
(New York: Praeger, 1965), Part IV.

scaled in less than a week. Instead of formal limitations, we must fall back on the hope that decision makers have been so inculcated with democratic values that they will not violate the trust which crises inevitably impose upon them. It is a matter of faith, and on this, as in most things, the people must take their chances.

Bibliographical Note

It is easier for a camel to pass through the eye of a needle than for a Pentagon spokesman to retain his integrity.

Anon.

Any researcher must beware of bias and ignorance in his sources. The student of foreign policy crises must be extraordinarily careful; for these events have attracted partisanship, secrecy, and lies like flies to a compost heap. I am tempted to repeat the warning "Be careful" till I drive the reader to paranoia—except that I recognize that such warnings are poor substitutes for a description of *how* to be careful. Here, I would suggest examining the author's background for signs of bias, checking his account for internal consistency, comparing and contrasting it with other accounts, and pausing to ask oneself in the privacy of one's own mind whether his facts and arguments seem plausible. These generalities, however, are hardly more helpful than my original injuction to be careful. And be careful of my book, too.

Certain sources will be essential to anyone planning serious investigation of any of this book's five crises: the "prestige" press (the *New York Times, Washington Post, Wall St. Journal,* and occasionally, *Christian Science Monitor*), the *Department of State Bulletin* (for the administration's views), the *Congressional Record* (for congressional reactions), and the periodicals of political opinion (such as the *New Republic, Nation, National Review,* and *I.F. Stone's Weekly*).

Analysis of the Kennedy crises inevitably relies heavily upon two monumental works of "court-history," Arthur M. Schlesinger's *A Thousand Days* (1965) and Theodore C. Sorensen's *Kennedy* (1965). Written by participant-observers, the books provide detailed accounts of events as seen from the "inside." In this same genre, but considerably more sophisticated and policy-oriented, is Roger Hilsman's *To Move a Nation* (1967).

Regarding the Bay of Pigs episode, useful journalistic reports include Karl E. Meyer and Tad Szulc's *The Cuban Invasion* (1962) and Haynes Johnson's *The Bay of Pigs* (1964). Also helpful are Paul W. Blackstock's *The Strategy of Subversion* (1964), and *The Real CIA* (1968) by Lyman B. Kirkpatrick, Jr., a former high-ranking CIA official.

The Cuban Missile Crisis provoked several book-length works, of which the best is Henry A. Pachter's *Collision Course* (1963). Robert Kennedy's *Thirteen Days* (1969) is very revealing, often unintentionally, as is Dean Acheson's critique of the Kennedy version in *Esquire*'s February 1969, issue. Superficial but sometimes factually helpful are Elie Abel's *The Missile Crisis* (1966) and *Facing the Brink* (1967) by veteran journalists Edward Weintal and Charles Bartlett. Several RAND Corporation Studies cited in my chapter on the crisis provide interesting analytical points.

Just as the Kennedy crises were too often analyzed by ravenous adorers, so the Johnson crises were too often treated by voracious haters. Neither emotional commitment, of course, served the search for truth. The Johnson cause has suffered also due to an absence of an impressive general history-apologia of the administration, comparable to the works of Schlesinger or Sorensen.

The Dominican Republic intervention, however, has produced an unusually fine body of source material. Tad Szulc's *Dominican Diary* (1965) and Dan Kurzman's *Santo Domingo: Revolt of the Damned* (1965) are excellent examples of eye-witness journalism, and portions of Philip Geyelin's *LBJ and the World* (1966) and, to a lesser extent, Rowland Evans and Robert Novak's *Lyndon B. Johnson: The Exercise of Power* (1966) are of real value. The administration's view of the tangled events is presented in Georgetown University's Center for Strategic Studies' *Dominican Action—1965: Intervention or Cooperation* (Special Report Series, No. 2, July 1966) and John Bartlow Martin's *Overtaken by Events* (1968), and is attacked broadside by Theodore Draper in *The Dominican Revolt* (1968). For fairness and balance, however, probably the best book on the crisis is *Intervention and Negotiation* (1970) by Jerome Slater.

With the two Vietnam crises, the researcher is not so lucky. Only one book of substance has been written on either—Joseph Goulden's helpful journalistic account of the Gulf of Tonkin incidents, *Truth Is the First Casualty* (1969)—forcing the investigator to depend greatly on other sources. For the Tet offensive, reliance must be placed upon newspapers and periodicals, and, fourtunately, the quality of reporting was very high. This was not the case concerning the Tonkin Gulf affair, but, here, one can make use of very valuable 1964 and 1968 Senate hearings: the

Senate Foreign Relations and Armed Services Committees' *Hearing on the Joint Resolution to Promote Maintenance of International Peace and Security in Southeast Asia* (1964) and the Senate Foreign Relations Committee's *Hearing on the Gulf of Tonkin, the 1964 Incidents* (1968).

All this provides merely the bare bones of an investigation into the crises. Readers desiring to inquire into these episodes in greater depth might find that the numerous footnotes in this study supply a sizable number of research "leads."

Index